Human Resource Management

Human Resources Management

H T Graham
DPA, Dip Soc Stud, FIPM, MBIM

R Bennett
BA, MSc (Econ), DPhil

Seventh Edition

THE M & E HANDBOOK SERIES

Pitman Publishing
128 Long Acre, London WC2E 9AN

A Division of Longman Group UK Limited

First published 1974
Second edition 1978
Third edition 1980
Fourth edition 1983
Fifth edition 1986
Sixth edition 1989
Seventh edition 1992
Reprinted 1993 (twice)

A CIP record for this book is available from the British Library.

ISBN 0 7121 0844 0

Founding Editor: P W D Redmond

Typeset by FDS Ltd, Penarth
Printed and bound in Singapore

Contents

Part two   Personnel management

Extract from preface to sixth edition

Human resources management is a subject which under various titles appears to an increasing extent in many professional and technical courses. It combines elements of industrial psychology, personnel management, training and industrial relations, therefore raising difficulties for the student because he or she is referred to a large number of textbooks, nearly all including much more detail than he or she needs and some not easily available or accessible. This *M & E Handbook* brings together in concise form the essential points the student requires and relates the various parts of the subject to each other by cross-references between chapters and sections. The book therefore provides a framework for the study of the subject and an aid to examination revision. In addition it may also be useful to managers who wish to have a convenient reference book covering the human aspects of their work.

Some of the examinations for which this book should be found useful are:

Association of Accounting Technicians;
Diploma and Certificate in Management Studies;
Fellowship of the Chartered Insurance Institute;
Institute of Management Services;
London Chamber of Commerce and Industry, private
   secretary's certificate;
National Examination Board for Supervisory Management
   (NEBSM);
Institute of Administrative Management;
Institute of Personnel Management;
Institute of Purchasing and Supply;
Institute of Chartered Secretaries and Administrators;
BTEC national and higher diplomas;
Chartered Building Societies Institute.

Preface to the seventh edition

This new edition contains a complete chapter on European Community dimensions of personnel management, including a discussion of recent EC Directives affecting human resources and the implications for personnel management of the possible implementation of the European Social Charter. The chapter on leadership has been thoroughly revised, and there is extensive fresh material on executive search (headhunting), the use of personnel management consultants, new work patterns (focusing on the increasingly important core/peripheral worker divide), salary administration, the demographic time bomb, and the contemporary debate on similarities and differences between 'human resources management' and personnel.

Sections on learning theory, psychometric testing, human resources planning and labour turnover, assessment centres, absenteeism and welfare services have been revised and extended, and the chapter on training is enlarged to encompass recent institutional developments, particularly the work of the NCVQ. Legal references have been updated, and the chapter 'What is personnel management?' now incorporates material on ethical issues in personnel administration and the 'future of personnel'. For the first time, the book has a wide-ranging glossary of key personnel management terms.

Thanks are due to Rosalind Bailey, who wordprocessed the manuscript, and to Jennifer Mair and Giovanna Ceroni of Pitman Publishing for their efficient processing of the book.

Roger Bennett

Part one

Industrial psychology

1
Elementary individual psychology

Introduction

1. Definition

Human resources management (HRM) concerns the human side of the management of enterprises and employees' relations with their firms. Its purpose is to ensure that the employees of a company, i.e. its human resources, are used in such a way that the employer obtains the greatest possible benefit from their abilities and the employees obtain both material and psychological rewards from their work. Human resources management is based on the findings of industrial psychology summarised in the first part of this book and uses the techniques and procedures known collectively as 'personnel management' which are described in the second part.

Personnel management (*see* Chapter 11) may be defined as that part of human resources management which is concerned with staffing the enterprise, determining and satisfying the needs of people at work, and the practical rules and procedures that govern relationships between employees and the organisation. Differences between personnel management and HRM are discussed in 11:**3**.

Everyone who has control over others shares in human resources management; it is not a function which the individual manager can avoid and leave to specialists. Human resources are much more difficult to manage than material resources, partly because conflict often occurs between the employer's and employees' wishes and partly because, to an increasing extent, employees try to share in making decisions about their working environment.

2.   Psychology and the manager

The above definition implies that managers, to be successful, must understand and be able to use personnel management techniques and in addition have some knowledge of the principles of industrial psychology on which they are based. They must be aware of the results of psychological studies of the employee as an individual, as a member of a working group and as a person whose behaviour is influenced to some extent by the technological environment. No one can lay down precise laws of psychology; we have to be content with tendencies, principles or theories rather than laws. It is possible to predict how the majority of people will behave in certain circumstances but almost impossible to foresee whether an individual will belong to the majority or the minority. The reason for this is the nature of psychology itself.

3.   Psychology as a science

In their investigations into natural phenomena, scientists try to follow accepted rules in order to reach well-founded conclusions. Scientific method, as these rules are called, requires the following.

(a) *Facts which are impersonal,* i.e. independent of any particular observer. Impression or opinions should be avoided.

(b) *Objective observations,* i.e. separate observers will agree when observing the same phenomenon simultaneously, or when it is repeated on different occasions. Subjective observations, i.e. those which depend on interpretation, surmise or judgment by an individual should not be used.

(c) *Investigation into all aspects of the problem,* rather than making assumptions. Every possible fact should be collected and considered.

(d) *Experimental controls,* so that changes in one factor (the subject of the experiment) are observed while other factors are kept unchanged.

(e) *Quantitative measurements and descriptions.* The need to provide measurements improves the design of an experiment, and numerical results can be classified and analysed, if necessary, by statistical methods.

A study of these rules of scientific method will show how

difficult it is to carry out truly scientific investigations into human behaviour.

(a) *Behaviour is very often interpreted* according to an observer's own experience and personality (*see* 10).

(b) Human behaviour has a quality which on any occasion *may please some judges and displease others*, or the same observer may form a different opinion of the same behaviour when it is repeated. Completely identical judgments rarely occur.

(c) Investigation of all aspects would include, for example, *complete knowledge of a person's heredity and environment (see* 4:2). This is never possible with human beings.

(d) *It is very difficult to control experiments with human beings* because it is impossible to know that all factors (except the one being investigated) are really stable. There may be unknown influences at work (e.g. dislike of the experimenter), and interference by various factors in the environment cannot in practice be eliminated.

(e) *Many aspects of human behaviour cannot be measured accurately or reliably,* for example personality traits (*see* 4:8–13).

4. Improving the quality of experiments

Psychological investigations can never therefore be truly scientific, though every effort should be made to follow scientific methods as far as possible. The following methods are often used to improve the quality of experiments.

(a) *Animals instead of humans* are sometimes the subjects of experiments, because their heredity and environment can be closely controlled and because they are available in large numbers. Obviously, it should not be assumed that animal behaviour is necessarily a true guide to human behaviour.

(b) *Large groups of experimental subjects* are used instead of individuals or small groups. Results from large groups will indicate a statistical probability of certain behaviour. For example, an experiment regarding a selection test might show that out of every 100 people reaching a score of X, about 75 will be successful in a certain occupation — but the identities of the successful and unsuccessful candidates in any group cannot be shown.

(c) As far as possible, people are studied in their *normal environment* and not in a laboratory or some other artificial situation which would make their behaviour untypical.

Psychology therefore does not give us infallible laws of behaviour, but instead suggests a series of principles, theories or tendencies which predict with a fair degree of accuracy how most people will behave in various situations, and can explain behaviour after it has occurred. In this and the following chapters the principles of psychology most relevant to industry and commerce will be considered.

Attention and perception

5. Sensation
People act on the basis of information received. The information coming from a person's environment reaches the individual through his or her *senses*, by messages called *sensations*. The following are the most important senses, nearly all of which need no explanation.

(a) Sight.
(b) Hearing.
(c) Smell.
(d) Taste.
(e) Skin (pressure, heat, cold, pain, etc.).
(f) Balance.
(g) Kinaesthesis (means of knowing the position and movement of limbs by messages received from muscles and tendons).

Therefore at any time a variety of information regarding the outside world is reaching a person's brain through his or her senses. The amount of information would be overwhelming and baffling unless some arrangement, called *attention*, was made to deal with the relevant and necessary part of it, discarding the rest.

6. Attention
The selection of certain sensations to be dealt with by the conscious mind may be either deliberate or involuntary.
(a) *Deliberate* — by an effort of will irrelevant, useless or distracting sensations are shut out. A student may in time develop the power of reading a textbook in a room where others are

watching television, or a worker may concentrate on a job disregarding background conversation. Certain sensations are only recognised if they are searched for deliberately, for example the ticking of a clock.

(b) *Involuntary* — a person attempting to concentrate on one thing may find that certain sensations relating to something else are forced on his or her attention by the subject matter of the information, or the form in which it is presented. The factors which govern involuntary attention are divided into two groups: subjective and objective.

7. Subjective and objective factors of attention

Subjective factors of attention are the elements in sensations which carry a personal message; for example, the sound of a long-awaited bus, or one's name mentioned in a conversation at the other side of a crowded room. Sensations which have a personal interest, or comply with current moods and needs, are likely to take precedence for our conscious attention over sensations which are impersonal, neutral or relevant to others rather than ourselves.

Objective factors of attention are those which lie outside the personality of the receiver; they are likely to have the same effect on everyone. They chiefly concern the form in which the sensation is presented rather than its subject matter. The objective factors are as follows.

(a) *Intensity* — the loudness, brightness or size of the sensation. Shouted words are more likely to receive attention than a whisper, vivid colours more than pastel shades, a stench more than a faint odour.

(b) *Change or movement* — constant variety in the shape, size or position of an object will cause it to be noticed. This factor applies particularly to the sense of sight.

(c) *Repetition* — something seen, heard, etc., over and over again is likely to receive conscious attention providing the repetition does not become monotonous and accepted as customary, like the lampposts along a road.

(d) *Systematic arrangement into patterns* — sensations presented in an orderly way, for example a notice set out with headings and sections, is more likely to receive attention than an untidy and confused arrangement. The completion of a pattern is also significant; for example, after a flash of lightning people usually listen to hear if a clap of thunder will follow, or a speaker may hold the attention of an audience by saying he or she will make five points and delaying exposition of the fifth until the end of the speech.

(e) *Novelty* — the unusual or unexpected event is always likely to receive more attention than the familiar. A person normally dressed quietly and conventionally will be noticed if he or she wears bright coloured bizarre clothes; a speaker, to obtain an audience's attention, may begin with an outrageous assertion which the speaker then knocks down.

8.   Conceptualisation

This means the linking together of items of information, objects, images, stimuli or events into a single mental category. The human brain receives so many messages that it needs a logical system for classifying items into groups that can be conveniently analysed. For example, apples, oranges, pineapples and bananas are all separate and unique entities, but the brain will combine them into the single concept of 'fruit'. Hence conceptualisation helps the individual arrange data, interrelate events and objects, identify similarities and differences between types of item, and compare and contrast elements of information received.

9.   Perception

Sensations are by themselves no more than colours, shapes, sounds, pains, pressures, etc. Something must be added to them before they have meaning and their source is identified. The mental function of giving significance to sensations is called *perception*; for example, one *perceives* black marks on white paper as words and sentences. The process of perception appears to follow the following principles.

(a) *The brain relates incoming sensations to its store of past experiences* and associates them with events or objects which in the past have provided the same or similar sensations.

(b) *A meaning is then perceived*; for example, a sound may be recognised as a train, another as a bus (perhaps mistakenly — it may be a lorry).

(c) *If the sensation does not appear to provide evidence,* confirmation may be sought by looking for other sensations to support the first. For example, if someone is not sure whether a sound represents a bus or not, they may look among the approaching traffic to see if a bus is there.

(d) *Perception may be made confidently and sometimes wrongly* on the basis of little sensory information. A slight change of facial expression is sometimes perceived as meaning approval, disapproval, interest, indifference, etc.

(e) *Perception may be influenced by suggestion.* It is difficult for one individual to perceive a sensation in a different way from a group or an influential person, because a certain perception is suggested to the individual concerned. Pre-conceptions can affect perception by suggestion; for example in a firm where industrial relations are poor, practically any action or statement by management may be perceived as hostile to the employees. Sometimes one sense may influence the perception of another sense; for example, a voice may seem to emerge from a ventriloquist's dummy.

(f) Perception is also influenced by a person's *motives* (*see* Chapter 2) and attitudes (*see* 7:**12**). Individuals tend to perceive sensations in ways which conform to their general outlooks, are welcome rather than unwelcome, and are familiar rather than unfamiliar.

10. The importance of perception

Since every individual is different, it is possible for one set of sensations to be perceived in different ways by different people, because they all interpret sensations through their own experiences, motives and attitudes. In the management of people, differences in perception can be the source of many difficulties and conflicts.

(a) *Communication* — a quite sincere and well-meaning communication from management to employees, or vice versa, may be perceived as a threat or a deprivation. Before the communication is made it may be necessary to reduce suspicion and allay fears so that the message may be correctly perceived (*see* Chapter 9).

(b) *Judgment of people* — the assessment of candidates for employment (*see* Chapter 5) or the appraisal of subordinates (*see* Chapter 18) is affected by the assessor's own preferences and prejudices. Interviewers tend to perceive candidates favourably whose backgrounds are similar to their own. Manager A, when appraising a subordinate who frequently offers suggestions for changing works procedures, may rate the subordinate as outstanding in initiative. Manager B might rate the same sort of person as uncooperative. It is much easier to gain agreement on the perception of a *ranking* of some quality (i.e. in what order individuals in a group should be placed for their possession of that quality — height, initiative, co-operation, etc.) than on the perception of the absolute degree to which one individual shows that quality. If several managers who knew a group of employees well were asked to rank them in order of dependability, quite close agreement would be obtained between the rank-orders, but if the managers were asked to say how dependable one person was, there would be considerable disagreement between them.

(c) *Training* — in manual tasks particularly, the object of a large part of training is to teach the trainee to perceive certain cues or signals in the process to which he must make an appropriate response (*see* 20:**5**). The training officer will not be successful without first identifying these 'perceptual cues' and devising exercises to facilitate their recognition.

(d) *Motivation* — people with the same need to satisfy may not perceive the same means of satisfaction (see Chapter 2). There may be different perceptions as to what motives are likely to be pre-eminent in a particular situation; management may expect employees to be motivated towards increased production by an incentive scheme, but find that the employees do not respond, as they put the unity of the group first (*see* Chapter 7).

(e) *Performance criteria* — it may be necessary to compare the actual performance of an employee with the standards of performance that the manager perceives to be reasonable. Unless performance can be objectively measured (for example, by quantity produced), differences in perception are almost bound to occur; managers will disagree as to which parts of a job are the most important and how quality of work can be judged, and the employees may well disagree with the managers.

Progress test 1

1. Why is it impossible to formulate scientific laws of human behaviour? **(2, 3)**

2. What are the subjective and objective factors of attention? **(7)**

3. What is the relationship between sensation and perception? **(9)**

4. In what ways can differences in perceptions cause difficulties for managers? **(10)**

2
Motivation in work

Needs and their satisfaction

The study of motivation — the reasons why people behave as they do — is of fundamental importance in the management of human resources.

1. Human needs

Psychologists make these basic assumptions when interpreting human behaviour.

(a) All human behaviour has a *cause*, which itself is the consequence of the combined effects of heredity and environment.
(b) At the root of human behaviour are needs, or wants or motives. Need is the term usually employed in this connection.
(c) Human behaviour is *goal-seeking*; people try to achieve objectives or goals which, when reached, will satisfy their needs. For example, food will satisfy the hunger need.

2. The hierarchy of needs

The American psychologist, A. H. Maslow, has divided human needs into the following classes.

(a) *Physiological or basic needs* — people must satisfy these needs just to keep alive. They include, for example, hunger, thirst and sleep. In the work environment, the fundamental purpose of a wage or salary is to provide the means of satisfying basic needs.
(b) *Security or safety needs* — these are concerned with self-protection, with the avoidance of harm and, to some extent, with provision for the future. Examples are the needs for shelter, warmth and self-defence. At work the wish for security of tenure,

the existence of restrictive practices, and many aspects of trade unionism show how employees try to satisfy needs of this kind.

(c) *Belonging or affection needs* — everyone, in various degrees, wishes to give and receive friendship. Companionship and association with others for recreational purposes are examples of these needs. Note that, for example, people may join with others partly to satisfy affection needs and partly for greater security.

(d) *Esteem or ego needs* — these include the needs to become independent, to receive the esteem of others, to dominate and to acquire possessions. As it is possible for needs of this kind to be satisfied through social activity, there is again overlapping between needs of groups (c) and (d). At work a position of authority, a company car, an office carpet or a special type of overall are means by which these needs are satisfied.

(e) *Self-actualisation needs* — this final group comprises the needs to make the fullest use of one's capabilities, to develop oneself and to be creative. In the working environment the majority of employees find few opportunities to satisfy needs in this class; skilled operatives, professional workers and managers are the most likely to be satisfied in this way.

Maslow has suggested that the classes of needs, in the order shown, form a hierarchy; people tend to satisfy their needs in a certain order of precedence. In general, when physiological and security needs have been satisfied, the higher needs (belonging, esteem and self-actualisation) become important, usually, according to Maslow, in the order of the hierarchy. For example, a manager who receives a substantial salary, and thus adequately satisfies his or her lower needs, regards status symbols like a well-furnished office as important, but a former manager who has been unemployed for a long time will eventually take any available job that brings a reasonable income, even though it is of low status.

3. Modifications to Maslow's theory
Maslow's theory is widely accepted, easy to understand and can be used to explain much, but not all, behaviour at work. Alderfer has proposed instead a modification of the theory, consisting of three levels of need.

(a) *Existence needs* — approximately equivalent to Maslow's physiological and security needs.

(b) *Relatedness needs* — including affection needs and that part of esteem needs which is concerned with personal relationships.
(c) *Growth needs* — including self-actualisation needs and that part of esteem needs which is concerned with individual effort.

The theory (often known as the ERG theory) agrees with Maslow in saying that as one level becomes satisfied the level above becomes important, but adds a further proposition that if one level is not sufficiently satisfied the level below becomes more important, e.g. a disappointment in promotion (growth needs) may produce a greater wish for social involvement (relatedness needs). Alderfer claims that his theory provides a more comprehensive explanation of behaviour than Maslow's.

4. Discussion of Maslow's work
Maslow's theory has been criticised on the following grounds.

(a) The theory asserts that people seek to achieve higher-level needs *after* lower level ones have been fulfilled. Yet some individuals feel strong desires to gratify higher-level needs *before* lower level needs have been fully satisfied. For instance, a poor person may yearn for status symbols even though his or her immediate physical and security requirements have not been properly met.
(b) Individuals might not rank the various types of need in the manner suggested. For some men and women, esteem needs are more important than needs for affection. Indeed, some of the needs in Maslow's hierarchy might not exist in certain people; and what is considered essential by one person might be trivial to someone else.

Note, moreover, that whether someone feels the need for something depends greatly on that person's perceptions, which themselves depend critically on the traditions, cultures and life-styles of the society in which he or she lives. Many desires are actually learned responses to environmental pressures with societal rather than physiological origins. For example, advertising can cause people to feel needs for things they never previously considered.

5.   Individual differences in need-satisfaction
People differ in the way they satisfy their needs in a variety of ways.

(a) *Cultural* — the manner in which for example hunger and sex needs are satisfied is surrounded by many customs and laws.

(b) *Perceptual* — in general, people perceive the world in terms of their least-satisfied needs; their perceptions tend to recognise goals which will help satisfy their needs (*see* 1:**9–10**). A starving person perceives an apple orchard as a source of food rather than an attractive feature of the countryside.

(c) *Individual* — people have different physical and intellectual capabilities and aptitudes; they also have different personalities. These are reflected in the various ways in which needs are satisfied; one person might achieve self-actualisation by an intellectual feat, another by sporting prowess.

6.   Conflict of needs
A person may wish to satisfy two needs simultaneously, but find that they are mutually exclusive; if one is satisfied, the other cannot be satisfied. For example, if the individual wishes to retain his or her job, duties may have to be carried out in a way disliked by the worker, or the boss may expect the individual to stay late frequently although this has adverse effects on the person's family life. A situation of this kind, where an individual is pulled in two ways at once, is called a *conflict of needs*. Until it is resolved, it may show itself in anxiety and irritability, or sometimes in what appears to be physical disorders like headaches or stomach complaints.

When an individual resolves such conflict, that is by accepting the situation into which he or she has been forced or finally making a choice between the needs he or she wishes to satisfy, the individual usually attempts to justify the decision made, e.g., by explaining to everyone the great benefits he or she will now gain and exaggerating the disadvantages of the choice that has been rejected.

At work, management should try to avoid putting employees into situations where conflict may occur; for instance, employees should not be promoted unless it is certain that they would welcome the promotion. A person promoted to take charge of a branch in a part of the country he or she dislikes would be torn between the wish to advance in the company and the wish to remain in a certain district. The resulting conflict might be difficult to resolve and its effects might not be beneficial to the company or the employee.

7. Achievement of goals

The assumptions regarding human behaviour set out in 1 may be shown in diagrammatic form as shown in Fig. 2.1.

The left-hand column shows the need-path-goal hypothesis in general terms. The other two columns show the ways in which actual needs might be satisfied.

The importance of *perception* (*see* 1:9–10) should be noted. Although people are in many cases motivated by the same needs, their perceptions of need-satisfying goals are different. A teetotaller, for example, would not perceive a public house as a means of satisfying thirst, and job-seekers do not all apply for the same job. Need-satisfaction is usually complex; a new job, if well chosen, can satisfy needs ranging over the whole of Maslow's hierarchy.

8. Frustration

A goal which is attempted may not always be reached; the individual may be *frustrated* when attempting to reach it. The *positive reaction* to frustration is to try to solve the problem, perhaps by finding a way round the obstacle that prevents the person from reaching the goal, perhaps by perceiving an alternative goal which will satisfy the need — though probably not to the same extent. The perception and achievement of an alternative goal is sometimes called *deprivation*, because the individual is deprived of the extra satisfaction he or she would have gained if the original goal had been obtainable.

Figure 2.1

Frustration may also produce various forms of *negative reactions* — exceptions to the general rule that all behaviour is purposeful and goal-seeking. A negative reaction may occur for various reasons.

(a) The goal being attempted seems unique and there appears to be no practicable alternative, e.g. there is no other public house for miles, and this one has just closed.

(b) There is a strong emotional attachment to the goal, e.g. the candidate has boasted to everyone of being certain to get the job applied for, and then hears that he or she has been turned down.

(c) The individual is by nature prone to react negatively.

Negative reactions can take several forms; the four found most often are as follows.

(a) *Aggression* — a physical or verbal attack on some person or object, e.g. abuse of the landlord of the public house.

(b) *Regression* — a reversion to childish behaviour, e.g. sulking or tears.

(c) *Resignation* — giving up, apathy, withdrawal, e.g. a person disappointed in promotion may come late, leave early and avoid making decisions.

(d) *Fixation* — persistence in useless behaviour, e.g. pushing on the public house door long after it is apparent that it is locked.

9. Frustration at work

Frustration may frequently occur among the employees of an organisation, for the following reasons.

(a) Their methods and speed of work may be closely controlled, and not what they themselves would choose.

(b) Their work may appear meaningless.

(c) Their grievances and problems may not be dealt with speedily or adequately by management.

(d) They may not be told, or cannot understand, the reasons for many management decisions which affect them.

When employees are frustrated at work they may react negatively, their behaviour taking the following forms:

(a) lateness, absence or eventually leaving the company;

(b) poor-quality work;

(c) unwillingness to take responsibility;

(d) quarrels with colleagues, disputes with management;

(e) accidents, damage to equipment and products.

10. Reducing frustration

Because frustration can have such serious consequences, every effort should be made to reduce it. A case may be made that the work situation is inherently frustrating because it implies that, for monetary payment, one person is putting him or herself under the instructions of another; however, the possibility of frustration at work can be reduced in the following ways.

(a) Designing jobs to give them greater meaning.

(b) Improving selection and training; a person will be more satisfied in jobs for which they are suitable and for which they have been trained.

(c) Recognising effort and merit, thus providing satisfaction of higher needs.

(d) Improving communications, consultation and disputes procedures so that potential causes of frustration may be identified and removed as far as possible.

11. Alienation

This is the feeling that work is not a relevant or important part of one's life; that one does not really belong to the work community. It is associated with feelings of discontent, isolation and futility. Alienated workers perceive themselves as powerless and dominated. Work becomes simply a means to achieve material ends. Great unhappiness can result from alienation; indeed, the mental or physical health of the employee can suffer. Alienation may result from lack of contact with other workers and/or with management, from authoritarian or paternalistic management styles, or simply through the boredom of routine work. Its consequences are numerous: poor quality output, absenteeism, resistance to change, industrial disputes, deteriorating inter-personal relationships, etc.

Expectancy theory

12. Vroom's expectancy theory

The motivational process may also be explained in another way. *Expectancy theory* states that effort to satisfy needs will depend on the person's perception that he or she can expect the effort to be followed by a certain outcome which will bring desirable rewards.

According to V. H. Vroom, an individual's behaviour is affected by:

(a) what the person wants to happen;
(b) his or her estimate of the probability of the thing happening;
(c) how strongly the person believes that the event will satisfy a need.

To illustrate this, suppose there are three employees who wish to obtain promotion in order to satisfy self-actualisation needs

(Maslow) or growth needs (Alderfer). The first employee perceives prominence in the firm's social club as the best route and spends much spare time there, confident that he or she will be voted into honorary office. The second employee perceives a professional qualification as the best way and works hard in the evenings to achieve one. The third also perceives the professional qualification as the best way, but does not make the effort to study because the person does not believe he or she would be able to pass the examinations; neither does the individual try to become an honorary officer of the social club because, unlike the first employee, he or she does not perceive this as a way of getting promotion.

Individuals normally base their predictions of what will happen in the future on what has occurred in the past. In consequence, new situations that workers have not previously experienced (e.g. job changes, new working conditions and environments) cause uncertainty and thus may reduce employee motivation, because the individuals involved have no prior knowledge of the likely consequences of altered circumstances.

13. Implications of Vroom's theory
The following implications emerge from Vroom's theory.

(a) Management should make clear to employees what exactly it expects from new working practices.
(b) Workers should be able to see a connection between their efforts and the rewards these efforts generate.
(c) Rewards should satisfy workers' needs.
(d) Complicated reward schemes (complex bonus schemes, for example) are unlikely to increase employees' effort because workers cannot relate harder work to higher wages.

14. Effort and performance: Porter and Lawler
The relationship between effort, reward and performance was further investigated by L. W. Porter and E. E. Lawler, who state that two factors determine the amount of effort put into a job.

(a) The extent to which the psychological and monetary rewards obtained from doing the job fulfil the worker's needs for:

    (*i*) security;
    (*ii*) esteem;
    (*iii*) independence;
    (*iv*) personal self-development.

(b) The worker's expectation that putting a great deal of effort into the job will lead to the achievement of satisfying rewards.

Thus, the more attractive an employee considers a particular reward, and the higher the probability that the exertion of effort will lead to that reward, then the more effort the individual will put into his or her work.

Work and need-satisfaction

15. Definition of work

Work may be defined as an activity which is directed by others as regards purpose, methods, materials, time and space. Its usual aim is to contribute towards the production of goods and services. In contrast to leisure, which is primarily concerned with the satisfaction of one's own needs, work is concerned with things that others require and are willing to pay for.

16. Satisfaction of needs at work

Although the above definition implies the opposite, it is still possible for needs to be satisfied at work to some degree.

(a) *The definition implies a passive acceptance of work* by an employee and does not indicate to what extent, if any, he or she will derive benefit from it. However, it must be assumed that since the great majority of people in western society are employees of some kind they must obtain some satisfaction of their needs from this arrangement. The normal contract of employment (*see* 14:**21**) states that in return for an employee's services given during a specified part of the employee's time, the employer will make a monetary payment and sometimes provide fringe benefits also (*see* 23:**13–19**). The employer is also expected by law to provide reasonable working conditions (*see* 23:**9–12**). Physiological and security needs may thus be satisfied.

(b) Some employers, particularly in the public sector, offer their employees a *steady wage or salary,* often with guaranteed increases according to length of service, generous fringe benefits and the prospect of almost complete security of tenure. Employees are expected to take the view that they have entered a family, and in return for the privileges and protection they receive are to fulfil the duties expected by the head of the family. This approach by an employer is usually termed 'paternalistic'; it emphasises above all the satisfaction of security needs.

(c) Another philosophy of employment is to attempt *to vary the employee's need-satisfaction* according to his or her merit and performance in the job. Additions to basic wage or salary are made according to management's assessment of these qualities, and employees who fail to reach certain standards of conduct or output are penalised by warnings, official reprimands, fines or dismissal. This approach, combined with particular attention to work study and specialisation of task, is usually known as scientific management, the name given to it by F. W. Taylor in 1910. Once more, it is concerned only with the satisfaction of physiological and security needs.

(d) More recently, influenced above all by Maslow's hierarchy of needs (*see* **2**), industrial psychologists have shown how work can be made more satisfying by giving greater attention to affection, ego and self-actualisation needs. The job is looked at not simply as a means of efficiently carrying out a specified function but as something which could be intrinsically satisfying to the worker. The rewards for work can go beyond pay or fringe benefits. This approach has also influenced thinking about leadership (*see* **8:1–10**), participation (*see* 8:**11–19**), management by objectives (*see* 18:**8–11**) and job design (*see* 4:**1**).

(e) Using Maslow's hierarchy, it can be seen that paternalism and scientific management can only satisfy physiological and security needs, except that under scientific management a high performance worker whose efforts were recognised by high pay might get some satisfaction of ego needs. The following table shows for each class of need the chief ways in which satisfaction may be obtained at work.

Needs	*Method of satisfaction at work*
Basic	Money, physical working conditions.
Security	Money, physical working conditions, pension and sick pay schemes, restrictive practices, trade union membership, company policy regarding security of tenure.
Affection	Companionship of fellow employees, group norms of production (*see* 7:8), trade union membership, company social activities.
Ego	Job title, possession of a certain skill or expertise, position of authority, status symbols — carpet in office, own parking space, etc., money as a sign of status.
Self-actualisation	A job that is satisfying for its own sake, self-regulation, the opportunity to be creative — to use all one's abilities and special talents, knowledge of results of one's work.

17. Herzberg's theory of motivational hygiene

The American psychologist Frederick Herzberg has propounded a theory of motivation at work which divides the factors of the work environment into two classes: motivators or satisfiers on the one hand; and hygiene factors or maintenance factors on the other.

Herzberg developed his theory by analysing the answers to two basic questions he and his collaborators put to engineers and accountants.

(a) What events at work have resulted in a marked increase in your job satisfaction?
(b) What events at work have resulted in a marked reduction in your job satisfaction?

The replies showed that, in general, the experiences which were regarded as exceptionally satisfying were not the opposite of those which were exceptionally dissatisfying. For example, someone might say that a job is disliked because of poor working conditions, but very rarely would that person say that a job is liked because of good working conditions.

From his analysis, Herzberg concluded that the elements in a job which produced *satisfaction* were:

(a) achievement;
(b) recognition;
(c) responsibility;
(d) promotion prospects;
(e) work itself.

He called these the 'motivators' or 'satisfiers'.

The elements whose absence or inadequacy in a job produced *dissatisfaction* were:

(a) pay;
(b) relations to others;
(c) type of supervision;
(d) company policy;
(e) physical working conditions;
(f) fringe benefits.

Herzberg called these hygiene factors (because, using the analogy of drains and refuse collection, they made the job environment fit to occupy), or maintenance factors (because they tended to maintain an employee in his or her job). He said that an employee might leave a firm because he or she disliked its working conditions or thought the pension scheme inadequate, but the employee would not be motivated to work harder or better if working conditions or the pension scheme were improved (provided they were already reasonably adequate).

On the other hand, the absence of achievement or responsibility, for example, would be unlikely to cause an employee to leave, but if these could be increased the employee would be more motivated at work. Herzberg recognised that individuals varied in the relative importance they attached to motivators or hygiene factors; some were very concerned to seek achievement, recognition, etc., in their jobs, while others were interested particularly in pay, personal relationships, etc.

18. Discussion of Herzberg's theory

When Herzberg's enquiries have been repeated using his methods, his findings have been confirmed to a large extent. However, when other methods have been used, for example questionnaires, different results have emerged. Very few enquiries appear to have been conducted with manual workers. Herzberg's method of investigation, which may be described as anecdotal self-report, is likely to produce answers of a certain type. People frequently describe good work experiences in terms which reflect credit on themselves — success, greater responsibility or recognition. Workers will always be tempted to attribute bad work experiences to things beyond their own control — uncongenial colleagues, an unpleasant boss or poor working conditions. Thus they will take the credit for the good experiences and blame others for the bad experiences.

The main application of the theory has been in the enlarging or enriching of the jobs of non-manual workers (*see* **20**). It would be possible to find theoretical justification for this in the hierarchy of needs without postulating a two-factor theory. Herzberg does, however, emphasise that improving fringe benefits or other conditions of work will not motivate employees; again the hierarchy of needs would explain this because working conditions are relevant to the lower needs (*see* **16 (e)**), which in modern industry and commerce are usually adequately satisfied.

19. Equity and control theories of motivation

The *Equity Theory* of motivation asserts that an employee's own assessment of whether he or she is being fairly treated is a major factor influencing motivation. Workers are assumed to compare their personal reward/effort situations with those of colleagues and to feel aggrieved if they believe they are *relatively* underrewarded. If returns are regarded as equal to those of other employees — proportionate to the effort expended by the individual — a state of 'distributive justice' is said to exist. Otherwise 'cognitive dissonance' occurs, whereby the individual perceives the reward/effort relationship as inconsistent and out of balance. Consequently, the worker feels uncomfortable and discontented, and his or her effort and motivation may diminish. Problems with Equity Theory include the subjectivity that employees typically apply to the assessment of their own and other workers' contributions to an organisation, the difficulty of accurately measuring inputs to and rewards from jobs, and the fact that group pressures can override equity considerations.

A development of this approach is the *Control Theory* of

motivation which suggests that workers compare their current job/task situations with desired ('referent') standards and are then motivated to behave in ways that will reduce discrepancies. Thus the theory suggests that motivation derives ultimately from how employees *perceive* the attractiveness of their work and the opportunities that exist for achieving improvements.

20. Job enlargement and job enrichment — definitions

A job is enlarged when the employee carries out a wider range of tasks of approximately the same level of difficulty and responsibility as before.

A job is enriched (or vertically enlarged) when the employee is given greater responsibilities and scope to make decisions, and is expected to use skills not used before. Both are examples of *job extension*.

Job extension

21. Effects of job enlargement and enrichment

Both are attempts to build opportunities into the employee's job for the satisfaction of ego and self-actualisation needs (*see* 2 (e)). A greater range of tasks or decisions will, it is thought, make the employee feel more important, give a sense of achievement and make more use of the person's abilities. The worker will therefore receive satisfaction from the job itself (intrinsic satisfaction) as well as money and fringe benefits (extrinsic satisfaction).

Many companies have introduced either job enlargement or job enrichment and increased the job satisfaction of their employees. In most cases it appears that non-manual workers (often managers) rather than manual workers are concerned. It is easier to extend the job of a non-manual worker, whose responsibilities and actions are very often not precisely described, than to change the job of a manual worker whose tasks may be highly specialised and precisely defined because they are part of a complex production process. There may be a conflict between specialisation and development of specific skills required for efficient operation of the process and the construction of a job sufficiently enlarged or enriched to give greater satisfaction to the employee. In order to make the job significant to the worker it may have to be extended so much that productivity is seriously affected. The result may be a compromise between efficiency and job satisfaction in which the worker, instead of doing one meaningless task, is now expected to do several meaningless tasks.

Extension of jobs may meet with trade union opposition because demarcation lines between skills are eroded. It will almost certainly necessitate increases in pay; wider or deeper responsibilities must be recognised by an increase in the monetary worth of the job, as measured by job evaluation (*see* Chapter 21). An employer might hesitate, therefore, before introducing job extension because the benefits to the employer would be somewhat uncertain, whereas the costs might be considerable.

22. Job rotation

Some of the difficulties the employee finds in job extension can be avoided if *job rotation* is used instead. Employees are trained in several minor skills and exchange jobs with each other at intervals. Greater satisfaction is obtained because the employee has a greater understanding of the work process through experiencing several jobs within it, and the increased versatility of the workers is useful to management when sickness absence is high. It is not necessary to redesign production methods, and rises in pay, if any, are small.

Not all individuals respond favourably to job enlargement, enrichment or rotation. Some do not appear to be motivated very strongly by the higher needs, or do not expect to satisfy them at work. Others resist any attempt to give them decision-making functions; they say that managers are there for that purpose.

Job satisfaction

23. The measurement of job satisfaction

Job satisfaction questionnaires are used to find out to what extent employees are satisfied at work. They may take several forms, some of which are described below.

(a) A series of questions covering different aspects of the job and working conditions. Against each question there are usually five possible answers; the employee is asked to indicate the answer he or she agrees with, e.g.,

I feel that my job is:
  (i) extremely boring;
  (ii) rather boring;
  (iii) fairly interesting;
  (iv) interesting;
  (v) extremely interesting.

It is possible to give a numerical score to this type of questionnaire by giving one point to answer (i), two points to answer (ii) and so on.

(b) A list of factors in job satisfaction which the employee is asked to rank in order of importance. This type of questionnaire is not directly linked to the conditions in which the employee works, or to the nature of the job, but its results may be used as a guide to future company policies, e.g.:

Consider the following factors in a job and put the figure 1 against the factor you think is the most important, 2 against the next most important and so on.

Security
Pleasant colleagues
Pay
Good boss
Efficient organisation
Fringe benefits (pension, sick pay, etc.)
Interesting job
Authority over others
Promotion prospects
Responsibility; freedom from close supervision
Pleasant working conditions

In such surveys pay is usually placed about fifth in rank order, behind such things as promotion prospects, responsibility, interesting job and security. When employees are asked instead to put the factors in the order in which the average person would place them, pay usually comes first (compare with the comment on Herzberg's questions, in 18).

(c) A free expression questionnaire, in which the employee is asked to write an essay on what is liked or disliked about the job and the employer. Sometimes the employee is interviewed and asked to reply orally instead of in writing.

24. The advantages of free expression questionnaires

(a) Employees can use their own words instead of those chosen by someone else.
(b) Employees can discuss topics which might not have occurred to the designer of a questionnaire of type **(a)** in **23**.

25. The disadvantages of free expression questionnaires

(a) Unless employees are quite sure that their remarks will be treated in complete confidence, they will not be frank.
(b) The analysis of a large number of completed questionnaires of this type is difficult and often subjective.
(c) Some employees find great difficulty in expressing themselves clearly, particularly in writing.

26. Comments on job satisfaction questionnaires

Although the results of questionnaires, especially of the type described in **23 (a)**, often correspond with actual behaviour, there must always be some doubt regarding their reliability. They are open to objection on the following grounds.

(a) The questions asked may be interpreted in various ways by different people.
(b) The form of the questions may call for a misleadingly definite answer, omitting conditions and qualifications.
(c) An individual's self-perception may lead to replies which are thought to be true, but which do not in fact represent that person's actual behaviour — a form of innocent self-deception.
(d) When responding to questions, people often give the answer they think will be most acceptable, or will show themselves to the best advantage.

The following conclusions regarding job satisfaction seem to be generally accepted, because they are confirmed by large numbers of questionnaires given to a wide variety of employees.

(a) Job satisfaction usually increases with age.

(b) Higher social class and status are related to greater satisfaction but, among those doing the same job, better education is associated with lower satisfaction.

(c) The less secure the job, the less the satisfaction.

(d) There is no firm relationship between job satisfaction and productivity (*see* 28).

27. Behavioural evidence of job satisfaction

A more reliable way of assessing job satisfaction should be through behaviour at work rather than replies to questions. Unfortunately, the interpretation of much working behaviour is highly subjective, e.g. whether the employees seem 'happy'. The most objective measures seem to be the extent of absence from work and the rate at which employees leave the company. It is logical to assume that if people are satisfied in their jobs they will tend to remain in that employment and have little avoidable time off. Of course, job satisfaction is not the only influence on leaving or absence; for example, suitable alternative jobs may not be easily found, or the employee may lose pay for absence.

When statistical correlations (*see Statistics* by W. M. Harper, in this series) are calculated between scores of job satisfaction and avoidable absence, a definite, though not high, negative correlation is found, i.e. the greater the satisfaction the less the absence. The correlation between job satisfaction and the rate of leaving is also negative, but lower.

28. The relationship between job satisfaction and productivity

Although common sense might lead us to expect that a worker who finds a job satisfying would produce more than one who is not satisfied, many investigations have shown that, generally speaking, productivity and job satisfaction are not related. It is possible for any degree of job satisfaction to be associated with any degree of productivity, i.e. a satisfied worker may have low productivity or a dissatisfied worker may have high productivity, or vice versa. Closer analysis may provide at least a partial explanation of this apparently irrational effect.

The expectation that a satisfied employee will work hard is basically a paternalistic attitude on the part of the employer. It implies either that the employee, grateful for being given a satisfying job, will show gratitude by complying with the employer's wishes, or that because the worker is satisfied he or she is inevitably enthusiastic, conscientious and persistent and therefore produces at a high rate. However, a more realistic assumption is that the employee may not have any feelings of gratitude towards the employer and that the worker's enthusiasm may either show itself in a form unwelcome to the employer, for example an overemphasis on accuracy, or may be tempered by other considerations, for example a wish to adhere to group norms of production (*see* 7:8). The interests of the employer and the employee do not always coincide.

From the employee's point of view, work brings many kinds of rewards: money, friendship, status and achievement among others. In some circumstances working harder may increase these rewards, in others it may reduce them. Status and achievement, which might be expected to favour higher productivity, are needs which have little appeal to some employees, or are needs which they do not expect to satisfy at work. It is quite possible for employees to work hard in jobs they dislike because they fear dismissal, are attracted by a high level of pay, or simply find hard work the best way of making the time go quickly. On the other hand, many employees, in particular professional and skilled workers and those who have a moral involvement in their jobs, combine high job satisfaction with high productivity, perhaps because they are motivated by loyalty towards a profession, craft or ideal rather than towards an employer. The relationship between productivity and the motivation of employees is extremely complex, and much research remains to be done.

29. Job satisfaction and costs
Although a manager who is successful in increasing the job satisfaction of employees may or may not benefit from an increase in their productivity, the manager will probably find that the costs of running his or her department are reduced. Labour turnover and absence (*see* **27** above and also Chapter 17) can be extremely expensive to the company and may well be reduced if jobs are made more satisfying. The manager should, however, be sure that the cost of redesigning jobs (which may include less efficiency in working methods and higher pay rates) does not outweigh the expected saving.

30. The concept of total rewards

An employee may receive extrinsic rewards (pay and fringe benefits) or intrinsic rewards (friendship, status and self-fulfilment) from work. The total reward is the employee's *perception* of the total value of all these. For example, individuals differ in the value they attach to achievement as compared with pay, or promotion opportunities as compared with security. For their part, employers recognise that some rewards compensate for the absence of others; a job which requires a strong moral involvement, e.g. social work, is often accompanied by a low level of pay, and a company which traditionally offers its employees almost complete security of tenure may have lower wage rates than a company with a 'hire and fire' reputation.

Employers and employees may have different perceptions of the rewards to be obtained from various jobs. Changes in working conditions regarded by the employer as improvements may not appear to be such to the employees, for example a new open-plan office instead of small separate offices. Sometimes the way in which the decision is reached and the change introduced is more significant than the change itself (*see* Chapters 8 and 9).

31. Absence from work

Absenteeism is a major source of cost and disruption in British companies. Currently, UK industry is losing 200 million working days each year to deliberate non-attendance. The average worker takes eleven days per year off, and on any given day up to 7 per cent of the workforce of a typical large British company will be absent — four times more than the rate among UK industry's leading international competitors. Losses attributable to absenteeism include reduced production, sick pay, the need for additional overtime to cover for absent workers, hassles resulting from having to reschedule projects, failure to meet deadlines, additional clerical and supervision expenses (telephone calls, administering statutory sick pay, etc.) and so on. Factors contributing to non-attendance include:

(a) *the nature of the job*: physical conditions, boredom, inconvenient working hours, stress, unsatisfactory interpersonal relations, poor supervision.

(b) *characteristics of the worker*: individual disinclination to work, age and sex (young people and females on average take more time off work than others), length of service (long-serving employees are less prone to absenteeism), a person's state of health, extent of family responsibilities, attitudes and perspectives concerning regular attendance, travelling difficulties.

(c) *motivating factors*: incentive schemes (bonuses, special awards for consistent attendance), availability of sick pay, extent of piece rate working (*see* 22:3–9), effectiveness of managerial exhortations aimed at persuading employees to turn up for work, the firm's readiness to apply disciplinary actions (formal warnings, deductions from pay, and other penalties short of dismissal, etc.).

Note how some of these factors interconnect, e.g. the fact that on average women take more time off than men but that women are also known to predominate in many tedious and low status occupations.

Measures for controlling absenteeism include job design (*see* 2:20) and job rotation intended to make work more interesting, increased employee participation in decision making (*see* 8:12–18), explicit consideration of job applicants' attitudes towards absenteeism during employee selection procedures, employee counselling, implementation of flexitime and job sharing arrangements, and careful record keeping to identify individuals and types of work with the highest absenteeism rates.

32. Grievances

Grievances can result from external circumstances — such as an employer imposing detrimental working conditions on employees, or from internal feelings of unhappiness and/or frustration. Externally created grievances may be remedied through altering the environmental circumstances that cause them: restoring a contractual right, improving conditions, increasing a benefit, or whatever. Grievances resulting from workers' hurt feelings might be best resolved through non-directive counselling (*see* 5:18).

Many grievances develop from misunderstandings rather than fundamental conflicts of interest, and a simple statement of facts may be all that is required to resolve the difficulty. Minor complaints can arise from breakdowns in communications, from petty jealousies, interpersonal rivalry, or from interdepartmental disputes. Such problems may usually be settled quite easily through increasing the flow of information within the organisation, by defining the authority and responsibilities of people and departments more carefully, and by generally promoting co-operation between sections.

No organisation is so well managed that its employees never need to complain, and even if a firm consciously seeks to be a good employer, staff may still *feel* that certain complaints are justified even if, objectively, they are not. Well-constructed grievance procedures enable firms to resolve complaints quickly, fairly, and without resort to industrial action on the part of employees. Formal procedures minimise the risk of inconsistent decisions: the employer is *seen* to be trying to be fair. And, of course, the absence of formal procedures will severely prejudice an employer's case if the grievance eventually results in legal proceedings.

A grievance 'procedure' is an established set of agreed rules for enabling management and the aggrieved employee to settle a complaint. Such rules restrain both sides from behaving irresponsibly, provided both are committed to their application and have confidence in their impartiality. Other advantages of formal procedures are as listed below.

(a) Both sides have a common understanding of how a grievance will be received and processed.

(b) The managers and union representatives who deal with grievances change periodically on account of promotions, resignations, retirements and staff transfers. However, the existence of written rules enables procedures to be applied consistently over time.

(c) Written rules clarify important matters such as who has authority to take decisions in settlement of disputes, the time-scale for registering a grievance, how an appeal should be lodged, etc.

(d) Formal records of grievance hearings avoid subsequent disputes about what was discussed and agreed in the hearing.

(e) Employees have the security of knowing that whenever major problems arise they can air their concerns to the highest levels of management within the firm.

There are, however, arguments in favour of *informal* procedures. Formalisation reduces flexibility, since precedents established through following formal rules must be adhered to in future cases. A mini legal system will build up around the policies, with its own protocol, norms, case law and rules of interpretation. It becomes impossible to 'turn a blind eye' to certain practices regardless of the circumstances in which they occur.

Progress test 2

1. What are the three basic assumptions underlying the study of motivation? **(1)**

2. What is the hierarchy of needs? **(2)**

3. Give an example of conflict of needs. **(6)**

4. Define frustration, and illustrate how it may produce either positive or negative reactions. **(8)**

5. Define the expectancy approach to motivation. **(12, 13)**

6. How may needs be satisfied at work? **(16, 17)**

7. Define, and give examples of, job enlargement and job enrichment. **(20, 21)**

8. How may job satisfaction be measured, and what is its relationship with **(a)** productivity and **(b)** costs? **(23–25, 28–30)**

9. What are the major sources of employee grievances? **(32)**

10. List the main factors that cause employers to be absent from work. **(31)**

3
Learning

Introduction

1. Definition

Learning is a relatively permanent change in the repertoire of behaviour occurring as a result of experience.

This definition implies that learning can only be said to occur when a person shows different behaviour, for example when he or she can prove the knowledge of new facts or do something the individual was not able to do before. Changes in behaviour due solely to ageing or injury would not be examples of learning. If, however, an injured person had found ways of adapting to a disability, this new behaviour would then have been learned.

Experiments with animals

2. Experiments in animal learning

Our knowledge of the psychology of learning is drawn partly from experiments with animals and humans, and partly from general observations of the human learning process. Experiments with animals, which have made a great contribution to psychological knowledge, have the following *advantages*.

(a) *Close control* — extraneous influences can be avoided, and the environment of the animals can be precisely supervised from birth. Even their heredity can be controlled. Thus any change in behaviour is due solely to the experimental situation and not to any other factors.

(b) *Large numbers* — laboratory animals can be readily obtained so that results can be seen not from a few but from many subjects. The reliability of experiments is therefore increased.

(c) *Freedom of action* — experiments with animals may be repeated many times or changes made in their environment at the wish of the experimenter, who is not concerned about the psychological or social after-effects on the animals and does not have to obtain their consent.

(d) *No communication* — the animal (presumably) is unable to deduce from the experimenter's words, facial expression, gestures or tone of voice what particular action is expected or desired. Any change in behaviour must therefore be due to the conditions the experimenter has contrived and not to his or her personal influence.

The *disadvantages* of animal experiments are as follows.

(a) *Limited motivation* — the motivation of animals is (very probably) limited in comparison with humans. We assume, for instance, that animals have no conception of ego and achievement needs. When humans learn, the higher needs are frequently very potent.

(b) *No verbal communication* — much human learning occurs through verbal communication. It is impossible to simulate this in animal experiments because animals cannot work from spoken or written instructions (apart from the monosyllabic words of command which a dog obeys), nor can they express their difficulties.

(c) *Lack of insight* — much human learning requires insight, the ability to see the connection between events or objects and from them mentally construct a significant pattern. As insight is probably possessed by the higher mammals only, e.g. chimpanzees, the value of experiments with most animals is limited to a certain extent.

(d) *Limited range of rewards* — humans respond to a variety of non-material rewards, like praise or the sense of achievement, when they are learning. Rewards of this kind cannot be introduced into animal experiments.

Using the results of animal experiments, and making due allowance for the differences between humans and animals, a great deal has been learned about the principles of human learning.

Conditioning

3. Important terms in learning

In studying the psychology of learning it is necessary to understand the meanings of four important terms — drive, stimulus, response and reinforcement. In the following definitions the word organism will be used to denote either a human being or an animal.

(a) *Drive* — the necessary condition of arousal or readiness for action or behaviour to begin. It is a condition in which the organism wishes to satisfy a need.

(b) *Stimulus* — the cue or signal which initiates a response. It is usually conveyed by sight, hearing, smell or touch. For example, the ringing of the telephone is the stimulus to pick it up, or the change of colour of the material is the stimulus to alter the application of paint.

(c) *Response* — the behaviour which is the result of stimulation (even though it may not be possible to identify the stimulus). Often a particular response becomes associated with a particular stimulus so that one almost automatically follows the other, for example changing gear when approaching a corner. The object of much industrial training is to establish these associations.

(d) *Reinforcement* — any event or object which strengthens a response, either by causing it to continue or increase, by providing the organism with some kind of reward. A dog after performing a trick may be rewarded either with food or with a pat and a friendly word. A learner-driver when he or she changes gear smoothly may be rewarded with the instructor's approval.

4. Classical conditioning

Experiments with animals have shown two important learning processes: classical conditioning and operant (or instrumental) conditioning.

Classical conditioning is associated above all with the Russian psychologist Pavlov. A typical experiment in this field would proceed as follows.

(a) *First stage* — a dog which is hungry (drive) is shown some food (stimulus). Its mouth waters (response). Eventually it is allowed to eat the food (reinforcement).

(b) *Second stage* — as before, but when the food is shown a bell is also rung.

(c) *Third stage* — the food is not shown, only the bell being rung. The dog's mouth waters at the sound of the bell.

The dog has now been *conditioned* to respond to a new stimulus. Since this response (watering of the mouth) is a reflex action, i.e. not consciously controlled, it is called a *conditioned reflex*.

By elaboration of this procedure Pavlov was able to show that dogs were colour-blind and that they could distinguish between a circle and an ellipse.

It is possible that certain superstitions and fears in humans may be due to a classical conditioning process. For example, an American psychologist was able to produce in his infant son terror of a teddy bear by making a loud noise whenever the child was shown the bear. Later he deconditioned his son by associating the bear with a favourite fruit jelly. Although classical conditioning may contribute to the development of certain personality traits, it is of only minor importance in learning within commerce or industry.

5. Operant (or instrumental) conditioning

This process, which is much more relevant to human learning, is associated with the American psychologist B. F. Skinner. A typical experiment would proceed as follows.

(a) A special cage is constructed which contains a lever on one side and a food receptacle on the other. Whenever the lever is depressed a piece of food is released from a container into the receptacle.

(b) An animal (very often a pigeon) which is hungry (drive) is placed in the cage. Eventually, during the course of random behaviour, it touches the lever with some part of its body and depresses it. This releases the food, which the pigeon eats. After some accidental repetitions of this sequence, the pigeon learns the connection between the lever and the food. The sight of the lever (stimulus) leads to the response of pressing it. The food is then eaten (reinforcement). This is an example of learning, because through experience the pigeon now behaves in a new way.

(c) Once behaviour is established in this way, the occasional reinforcement gets better results than the reinforcement of every response (compare people who are told continually while they are learning that they are doing very well).

(d) Behaviour can be *shaped* by operant conditioning, that is, gradually made more precise and less general. For example, pigeons have been trained to play table-tennis with each other, to play simple tunes on a toy piano, and even to reject misshapen tablets in a pharmaceutical factory by pressing levers with their beaks as the tablets go past on a moving belt.

Operant conditioning is *different* from classical conditioning in the following respects.

(a) The animal is not passive but active (hence operant).

(b) Its behaviour is *instrumental* in obtaining a reward or reinforcement; in classical conditioning the reward is not important.

(c) It learns new behaviour instead of providing an existing response to a new stimulus.

(d) Its behaviour is consciously controlled, not a reflex action.

There are, of course, a number of criticisms of operant conditioning theory, especially the assumption that probable human behaviour can be inferred from observing the behaviour of non-human animals. Experiments on animals may reveal much about the psychology of cats, dogs, rats and pigeons, but not be relevant to the psychology of human beings. Animals possess motivations which are possibly quite different from those of humans, and mute animals cannot be asked *why* they chose to act in a particular way. Also, the operant conditioning model says little about how insight and understanding develop, about how people 'learn how to learn', or about the best means for transmitting basic intellectual concepts of space, time, logic or fundamental philosophy. Moreover, it ignores the issue of *who* should devise training courses and which topics should be covered in a course.

Animal and human learning

6. The application of animal experiments to human learning
Classical conditioning is not appropriate to learning in commerce and industry since it does not deal with consciously determined responses. Operant conditioning has had one very specific human application, programmed learning (*see* 20:**11**), but it has been valuable above all in emphasising the patterns which must be followed if any human learning is to be successful, though it must be borne in mind that operant conditioning with animals as subjects is a form of trial-and-error learning, whereas most human learning occurs by copying and by receiving explanations in words or diagrams. Taking training in a manual skill as an example:

(a) the trainee must be motivated (cf. drive) to complete the course and must see some benefit from it, for example an increase in pay, a different job title, or the satisfaction of possessing a skill that few have.

(b) Individual motivation must be maintained during training by various methods:

- (*i*) intermediate goal-setting — dividing the whole task into self-contained units or elements, each with a given standard of performance the trainee tries to achieve;
- (*ii*) competition — though it should not be carried too far, competition between trainees is frequently motivating;
- (*iii*) indicating relevance — the purpose of any theoretical knowledge or exercises that are given should be explained;
- (*iv*) factors of attention — the subjective and objective factors of attention (*see* 1:**7**) are relevant in maintaining motivation.

(c) In designing the programme, the stimulus and response must be made very clear. Recognition of the appropriate stimulus among many incoming sensations, or the appropriate response to a particular stimulus, can be very difficult for a trainee to learn unless the training programme is carefully designed.

(d) At frequent intervals during the training programme the trainee's responses should be reinforced, not of course by pieces of food but by much less tangible rewards.

(*i*) Knowledge of results is an extremely powerful reinforcement for humans. A trainee should very frequently receive reports of the progress he or she is making, either from the instructor of by feedback of a score against a target. The Cambridge psychologist, F. C. Bartlett, said: 'That practice makes perfect is not true. But it is true to say that it is practice, the results of which are known, which makes perfect.'

(*ii*) Praise by the instructor is strongly reinforcing. Strong criticism or penalties for incorrect responses should be avoided; they tend to emphasise wrong methods unduly, encourage unadventurous behaviour and may cause the trainee to dislike the instructor and the task.

The principles of operant conditioning, therefore, indicate how the best results can be obtained from training in industry and commerce. Other important factors in human learning, not derived from animal experiments, are described in the next paragraph.

7. Other factors in human learning

The principles described below are generalisations and tendencies rather than scientific laws; their truth varies according to the qualities of the learner and to the type of subject-matter which is being learned.

(a) *Whole* v. *part learning* — a task to be learned is usually taught in parts if it involves difficult perceptions or unusual stimulus-response associations. Motivation is stronger when the whole, rather than parts, is taught, particularly when the learners have relatively high intelligence. Whole methods are also preferable where the task loses much of its meaning unless it is dealt with as a complete unit. The teacher must therefore decide which method to follow by weighing difficulty against motivation. If a task is learned in parts (A, B, C, etc.), the following procedure has been found to give the best results:

Learn A, then practise A.
Learn B, then practise A + B.
Learn C, then practise A + B + C, etc.

In this way the early parts are not forgotten when the later parts are learned, and the task has more meaning as it is gradually built up.

(b) *Distribution of practice* — continuous learning should be avoided; either rest periods should be given or practical training alternated with theoretical training. In general, training sessions should be shorter at the beginning of a training programme and longer towards the end. Another generalisation is that complex or difficult material requires shorter sessions than straightforward and simple material.

(c) *The learning plateau* — graphs showing the relationship between performance and training time are called *learning curves*. Figures 3.1 and 3.2 show learning curves for easy and difficult tasks respectively. The curves can, of course, be interpreted in terms of the learner's ability or motivation. Figure 3.3 shows that during weeks 2 and 3 the learner has apparently been at a standstill; from week four onward he or she again makes progress. The horizontal part of the curve (in weeks 2 and 3) is called the *learning plateau*; it can be found in many learning situations where the learner appears to mark time for a period after the programme has been started. The learning plateau has been explained as follows.

Figure 3.1   *Learning curve — easy task*

Figure 3.2 *Learning curve — difficult task*

Figure 3.3 *Learning curve showing plateau*

(*i*) The trainee is temporarily discouraged by the increasing difficulty of the task; he or she has lost motivation.

(*ii*) The trainee has acquired some incorrect responses during the first part of the learning programme which he or she must lose if further progress is to be made.

(*iii*) The trainee wishes to look back over the material learned so far and discover its significance.

(*iv*) In the case of manual training, the task may include some difficult perceptions or stimulus-response associations. Up to a point the trainee can make progress simply by copying, but beyond this point, he or she must understand and mentally organise these difficulties. The individual must see the significance of the various cues and responses and realise how one movement is co-ordinated with another. When this level of understanding has been attained, then he or she is able to make progress once more.

The learning plateau can be shortened or removed altogether if the material to be learned is carefully analysed and a method devised which anticipates the learner's difficulties instead of leaving the individual to solve them. Skills analysis (*see* 20:5) is an example of this approach).

8. Other theories of learning

Not everything is known about learning, and the operant conditioning (behaviourist) model previously outlined is just one of several approaches to the subject. According to operant conditioning, learning is a *responsive* process with learners taking no part in deciding what should be learned or the methods of training to be applied. The usefulness of this model is contested by the *action learning* school, which regards learning as an essentially participative process that actively connects individuals to their environments. Learning is regarded as a *manifestation* of general intellectual development that need not depend on stimulus-response factors. For example, people learn about time, space and logic through means not at all connected with operant conditioning.

Advocates of action learning assert that learning occurs as people adjust their attitudes and perceptions in consequence of their attempts to relate to the outside world. The mind is said to perform a function similar to that of the digestive system: constantly assimilating, interpreting and accommodating new material.

Another approach to learning is the *social learning* model, which assumes that the individual possesses an intellect which from the very first day of life attempts to understand events and surroundings. The social learning approach has the following implications.

(a) Much human learning results from the observation of other people. At work, individuals learn to behave, feel and perceive the world in the same way as other employees occupying similar work roles and positions.
(b) Failure of trainees to learn typically results from mismanagement of the learning process rather than from trainees' personal inadequacies.
(c) Individuals interact with, and hence learn from, social as well as material environments.

The *cognitive* model of learning is a further alternative to operant conditioning. 'Cognition' is the mental process that governs the acquisition of knowledge. It involves intuition, perception, imagination and reasoning, and concerns how people acquire ideas and how perceptions are organised. Accordingly, the cognitive model regards learning as the process whereby individuals come to make sense of their experiences, which they constantly re-evaluate in order to understand better the environments in which they function. This has the following implications.

(a) For learning to occur, learners need to be continually and actively involved with learning materials, which they should perceive as valuable and directly relevant to their training requirements.
(b) Since cognitions derive from complex interactions of thoughts, emotions, observations and experiences, the learning process cannot be dismembered into simple stimulus-response components as suggested by the behaviourists.

Transfer of learning

9.   Transfer of learning

If someone learns task A and then task B, which is somewhat similar, to what extent will his or her learning of task B be affected? If it is made easier, then it is said that there is *positive transfer of learning*; if it is made more difficult there is *negative transfer*. There are two theories regarding transfer of learning — *identical elements* and *transfer through principles*.

(a) *Identical elements* — this theory states that if parts of task A are the same as parts of task B there will be positive transfer of learning for those parts of task B. For example, two office jobs may be different from each other except that they both include telephoning and alphabetical filing. A clerk who has been transferred from the first job to train for the second job will have an advantage over someone who has been transferred from a completely different job, because he or she will benefit from a carry-over of the learned skills in telephoning and filing.

Unfortunately this theory, although apparently attractive, has difficulties in practice. The elements may not in fact be as identical as they appear at first sight. There are, for example, differences between telephoning to collect debts and to give advice, and between alphabetical filing by company name and by name of town. The clerk may therefore not learn the job as quickly as was hoped, possibly even more slowly than someone whose previous job contained no identical elements. Quite possibly, perception is again important; an operation which outwardly looks the same within two jobs may be perceived differently by the worker because it occurs in different contexts.

(b) *Transfer through principles* — according to this theory, transfer of learning is facilitated not because identical elements are present but because the learner applies to the new task general principles derived from experience in the previous task. Thus a clerk is likely to learn a different clerical job more easily than, for example, a manual worker because he or she can bring to the new job experience of organising documents in an orderly manner.

There is some common ground between the two theories, especially at the point where an element becomes a principle. The second theory, however, encourages an approach to industrial training which is more in accordance with other trends in industrial psychology. It suggests that instead of a rigid training programme run authoritatively, training methods which enable the employee to understand the purpose of the task and its context will help the trainee to adapt in the future to new jobs more easily. The principles discussed in 2:28 also suggest that such methods will increase the employee's motivation during training and subsequently.

Negative transfer, that is increased difficulty in learning a new task because of knowledge of a previous task, is frequently found. Drivers often report difficulty when first driving a car with an automatic gearbox; quite possibly a novice driver would have much less trouble with it. A typist who has learned to type using two fingers finds a course in touch-typing more difficult than someone who has never used a typewriter before. On the other hand, a touch-typist who is used to copying from documents has little difficulty in learning to type from a dictating machine.

The general rule seems to be that negative transfer between tasks is particularly probable where the same stimulus occurring in both tasks is followed by a different response in each case, e.g. for the same driving conditions one action is required for a manual gearbox, another action for an automatic. Where the stimuli are different, but the responses are the same, there will probably be some degree of positive transfer, e.g. a driver who has learned to stop suddenly to avoid a pedestrian will just as easily be able to stop when confronted by a red light.

10. The importance of transfer of learning

The possibility of negative transfer makes it very important for new employees to be taught correct methods of work from the very beginning, rather than be allowed to pick up incorrect methods which they might find difficult to lose.

Positive or negative transfer may occur when an employee moves to another job, depending on the similarities and differences between the two jobs. Transfer may also be significant when an employee leaves a training environment and begins productive work. The ex-trainee often finds adjustment very difficult, in consequence of having been taught methods which are different from those which other workers are using, or the equipment the person has been trained on may not be similar. The social atmosphere and working conditions in a training school do not usually resemble those in a productive workshop or office, again giving the trainee problems of adjustment. For this reason on-the-job training is sometimes held to be preferable to off-the-job (*see* Chapter 19), but the difficulties can be reduced by continually reviewing training methods and equipment, emphasising principles as well as methods, and introducing the trainee gradually to the training environment instead of giving that person the sudden plunge.

Progress test 3

1. What are the advantages and disadvantages of using experiments with animals as a guide to human behaviour? **(2)**

2. Define and show the connection between drive, stimulus, response and reinforcement. **(3)**

3. What are the differences between classical and operant conditioning? **(4, 5)**

4. Describe how the results of experiments in animal learning can be applied to human learning. **(6)**

5. What is the learning plateau? **(7)**

6. Define and give an example of transfer of learning. **(9, 10)**

4

Individual differences

Introduction

1. Fitting the person to the job

In Chapter 1 reference was made to the importance of achieving a good fit between worker and job; one of the aims of human resources management is to see that employees are working in jobs which are suitable for them and that their jobs are designed with due regard to the abilities and limitations of the employee. The design of jobs is dealt with elsewhere in this book under the following headings.

> Physical conditions of work — Chapter 6
> Satisfaction of human needs — Chapter 2
> Job analysis and job specifications — Chapter 13

The methods by which employers try to make the best use of their employees and satisfy their needs are covered under the following headings.

> Recruitment and selection — Chapter 14
> Transfer and promotion — Chapter 15
> Development — Chapters 18–20
> Pay — Chapters 18 and 22

A manager must have some understanding of the important differences that exist between individual employees. Managers must know how these differences can be identified, to what extent they can be measured, and how they can be related to job performance.

2. Heredity and environment

In the preceding chapters the psychological principles of

perception, motivation and learning have been discussed on the assumption that they have universal application and that everyone's behaviour is influenced by them. However, although in one sense people are alike in following the same psychological rules, they are different in the way they put these rules into practice. These variations in behaviour are due to differences between individuals, which in turn derive from differences in heredity and environment. Since there are countless possible combinations of these two factors, the differences between individuals are infinite in number and degree — a fact which makes life interesting, though sometimes difficult, and presents the manager with the opportunity to use the differences in a productive way. When they are thoughtfully used they can help to increase productivity and job satisfaction; badly used, or ignored, they can reduce efficiency and bring about unhappy relationships at work.

It is usual to deal with individual differences under three headings — physique, intelligence and personality.

Physique

3. Physique
This can be defined as the attributes of the body; its size and shape, its speed and strength of movement, the efficiency of its senses. Physical qualities are basically determined by heredity, though they can be developed or suppressed by upbringing or training. For example, there are inherited tendencies to be short or tall, fast or slow, but a poor diet will cause a person to be shorter than otherwise might have been the case, and appropriate training will enable an athlete to run longer and faster than before.

It is easy to measure most physical characteristics objectively, i.e. measurements of height, weight, eyesight, reaction speed, etc., can be quickly and simply made, independent observers producing identical results. Under modern conditions physical differences are not very important in placing individuals in appropriate jobs. The advance of technology has greatly reduced the number of jobs in which great physical endurance or strength is required, and instrumentation often decreases the need to rely on the senses of touch, hearing, etc.

Eyesight is the most important physical factor in the employment field; in some manual jobs it is necessary for employees to have above-average eyesight or perfect colour vision. In other jobs, co-ordination of limb movements or speed of reaction may be important. Tests are available to measure these qualities.

A small number of candidates for jobs have disabilities which exclude them from certain occupations or compel them to work only in sheltered conditions. The Disabled Persons (Employment) Acts 1944 and 1958 place obligations on employers in this respect (*see* 14:20)

Ideally, an employer should arrange for every candidate to have a medical examination before an offer of a job is made so that no one is asked to do work for which they are physically unsuited. In practice, medical examinations are given only in a minority of cases because employers assume that physical unfitness for work is so rare that the expense of examining all candidates is not justified. This matter is discussed later in 14:19.

Intelligence

4.   Definition

Intelligence is the capacity to make effective use of the intellect, which is the sum total of the mental functions of understanding, thinking, learning, observing, problem-solving and perceptual relationships. It is sometimes called mental ability.

The structure of intelligence is still the subject of intense controversy among psychologists. It is not necessary to recount the various theories that have been put forward; in simple terms, most British psychologists believe that there is a general factor of intelligence which enters into all functioning of the intellect and influences the performance of all tasks. Subordinate to general intelligence are a number of specific mental abilities which enter into the performance of some tasks but not others, e.g. verbal fluency, spatial ability, mechanical aptitude, numerical ability.

5.   Intelligence tests

If they are to be useful, intelligence tests must be *reliable* and *valid*.

(a) *Reliable* means that the test gives consistent results when repeated.

(b) *Valid* means that the test measures what it claims to measure, i.e. intelligence and not general knowledge.

Most intelligence tests used in commerce and industry are group written tests, i.e. they may be given, if necessary, to several candidates simultaneously, and consist of a number of printed questions to which the candidates must give a written reply. The test is then scored with the use of a key.

Publishers of tests usually restrict their sale to people who have been trained in their use. They must be given in precisely the manner described in the test manual, and the results interpreted by a qualified person. Critics of this practice allege, however, that in so doing publishers and psychologists conceal the foundations upon which tests are constructed and the validity of their assumptions, and thus exclude all possibilities for external scrutiny, criticism and academic debate. And people who take such tests but are then not happy with the scores they are awarded cannot challenge the marking criteria and propriety of the test.

6. Types of questions

Some intelligence tests contain questions of only one kind, e.g. verbal, numerical or spatial (i.e. diagrammatic) questions. Most tests used in industry contain a mixture of all three types, the candidate being asked questions along the following lines.

(a) Identify a word or phrase which has the same or opposite meaning as the one given.
(b) Solve anagrams or decode words.
(c) Perform addition, subtraction, multiplication and division.
(d) Identify one or more shapes which match or complete others.
(e) Write down a number in a series.
(f) Solve a problem in logic.

Intelligence tests have a time limit (usually between 20 and 60 minutes), and very few candidates indeed complete a test within the limit.

7. Intelligence quotient

The early work on intelligence testing conducted in the first half of this century was done with children, and it was found convenient to introduce the concept of *mental age*. If a child was able to accomplish tasks which were considered appropriate to a child of average intelligence aged x, he or she was said to have a mental age of x which could, of course be higher or lower than the child's chronological age, or the same. An easy measure of intelligence was then possible by expressing a mathematical relationship between mental age and chronological age, as follows:

$$\frac{\text{Mental age}}{\text{Chronological age}} \times 100$$

This formula is known as the *intelligence quotient*, usually abbreviated to IQ. A person of average intelligence will obviously have intelligence quotient of 100.

It is found that the mental age shown by intelligence test scores does not increase beyond a certain point; for some people the maximum mental age is as low as 13, for others as high as 20. Therefore, in order to avoid an apparent steady decrease in intelligence with age, chronological age in the IQ formula never exceeds 15. Although mental age may not increase, adults may perform many tasks better as they get older because they have learned from experience.

To compute intelligence quotients for adults, testers give a series of problems to a large number of people and compute the average score which then represents average intelligence, or IQ = 100. People scoring above or below level 100 in the tests are regarded respectively as above or below average intelligence.

Intelligence testing is a highly specialised skill for which extensive training is necessary. And trained psychologists themselves are the first to cast doubt on the usefulness of attempts to measure IQ. The questions asked need to be culturally neutral, independent of general knowledge and past training (otherwise people could learn to become intelligent), while answers given should not depend on environmental factors or be related to the circumstances of the test. In reality, however, results are often sensitive to how people feel at the time the test is attempted — whether they are tired, nervous, have the flu, or whatever; and quite often candidates do not take the exercise seriously. Intelligence tests should give consistent results when they are repeated and outcomes compared with other indicators of ability and records of actual performance.

Success in an intelligence test does not guarantee that a candidate will perform well in a job. The demands of a particular type of work could be much greater or less than the level of intelligence required by an IQ test. Also candidates who are told they scored highly might wrongly assume that they possess exceptional ability for their work.

Personality

8. Definition
Personality may be defined as the sum total of the various qualities that are shown in behaviour. Although this definition taken literally includes intelligence and physique, the term personality is usually taken to include above all emotions, motivation, interests and social qualities. It is incorrect to use the word personality as a synonym for charm or dominance; everyone has a personality, just as everyone has weight, height and intelligence.

9. Personality judgments
We assess the personality of someone we know well by recalling their behaviour in different circumstances, usually describing it in terms of traits, e.g. they are judged to be sociable, enterprising, tolerant, etc. As an individual passes through adolescence into adulthood, the personality becomes more consistent in the sense that behaviour in various circumstances becomes more predictable.

It is dangerous, however, to describe personality in terms of traits because they are affected so much by the situation at the time, as well as by personality. A person may be dominant when dealing with subordinates but submissive when speaking to his or her boss. Co-operation and honesty are other traits which are often highly dependent on the situation at the time.

10. Self-report personality tests
Most personality tests are written questionnaires of the self-report type, asking subjects for their views about their behaviour in various hypothetical situations or their opinions about other people. Although tests of this kind are used as one of

the tools of personnel selection by a few consultants and large companies, the general opinion in this country is that personality questionnaires are unlikely to be useful and reliable in industry, for various reasons.

(a) Self-report is inherently unreliable when people answering the questions have a strong reason for presenting themselves in the best light. The prospective employer can never be sure which answers are genuine and which have been faked.
(b) Even when the candidate tries to answer the questions sincerely, a misleading impression might be given because the person's self-image and self-perceived personality may not correspond with his or her personality as seen by others.
(c) Experience has shown that personality questionnaires are not reliable predictors of success in a given job and that the scores are unstable — when a test is repeated with the same candidates, different scores are obtained.

11. Other tests of personality

These seek to identify individual traits such as introversion, extroversion, personal assertiveness, or ability to cope with stress and/or expected future patterns of behaviour (management style, potential for leadership, etc.). Personality covers very many aspects of individual identity — emotions, motivations, needs, interests, attitudes, social relationships, many of which are environmentally or culturally determined. A personality test tries to discover whether the candidate really wants to do certain things, rather than simply whether he or she is technically capable of doing them. Interpretation of results is of course highly subjective. Specific problems are that:

(a) candidates, knowing their personalities are being examined, will attempt to present themselves in ways that create favourable impressions;
(b) individual attitudes and behaviour can change drastically over time and according to circumstances;
(c) assessments relate to observed behaviour and expressed opinions at a particular moment. These might be untypical, so average behaviour is largely ignored;

(d) because of the subjectivity in interpreting results, candidates might be given very different personality descriptions by differing assessors.

Techniques for personality testing include **(a)** projective tests, where candidates supposedly project their personalities by describing what particular shapes or objects (ink blots, etc.) mean to them; **(b)** assessment of candidates' contributions to leaderless group discussion; and **(c)** self-analysis sessions where candidates state their own interpretations of their personal behaviour and motivation. All these are prone to the problem that subjects can (and do) behave abnormally when being observed, and they all rest on subjective, intuitive interpretations of candidates' performances.

12. Physical indications

Many people when selecting employees are influenced by intuitive first impressions, based perhaps on an interpretation of body-build, manner and speech and affected by prejudices about dress and hair style and by the mood of the moment. Some claim to be able to judge a person as soon as he or she enters a room. Occasionally, such judgments have turned out to be surprisingly accurate; usually they are not. In some jobs the first impression a person makes is very important, e.g. sales representative, but in most jobs it is irrelevant. In any case, training can often greatly improve the first impression a person makes.

13. Situational tests of personality

In tests of this type, the personality of the candidate is not judged indirectly from answers to questions or interpretation of appearance but more directly from the observation of actual behaviour under controlled conditions.

The armed forces were the pioneers of situational testing during the 1939–45 war. Candidates for commissions were formed into groups and asked to cross ditches with apparently inadequate means, or to transport heavy objects across obstacles. Sometimes a leader was appointed for the group, whose abilities as an organiser and leader would then be assessed. Sometimes no leader would be appointed, and the observers would watch to see if any natural leader or leaders emerged.

This method is still used in officer selection, and in modified form has been taken up by the Civil Service and by some industrial and commercial employers. In its civilian applications, the candidates are still dealt with as a group (usually from five to ten in number), but their task is intellectual rather than practical. They are asked to discuss a topic of current interest for about 30 to 45 minutes without a chairman; hence its title 'leaderless group discussion'. Several observers are able to watch and listen, but they do not intervene except to bring the discussion to an end or introduce a new subject.

Misleading results can, however, sometimes occur. Some candidates, normally quiet and retiring, can for the day of the test successfully act the part of the self-assertive leader; and frequently the performance of individuals is affected by the composition of the group — if it contains one or two uncongenial members the remainder may behave out of character.

14. Examples of psychometric tests

Tests of intelligence, personality, motivation and other aspects of an individual's psychological make-up are collectively known as 'psychometric tests'. Typically, test subjects complete a checklist questionnaire which asks them to express their preferences in relation to various issues and situations, e.g. by requiring candidates to state which outcome to a problem they find most desirable, or to select words and phrases (such as 'persuasive', 'gentle', 'innovative') which they regard as describing aspects of their personalities most and least accurately. Tests that require subjects to choose between several alternatives when answering each question are referred to as 'ipsative' tests.

Examples of psychometric tests commonly used by UK companies include:

(a) *The 16 PF test*, which assumes the existence within people of 16 clusters of behaviour ('factors') relating to such matters as a person's excitability, assertiveness, emotional stability, conscientiousness; whether he or she is extrovert or introvert, cheerful or depressive, etc.

(b) *The Myers–Briggs type indicator*, which seeks to categorise test subjects under four main headings: objective/intuitive, logical/emotional, decisive/hesitant, introvert/extrovert.

(c) *The DISC test,* which aims to identify the extents of 'dominance', 'influence' (or 'inducement'), 'submission' (or 'steadiness') and 'compliance' in test-subjects' personalities. Test results are plotted onto star-shaped graphs which purport to show a person's self-image, actual personality, and ability to cope with pressure.

(d) *The Eysenck personality inventory,* which consists of a simple questionnaire involving yes–no answers to questions intended to measure candidates' introversion/extroversion and stability/neuroticism. Each of these dimensions is then broken down into sub-categories. For example, 'stability' segments into 'phlegmatic' and 'sanguine'. 'Phlegmatic' is then split into categories for passive, careful, thoughtful, peaceful, controlled, reliable, even-tempered, and calm. The term 'inventory' (rather than 'test') is used here to indicate that there is no pass/fail cutoff. Rather, the exercise aims to isolate personal strengths and weaknesses in specified psychological dimensions.

15. Usefulness of psychometric tests
Advantages to using psychometric tests for employee selection include the following.

(a) Tests are cheap to administer. A single person can give a test to (say) 30 or 40 people at each sitting. This makes testing useful for situations where large numbers of employees have to be engaged within a short period.

(b) It enables distinctions to be made between candidates with exactly the same academic qualifications and work experience.

(c) Objective information about a candidate's psychological characteristics can be a valuable adjunct to other selection procedures. This additional information should help remove subjectivity in selection.

(d) There is little point in (expensively) training employees who are not mentally capable of absorbing relevant information. Psychometric testing, its advocates argue, can weed out such individuals.

(e) People of genuine intellectual ability who, nevertheless, have received minimal formal education may be identified.

Arguments against the use of psychometric tests are that:

(a) it may be unfair. People might be arbitrarily labelled as outstanding or mediocre on the basis of a (perhaps ill-conceived and poorly-validated) 20-minute test, while ignoring their overall achievements and educational backgrounds.

(b) workers may be allocated to (inappropriate) roles and occupations in direct consequence of inaccurate information about their psychological characteristics.

(c) practice at psychometric tests can lead to improved test performance; indeed, there exist publications on 'How to Pass Psychometric Tests'.

(d) a candidate's motivation and state of mind at the time a test is taken (e.g. if the person has just suffered a bereavement) can affect results significantly.

(e) the total worth of a person depends on so many factors that any selection of a sub-set of them is bound to be arbitrary.

(f) requiring a job applicant to take a test can itself cause that person to feel nervous and to fear the humiliation of possibly doing badly. This can create a self-fulfilling prophecy; the individual loses self-confidence, which leads to poor performance in the test!

Aptitude and achievement tests

16. Aptitude tests

Quite frequently a candidate applies for a job in which he or she has had no previous experience. The employer accepts that training will be necessary, but wants to ensure as far as possible that the candidate is suitable for training. The employer wishes to know whether the candidate possesses an aptitude for the job, i.e. the basic mental and physical qualities which can be developed into the specific skill.

An aptitude seems to be made up of several components: general intelligence, one or more specific mental abilities, physical attributes (such as muscular co-ordination), experience in a related activity and possibly personality factors like interests and motivation.

Some aptitudes, e.g. managerial or selling aptitudes, are so complex and controversial that no satisfactory way of testing for them has yet been discovered.

Some of the simpler aptitudes, for which tests have been shown to give worthwhile results, are as follows.

(a) *Verbal aptitude* — a good command of written or spoken English.

(b) *Arithmetical aptitude* — ability in addition, subtraction, multiplication and division.

(c) *Spatial aptitude* — facility in judging shapes and dimensions important in e.g. drawing, packing or driving.

(d) *Mechanical aptitude* — understanding of mechanical principles.

(e) *Manual dexterity* — more accurately called psychomotor dexterity.

Tests are available for these aptitudes, but their construction and interpretation is a skilled task, only to be carried out by psychologists or under their guidance.

17. Achievement tests

In contrast to aptitude tests (which measure potential ability after training), achievement tests measure the skill and knowledge that the candidate already has. They are the most common of all tests; every candidate during his or her interview is asked at least one question about previous experience.

Construction of achievement tests is usually quite simple; generally they are either *work-sample* or *symbolic*.

(a) *Work-sample tests* consist of a carefully-chosen part of the actual job. If the candidate fails to reach the required standard of performance in this part it is assumed that his or her performance in the whole job will be inadequate. Examples are the shorthand and typing tests nearly always given to candidates applying for secretarial posts, the vehicle-handling test for road transport drivers, and the test piece of work for engineering craftsworkers.

(b) *Symbolic tests* are used when a work sample would be impracticable; they represent aspects of the job in symbolic, usually verbal, terms. They may consist of questions to probe the candidate's knowledge, circuit diagrams or technical specifications to be interpreted, or occasionally in-tray exercises in which the candidate is confronted with a batch of incoming letters and memoranda to be answered.

Advantages of achievement tests are that (a) they can expose candidates who claim to possess abilities (typing speeds, machine skill, etc.) they do not actually have, and **(b)** tests are directly relevant to the work the successful candidates will have to perform in the job. Note, however, that a test will necessarily cover only a part of the successful candidate's eventual duties. A candidate who fails the test might be assumed incapable of doing the entire job, which need not be true. A secretary, for example, might fail to achieve a predetermined minimum speed under test conditions, but this does not necessarily mean the candidate is an inadequate secretary overall.

Also, tests are undertaken in specific test conditions. Success in a driving test proves that the candidate did well over the test circuit, yet this person may not be a good driver elsewhere. Job applicants will feel nervous during a test, and this may cause them to do badly. It is a fact that people who have done a particular test previously do better on average than people attempting it for the first time. Thus, candidates who have already taken and failed a similar test will have an advantage, yet these might be precisely the sort of candidates the test was originally intended to weed out. Further problems are outlined below.

(a) Candidates who have passed a test might assume they possess knowledge or ability which in fact they do not have. Supervisors also might conclude that new entrants are fully competent simply because they did well in a single test, conducted in highly specific conditions.

(b) An internal candidate for promotion who is given and fails a test might lose self-confidence and hence underperform in a currently held job. That person will, moreover, be identified by colleagues as a failure and in consequence the worker's morale might collapse.

(c) Some ethnic and other minority groups consistently do badly in certain types of achievement test because they have not had access to educational and training programmes necessary to equip them with the basic skills expected of test candidates.

(d) High marks obtained in a test do not guarantee that the successful candidate will do well in the vacant post. In particular, high marks do not say why the candidate passed. Knowledge of the causes of success or failure might be as valuable to management as identification of individuals capable of obtaining high marks.

(e) Achievement tests do not evaluate the whole person; only a small sub-section of his or her characteristics. Note that a formal educational qualification awarded after perhaps several years' study should in principle offer much more information about a person overall.

Validating tests

18. Methods of validation

All tests used to measure individual differences should be validated, i.e. an investigation made to see if the test measures what it is claimed to measure, or predicts what it is claimed to predict. During this investigation the text may also be standardised, i.e. a cut-off score decided, below which a candidate is to be rejected.

There are four types of validity, the last two being particularly relevant for personnel selection.

(a) *Content validity* — an inspection is made of the subject-matter of the test to see if it is relevant to the quality being measured.

(b) *Construct validity* — the results of the test are compared with the results obtained by the same group of candidates who have taken another test, the validity of which has already been established.

(c) *Predictive validity* — a group of candidates is given the test. They are all engaged, and their subsequent job performance compared with their test scores. If there is a reasonable relationship, the test is valid and it can be standardised, i.e. a score identified which will cut off the unsuitable and admit the suitable candidates. There are possible disadvantages with this method:

   (i) job performance may be difficult to assess objectively;

   (ii) the process of validation may be lengthy; adequate assessment of performance may not be possible until a long time after the test has been given and a large number of results will be necessary before validation is complete;

   (iii) in practice it is rarely possible to engage *all* candidates, but if the results of the test are compared with the performance of a selected group only it is not completely validated.

(d) *Concurrent validity* — the test is given to present employees in the job in question. If the test is valid, then the more proficient the employee, the higher the score. This method is quick, but has the following disadvantages:

    (*i*) standardisation is difficult;

    (*ii*) the test is validated against a non-typical group, i.e. present employees rather than candidates for employment;

    (*iii*) the employees may not behave normally when they do the test. They may be suspicious and deliberately give a poor performance, or they may be anxious to excel themselves and give an unusually good performance.

A common method of validation is to combine predictive with concurrent validity. The test is first tried out on present employees, after reassuring them that it is not in their interests to falsify their performance. Prima-facie validity can be established and standards approximately found. The test is then used on candidates for the job concerned, their subsequent progress being compared with their test scores. Validity can therefore be confirmed and the standard fixed more precisely. It is in any case good practice to make a continual review of test scores and proficiency because many jobs gradually change in character, thus reducing the validity of the test.

Progress test 4

1. In what way is the measurement of physique different from the measurement of intelligence or personality? **(3)**

2. Define 'intelligence'. **(4)**

3. What does 'IQ' stand for? Define the term **(7)**

4. Why is a high intelligence test score not a guarantee of success in a job? **(8)**

5. Define 'personality'. **(9)**

6. What are 'self-report' personality tests? What is their value in personnel selection? **(10)**

7. Should personality be judged by first impressions? **(12)**

8. What is 'leaderless group discussion'? **(13)**

9. What is the difference between an aptitude test and an achievement test? **(16, 17)**

10. Describe one way in which a test may be validated. **(18)**

5
Interviewing

The selection interview

1. Description

A selection interview is an extension and development of the inevitable meeting which takes place between an employer and a prospective employee. It includes questions designed to test achievement or aptitude, and is at present the most commonly used method of personality assessment.

2. Reliability and validity of the selection interview

There is much conflicting evidence here. Some studies have shown how easily interviewers can disagree about a candidate, and how predictions made on the basis of an interview are often not fulfilled. Other studies, however, provide evidence of agreement between interviewers, and of predictions coming true. The majority opinion is that the selection interview is in any case unavoidable, so the best possible use should be made of it. Reliability and validity can be greatly improved if the following conditions are observed.

(a) Interviewers are not rigid or authoritarian in their views and are reasonably sensitive to other people.
(b) The job is thoroughly studied and described.
(c) Interviewers plan their questions in advance.
(d) They are trained in interviewing.

3. The philosophy of the selection interview

There are two schools of thought regarding the way a selection interview should be conducted.

The first makes the assumption that an individual's general

behaviour has become stable by the time he or she has reached adulthood, i.e. that the individual's personality has now become established. At the interview, therefore, questions should be asked about the candidate's past behaviour, in particular his or her motivation, how he or she dealt with crises and about the person's social adjustment. The pattern that emerges from the candidate's answers will be a reliable guide to his or her future behaviour, after making allowances for a different environment. In order to obtain this information the interviewer must establish a good personal relationship with the candidate (establish rapport, as it is sometimes called) and encourage the candidate to speak freely and frankly. This is the approach favoured by most employers.

The second view is that candidates attending a selection interview will intentionally or unintentionally distort their answers, exaggerating points in their favour and minimising others. Since none of the information they give about their past lives can be relied on, the interviewer must draw conclusions based on candidates' present behaviour only, i.e. the way they react to situations contrived and controlled by the interviewer. Testing is, of course, a special example of this attitude with which no one would quarrel; a test taken away by the candidate to be done at home and unsupervised would be valueless. Leaderless group discussion (*see* **4:13**) is another example where candidates are observed in a controlled social setting. When this philosophy is applied to the interview its outcome is usually a situation where mental stress is applied; for example, the candidate may not be invited to sit down, his or her answers may be ridiculed or the interviewer may remain silent and expressionless for long periods.

The stress-interview is intended to provoke the candidate into displaying his or her true personality rather than the facade the candidate is trying to maintain to impress the prospective employer. Though superficially attractive, this approach is rarely used by reputable employers for the following reasons.

(a) Behaviour under the created stress conditions will probably not be typical of the candidate's behaviour under genuine stress. All the interviewer will learn is how the candidate behaves when he or she encounters some rather foolish and annoying events at a selection interview. The candidate's responses will largely depend on how badly the person wants the job.

(b) The employer's good name will suffer and candidates may withdraw their applications.

(c) A stress interview, by concentrating entirely on personality, is incomplete. It makes the candidate unwilling to talk freely about his or her experience.

4.   Purposes of the selection interview

A well-conducted selection interview fulfils three functions.

(a) To elicit information about the candidate's motives and behaviour in order to assess personality.

(b) To check the factual information the candidate has already given about him or herself, to examine the value and relevance of experience and qualifications, and often to give an achievement test in symbolic terms (*see* 4:**17**).

(c) To give information to the candidate about the job and company. This part of the interview is very often omitted or skimped, but it is quite essential. Selection is mutual; the employer selects the candidate, and the candidate must be given the information needed to select the employer.

5.   Preparing for the interview

It is impossible for an interview to be done well unless thorough preparations have been made.

(a) The job is analysed and described (*see* Chapter 13). If a job specification already exists, it should be brought up to date. It is impossible to say if a candidate is suitable for a job unless the job is thoroughly known.

(b) Written information about the candidate is obtained (*see* 14:**15**).

(c) The candidate's written statement is compared with the job specification so that the interviewer can decide where clarification or further information is needed. The interviewer makes a note of the key questions to be asked.

(d) The interviewer makes sure that the interview will not be interrupted by visitors or telephone calls.

(e) Interviewing across a desk which is cluttered up with filing trays, telephones, ornaments and other objects is avoided, because a physical barrier between two people seems to create a psychological barrier. The candidate is placed at the side of the desk, or better still the interview takes places away from a desk, using perhaps two chairs with a low table between them.

6. Conduct of the interview

Most experienced interviewers begin the interview with a few remarks and questions designed to welcome and set the candidate at ease. For example, a question about the candidate's journey to the place of the interview not only breaks the ice but provides the interviewer with useful information.

It is often easier to get the candidate to talk freely if the early questions are about that person's present job rather than about his or her schooldays followed by a laborious plod in strict chronological order. The order in which topics are dealt with is not important as long as they are all covered. Maintaining an easy conversational tone should have precedence over a rigid programme of questions.

The object of the questions is to get candidates to talk about their experience and reveal their motivations, social adjustment and the ways in which they have dealt with any difficult episodes in their private or working lives. These rules should be followed when framing questions.

(a) *Questions should not suggest their own answers* (e.g. 'I'm sure you have had experience in stocktaking, haven't you?') or be answerable in a very few words (e.g. 'I see from your form that you've passed GCSE in four subjects'). Open-ended questions are best; they suggest no particular answer and encourage the candidate to talk at some length. Examples are: 'Tell me about any stocktaking experience you have had', or 'What were your best subjects at school?'

(b) *The meaning of questions should be clear* and they should be expressed in a way appropriate to the candidate's experience and education. The interviewer must try to adapt his or her manner and choice of words to suit the candidate, though not to a ludicrous degree.

(c) *Probing questions should be used.* If a candidate says he or she was responsible for a certain activity, this must not be taken at its face value — further questioning may show that the responsibility was confined to keeping records about it. Similarly a candidate's impressive list of hobbies and interests may be merely things the person has done once or watched others do.

(d) *The interviewer should unobtrusively guide* the course and subject-matter of the interview by questions which introduce new topics, linking them to what has been dealt with before. The candidate should do most of the talking, but on subjects which have been chosen and introduced by the interviewer.

(e) *A very large number of questions* should begin with the words how or why. The reasons behind the candidate's actions and the way he or she goes about getting things done are invaluable clues to personality.

(f) *Rude, insensitive and irrelevant questions* should not be asked. Critical remarks that might upset and fluster the candidate (thus causing the interviewee to 'clam up' and not reveal important information) should not be made during the interview.

(g) *Interviewers should not compare candidates with themselves*, since interviewers may hold overinflated opinions about their own abilities, and might wrongly assume that candidates most like themselves are necessarily best suited for *any* vacant position.

(h) *Inappropriate selection criteria must be avoided*, particularly the 'halo effect', whereby interviewers assume that one desirable characteristic in an applicant necessarily means the candidate is equally worthy in other respects. For example, an attractive physical appearance does not imply that an applicant for a secretary's job will be a good typist. Note how this phenomenon can work in reverse: an interviewer may conclude incorrectly that weakness in one area means low calibre overall.

During the interview the job, company and working conditions, e.g. hours, holidays, pension scheme, etc., should be briefly described, and the candidate if possible be shown the place of work. The candidate should be given plenty of opportunity to ask questions.

The interviewer should indicate clearly to the candidate when the interview is at an end, and what the next step will be, e.g. the candidate will receive a letter or should telephone the company on a certain day.

Assessment

7. Recording the interview

Note-taking during the interview should be avoided because it seems to inhibit the candidate from speaking freely; exceptions may be made, however, for information which must be recorded exactly, such as a change of address or the candidate's present salary. A full note should be taken *immediately after* the interview and certainly before the next candidate is seen.

It is essential for the record to be made in a systematic way to be sure that comments have been made on all important points and to enable comparisons with other candidates to be made more easily. There are many systems for describing candidates, two of which are as follows.

(a) *The seven-point plan of the National Institute of Industrial Psychology*, which suggests that the candidate should be assessed under the following headings:

(*i*)   physical make-up;
(*ii*) attainments;
(*iii*) general intelligence;
(*iv*) special aptitudes;
(*v*)   interests;
(*vi*) disposition;
(*vii*) circumstances.

(b) *The five-fold grading*, devised by John Munro Fraser, which uses the following classification:

(*i*)   first impressions and physical make-up;
(*ii*) qualifications;
(*iii*) brains and abilities;
(*iv*) motivation;
(*v*)   adjustment.

The second scheme is perhaps more realistic for adult candidates, particularly as it draws attention to the main fields an interview should cover. It is usually advisable to add a sixth heading, circumstances, since a candidate's domestic life, travelling problems, etc., are sometimes relevant to his or her suitability.

Two problems arise when applying these systems.

(a) Subjective and incorrect allocation of people to categories, e.g. what seems a pleasant disposition to one person may appear as surly and aggressive to someone else.

(b) Applying the same categories to candidates of widely varying background, experience and educational qualifications.

To illustrate the latter problem, consider the comparison of an older female applicant (who possesses certificates and diplomas with titles quite different to those obtained by younger people) with a male applicant who recently left college. The woman may have been out of employment for several years in order to raise children, and then may have worked in an industry quite different to that in which the recruiting firm operates. Interviewers will, of course, have to deal with this situation increasingly frequently as more and more women return to work through the 1990s in consequence of social trends and, in particular, of the projected shortage of skilled and qualified young people. This phenomenon may alter fundamentally the ways in which employers structure the interviewing process, competing with each other to obtain the best female returners available.

Comparing candidates with widely differing backgrounds
It is usual in these circumstances to look for common factors among candidates. For example, has the applicant a good record of passing examinations first time, or were several attempts required? Are there any observable gaps in particular subject areas (mathematics or English, for example)? Did the candidate drop out of particular courses? How much responsibility did the candidate carry in his or her previous post? Is there evidence of the candidate's willingness to attend courses and update skills? Did the applicant remain long with any one employer without being promoted? The fact that any of these are true does not necessarily mean the candidate is unsuitable, only that the issue should be further explored during the interview.

Many experienced interviewers evolve their own systems, often because they deal almost exclusively with a particular type of candidate, e.g. university graduates or manual workers, and wish to give attention to some points rather than others. Either of the two systems described above may be used as the basis of one's own scheme.

8. Assessing the candidate

The information given by a candidate and recorded by the interviewer must now be interpreted so that suitability for the job can be assessed. It is comparatively easy to make an objective judgment about the candidate's experience and qualifications, particularly if questions on these subjects have been carefully thought out in advance. It is often possible, in addition, to give an achievement test (*see* 4:17).

Assessment of personality is much less reliable. The candidate's replies are interpreted by the interviewer, who has his or her own prejudices and preferences, and will be guided by perceptions unique to that individual. It is impossible to eliminate the effects of bias on the part of the interviewer, but they may be reduced by the following means.

(a) The interviewer should keep an open mind until the end of the interview; first impressions, though important in some jobs, can be extremely misleading.

(b) The interviewer must try to become aware of his or her prejudices, and allow for them.

(c) The candidate's statements are analysed to look for recurring patterns of behaviour, e.g. constant rebelliousness against authority or a tendency to avoid decision making. Any conclusions reached about personality are justified by reference to incidents the candidate has described, so that no personality assessment is made without evidence.

(d) Doubts about a candidate's personality can often be resolved by deferring a decision for 24 hours or by asking the candidate to return for a second interview.

(e) Several experienced interviewers are more likely to make a reliable assessment than one alone. There are, however, some practical difficulties in arranging this (*see* 10–13).

(f) The interview is validated by following up the successful candidate's progress and behaviour after he or she has been working in the job for some time (*see* 14:23). Unfortunately it is not possible to follow up the candidates who are judged unsuitable, so that interview validation will always be incomplete.

9. Final rating

It is useful to conclude the written assessment of the candidate with a final rating, particularly if a number of candidates are to be seen over a period. Selection is then made easier by comparing the final ratings. A five-point scale can be used:

A — Outstanding candidate.
B — Very good candidate but . . .
C — Good candidate but . . .
D — Needs further consideration because . . .
E — Unacceptable because . . .

The 'buts' in grades B and C indicate that the candidate may need some special training or that the job may have to be modified in some way. The 'becauses' in grades D and E are important in that they show the quality of candidates coming forward and the reason for rejection; the latter may sometimes be required by some outside body, e.g. an industrial tribunal.

Multiple interviews

10. The use of several interviewers

In most organisations it is unusual for employees to be engaged on the authority of one person, e.g. a personnel manager, a departmental manager and his or her deputy might wish to be involved. The use of several interviewers enables a wider and more expert range of questions to be asked, and reduces the effects of personal bias. On the other hand, a single interviewer is more likely to establish rapport and develop a connected line of questioning to explore motivation and social adjustment.

There are three ways of arranging for a candidate to be seen by several selectors: successive interviews; panel interviews; and board interviews.

11. Successive interviews

In this method the candidate is seen by one interviewer, then by a second and then by a third (rarely more). This method preserves the one-to-one relationship but has disadvantages.

(a) The candidate often finds the procedure very tedious, particularly when asked the same question by all the interviewers.

(b) An inexpert interviewer can cause damage.

(c) The candidate's responses may change as he or she goes from one interview to the next because the person learns to expect certain questions and becomes more adept at giving acceptable answers to them.

12. Panel interviews

These are interviews in which the candidate is seen by a comparatively small number of people simultaneously. The usual membership of a panel is three or four; anything larger than this would best be described as a board.

A panel interview has the following *advantages*.

(a) The candidate's time is saved as compared with successive interviews.

(b) Each interviewer can specialise in asking questions in which he or she is expert.

(c) There is time for each interviewer to ask several questions.

(d) All the interviewers are able to take part in the joint assessment of the candidate and express their own views.

(e) Inexperienced interviewers can be trained by including them in panels.

The *disadvantages* of the panel interview are as follows.

(a) It is less easy to establish rapport with the candidate than it is in a one-to-one interview.

(b) The questioning may be disorganised and repetitive.

(c) Occasionally, the interviewers transact company business during the interview.

(d) Certain panel members might not be genuinely interested in the proceedings, attending simply to fill out their time and/or appear important and influential.

These disadvantages can be overcome with some forethought. The interviewers should agree among themselves which one of them is to carry out the main part of the interview — the biography, the exploration of motivation, etc. The other interviewers arrange to join in later with prepared questions in their particular fields. The principal interviewer acts as chairperson, controlling and directing the proceedings. It is preferable to have the interviewers and the candidate sitting round a table rather than the common arrangement in which the interviewers sit on one side of a table and the candidate on the other.

For a panel interview to be effective it is necessary that:

(a) each member have something definite to contribute;
(b) the panel establish an interview plan and definite criteria for assessing candidates;
(c) the majority of panel members be trained, skilled or experienced in interviewing methods;
(d) each member have a predetermined role in the proceedings.

13. Board interview

In this method the candidate is seen by a comparatively large number of selectors simultaneously, i.e. five or more. The board interview is used above all in the public sector of employment, where boards of 30 or more members are not unknown.

Advantages

(a) It enables many people to see the candidate on one occasion.
(b) It shows the candidate's behaviour under stress.

Disadvantages

(a) Rapport between the board and the candidate is impossible.
(b) The candidate's behaviour may not be typical of his or her conduct under more normal kinds of stress.
(c) When so many wish to ask questions, any connected line of enquiry is impossible.
(d) The interviewers are seldom expert.
(e) With such large numbers, it is very difficult for the chairperson to agree and control an interviewing plan.
(f) Rivalries and disagreements among members of the board often appear, putting the candidate in an awkward position.
(g) It is difficult for a board to have adequate knowledge of the requirements of the job.
(h) The final assessment of candidates is very difficult.

As a means of selection there is very little to commend in the board interview. It has been suggested that if a large group wishes to be involved in selection it should delegate the actual interviewing to a panel drawn from the group, the rest observing the interview by a closed circuit television. This would be an improvement, but it would still not avoid the difficulties caused by lack of knowledge of the job and by the large number from whom agreement must be reached.

14. Other approaches to selection

Critics of the interview method of employee selection allege that so many biases creep into the interview process that it can never be a truly objective selection technique. They suggest that in too many cases it is a candidate's *demeanour* during an interview that actually leads to his or her selection. Managers who conduct interviews often have inappropriate and/or unrealistic expectations of what candidates should be like; assumptions based on their *own* life experiences, social backgrounds, outlooks, etc. These and other anxieties have created interest in alternative approaches to recruitment and selection, notably the application of psychometric testing (*see* 4:**4–14**), assessment centres (*see* 18:**13**), board interviews (*see* **13**), and in-tray and other work-related selection methods (*see* 20:**10**). Further possibilities include the following.

(a) *Use of biodata*. Here, biographical data is assembled (usually *via* a multiple choice form) on each candidate's family background, upbringing, and lifetime experiences. Examples of questions asked are the number of brothers and sisters a candidate has, whether he or she is the oldest or youngest child, the person's social activities and outside interests, domestic circumstances, etc. The backgrounds of a sample of existing 'successful' employees currently undertaking work similar to that involved in the vacant position are then analysed, and the candidate whose biodata most closely matches that of existing successful workers is offered the job. This assumes that a person's characteristics are the consequence of certain lifetime experiences (being the youngest of a large family, for example). Advocates of the biodata method assert that it uses objective information, that the same questions are asked of all candidates, and that answers are scored in an identical manner. It is a cheap method of recruitment: anyone can undertake the scoring. There are, however, a number of problems with the technique, as follows:

(*i*) it rests on unproven psychological foundations;

(*ii*) there is no obvious way of choosing the criteria for evaluating candidates (i.e. for identifying the *particular* lifetime experiences that caused current employees to succeed);

(*iii*) the possibility of candidates not telling the truth about their personal details;

(*iv*) selection *via* biodata might be used to circumvent equal opportunities legislation;

(*v*) collecting biodata from large samples of existing employees is time consuming and administratively inconvenient;

(*vi*) lifetime experiences such as type of school attended (state or private), area of residence, nature (and hence the cost) of childhood hobbies pursued, etc., typically depend on the economic status of a person's parents. Hence, the use of biodata for selection might unfairly discriminate against candidates from poor families.

(b) *Open-door recruitment.* This means appointing the first applicant who presents him or herself and who possesses all the attributes necessary to complete the job. It has been used by large department stores needing to appoint many staff simultaneously (immediately prior to Christmas, for instance) and for hiring production operatives. There is no interviewing or testing. Rather, the firm drafts detailed and extremely precise person specifications (*see* **7**) containing definitive listings of all the personal and other qualities needed to perform the vacant job. The first candidate to satisfy the specified criteria is automatically accepted. If the appointee subsequently fails, then the listing of necessary personal attributes is deemed unsatisfactory and amended prior to the next appointment.

Advantages to the open-door method are its low cost, its avoidance of tedious administrative routines, the removal of many sources of unfair discrimination, and the fact that management is forced to predetermine clearly and exactly the criteria to be applied when filling a vacancy. Equally, however, the appointed person might not fit in with the prevailing culture of the organisation, or be able to get on socially with colleagues.

15. Unconventional approaches

Interesting research has been conducted into the use of astrology and graphology as devices for employee selection. While the results are inconclusive, they do provide fresh insights into the fundamental nature and problems of the recruitment process.

Graphology
This is the study of the shape, size and manner of a person's handwriting, including closure of letters, positioning of words on paper and slope of lines, pressure exerted, etc., in order to predict personality characteristics such as attention to detail, persistence, etc. Advocates of graphology argue that it provides an objective base for assessing candidates (a person's handwriting does not change much over time) and that different graphologists typically give similar analyses of the same person's handwriting. However, there is little hard scientific evidence to support the method, and people can change their style of handwriting (making it neater and more consistent) in order to create a good impression if they know their handwriting is to be analysed.

Astrology
Although there are no known scientific links between star sign and individual behaviour and personality, popular interest in astrology is extremely high. Horoscopes are published in numerous magazines and newspapers and are known to be read avidly by large numbers of people. Arguably, the publication of so much material on astrology *itself* creates self-fulfilling prophecies, since most people know their own star sign and what this is supposed to mean in relation to their personalities. Consequently, individuals might describe themselves in these terms when asked about their thoughts, feelings and behaviour. Indeed they might even answer questions in psychometric tests according to how they believe someone of their star sign *ought* to respond. This could create fallacious observed relationships between test results and the signs of the zodiac.

The counselling interview

16. When counselling is used
In general, counselling interviews are used for present employees of the company rather than candidates for employment. They are not primarily intended to obtain information, like the selection interview, but instead they are used

to give advice and information and to discuss problems. Compared with a selection interview a counselling interview is unstructured, little preparatory work being necessary or possible because the interviewer's role is mainly to react to the interviewee.

Sometimes, particularly in appraisal or grievance interviews, the manager who conducts the interview makes up his or her mind to some extent to follow a particular line before he or she has seen the employee and then conducts a telling interview, rather than a problem-solving interview, in which the interviewer listens and responds to the employee's statements and attitudes. When the manager is highly respected and very knowledgeable, a telling interview may be successful because the employee learns clearly what the manager thinks of the employee and what is now expected, but in this type of interview the telling is one-sided; the manager is told very little about subordinates.

17. What counselling is

Counselling is the process of helping people recognise their feelings about problems, define those problems accurately, find solutions, or learn to live with a situation. Counselling situations arise when managers listen to grievances, handle disputes, deal with employees accused of improper behaviour, or assist people undergoing excessive work-related stress. A counselling session might involve:

(a) giving advice;
(b) encouraging a change in behaviour;
(c) discussion of a problem not previously recognised or accepted by the counsellee;
(d) helping someone take a difficult decision;
(e) gaining acceptance of a situation that cannot be changed;
(f) altering someone's perceptions of an issue.

The aim is not to impose solutions but rather to induce people independently to learn how to overcome difficulties and take appropriate decisions. Counselling should always occur in private, and without interruption from ringing telephones, secretaries with messages, etc.

18. Counselling methods

There are two approaches to counselling: directive and

non-directive. With *non-directive* counselling, the manager conducting the interview will make the following assumptions.

(a) Only the counsellee is capable of defining accurately his or her own problems.
(b) The most effective way of getting to the heart of a problem is to encourage the other party to talk about what he or she wishes to discuss.
(c) Solutions to problems will not be implemented unless counsellees wholeheartedly agree with solutions that emerge from the interview.
(d) Managers must accept situations as they are rather than as they would like them to be. Thus the aim is to understand and explain events rather than seek immediate change or remedy.

Directive counselling, conversely, requires the counsellor to take the initiative and suggest ways of solving a problem. This involves:

(a) outlining the implications and possible consequences of various courses of action;
(b) suggesting a range of solutions to be considered;
(c) charting a path towards the correct decision.

The counsellee is encouraged to rely on the expert knowledge and experience of the other party, while gradually responding to the latter's conversation and advice. Ultimately, however, it is the counsellee who makes the final decision.

19. Problem-solving interviews

Although many managers find such an approach inconsistent with their usual management style (*see* Chapter 8), the problem-solving method is much more likely than any other to increase an employee's job satisfaction. Whether the purpose of the interview is to appraise the employee or to deal with a complaint, an approach which encourages the employee to state his or her own point of view and, with the manager's prompting, work out a plan of action is more likely to have a satisfactory sequel than an interview where the manager attempts to dictate to the employee a course of action based on insufficient information.

Problem-solving interviews are often difficult because the normal manager–subordinate relationship may inhibit frank speaking. The best way to overcome this is to remove the physical signs of this relationship, e.g. to conduct the interview in chairs side by side rather than across the manager's imposing desk.

The manager should try not to express his or her own point of view during the early part of the discussion; if this happens, the subordinate will tend to say things which conform with this point of view instead of what is really in his or her mind. In extreme cases the grunting technique may be used; in order to encourage the subordinate to talk the manager merely grunts or murmurs to show he or she is listening, with occasional remarks encouraging the subordinate to continue or summing up what has already been said.

The disciplinary interview

20. Definition

A disciplinary interview enquires into a complaint made about the work or conduct of an employee in order to see if the person should be reproved, warned or threatened. The dividing line between a disciplinary and a counselling interview is not always clear; an investigation into a complaint may end with the employee being given advice rather than a warning. Some counselling interviews may contain a veiled threat from the manager that he or she does not want the problem in question to occur again.

21. Conduct of the disciplinary interview

This is best illustrated by assuming that a manager has learned that an employee's work has become unsatisfactory. The manager should not automatically take disciplinary action but follow this procedure.

(a) Check the facts; on what basis and by whose judgment is it said that the employee's work has deteriorated?
(b) When interviewing the subordinate state the accusations clearly and the source of the manager's information.
(c) Give the employee every opportunity to reply; in some firms it is customary for a shop steward to assist the employee in stating his or her case.

(d) At this point it may be apparent that the information is not as reliable as appeared at first, or that there are extenuating circumstances. The manager may then in the first case promise to investigate further, or in the second case continue the interview on a counselling basis.

(e) If the manager considers the employee has been at fault, this is communicated to the worker, giving reasons (if possible) in objective, quantitative terms, e.g. 'Your output is x per cent below the average for the department.'

(f) The manager then tells the employee what he or she proposes to do, e.g. give a warning that an improvement must occur within one month. This warning is recorded in writing.

(g) After a month the employee is seen again, whether or not his or her work has improved.

This procedure may seem cumbersome but it follows the rules of justice and obviates the awkward situation in which disciplinary action has to be withdrawn because the employee's case has not been properly heard. It should also improve industrial relations within the organisation.

Note that for serious cases of indiscipline and/or underperformance (i.e. cases where if a warning is unheeded the worker could be dismissed) it is necessary to follow up the interview with a letter formally advising the employee of the need to improve and of the possible consequences of ignoring the warning. This letter (which is required under the ACAS Code of Practice on disciplinary proceedings, *see* 16:18) should specify details of alleged inadequacies and of what the employee must do to overcome them.

Progress test 5

1. How can the reliability and validity of the selection interview be improved? **(2)**

2. What is a stress interview? **(3)**

3. What are the purposes of a selection interview? **(4)**

4.   What kinds of questions should be avoided in a selection interview?   **(6)**

5.   How should an interviewer assess personality?   **(8)**

6.   What are the advantages and disadvantages of panel interviews?   **(12)**

7.   Define biodata. How might biodata be used?   **(14)**

8.   What is a problem-solving interview, and what is it used for? (16, 19)

9.   What are the key differences between counselling and other types of interview?   **(17)**

10. State the procedure to be followed in a disciplinary interview.   **(21)**

6
Physical and psychological conditions of work

Fatigue

1. Definition
Because it is used rather loosely in industrial psychology the term fatigue is difficult to define. The most satisfactory definition appears to be 'a reduction in the energy available to perform a task'. Fatigue is used to explain physical changes occurring in the body as a result of effort, the subjective feeling of tiredness and the cause of an otherwise unexplained reduction of output during a working spell.

2. Physical fatigue
Towards the end of the nineteenth century the Italian scientist Mosso, using a device known as the ergograph, formulated some laws of physical fatigue, i.e. the fatigue occurring as the result of muscular effort. The most important of his laws are:

(a) light loads lifted frequently cause less fatigue than heavy loads lifted infrequently;

(b) rest pauses can give complete recovery from fatigue.

To illustrate the first law, moving a heap of sand by 100 movements of a large shovel will be more fatiguing than moving the same amount by 200 movements of a shovel half the size. Jobs which involve lifting should therefore be designed in such a way that heavy loads are avoided and lighter loads used instead.

The second law has been verified in industry many times, particularly by the work of the Industrial Health Research Board in the 1914–18 war. It is found that the output of employees engaged on manual work gradually rises at the beginning of an uninterrupted working spell until it reaches a steady amount; after a time output begins to decrease until the spell is over. The periods when output is increasing, stable or decreasing vary in their length according to the characteristics of the job and workers, but the pattern remains the same.

If a rest pause is introduced before production begins to fall, the period of stable production will usually continue after the pause, and the period of decreasing production will be shorter. The more physically taxing the job, the more frequent the rest pauses that are required.

Physical fatigue shows itself in ways other than reduced output and a feeling of tiredness. Evidence of an objective kind can be found in the changed chemical composition of body fluids and in the accumulation of waste products of muscular exertion, particularly lactic acid. The physiological effect of a rest pause is to allow the body fluids to return to their normal state and for the waste products to be removed from the vicinity of the muscles, but the recovery will take longer if the rest pause occurs after the physiological changes have started.

Experiments can be made to determine the number and timing of rest pauses which give the best results; it is not advisable to allow workers to rest when they feel tired, because by then fatigue will be well established and a comparatively long rest pause will be necessary before they feel refreshed and are able to put out their normal amount of energy. To obtain the greatest benefit, therefore, the rest pauses should be compulsory and occur before the worker begins to feel tired. Study of the rate of output will show a decrease or irregularity occurring before the feeling of tiredness arrives; the rest pause should be taken at the average time of this change in output.

Stress

3. Stress at work

Stress has both positive and negative aspects. Some employees thrive on pressure; it helps them draw on physical and emotional resources and they actually enjoy tense and challenging situations. Stress triggers in these people the adrenalin needed to sustain intense effort and to be able to cope with several different problems all at the same time. Continued exposure to stress, however, can cause extreme tiredness, irritability, physical upsets such as headaches and rashes, insomnia and, possibly, aggression towards fellow employees.

Individuals react to stress physiologically. On encountering a threatening situation, a person experiences a release of hormones which drains blood from the skin and the digestive system; glucose and fat are released into the bloodstream, and breathing becomes more rapid. Whether this is harmful or beneficial depends on the background to the event and its duration — initial excitement can quickly develop into serious long-run distress. Causes of stress at work include the following.

(a) Not knowing which tasks should assume priority and thus trying (unsuccessfully) to complete all of them simultaneously.

(b) Unclear job descriptions and organisation charts/manuals leading to ambiguity about who should do what.

(c) Feelings of personal inadequacy and insecurity.

(d) Frustrations at not being able to get things done.

(e) Lack of communication with superiors, and conflicting demands placed on the individual by superiors who impose incompatible goals. For example, technical managers may demand high-quality output from a certain section, while the firm's accountant concurrently insists that the head of the section drastically reduce its operating costs.

(f) Bad personal relationships with other workers.

(g) Overwork, which may be quantitative (having too much work to do) or qualitative (finding work too difficult). Moreover, long working hours are frequently connected with a poor diet, lack of exercise and inadequate relaxation.

The symptoms of stress can be physical, psychological and/or behavioural. Physical manifestations include restlessness, hyperactivity, impatience, high blood pressure, headaches, weight loss and skin complaints. Stress might also cause other illnesses which result from its effects — excessive smoking, drinking, poor diet, and so on. Severe exhaustion, cramp and backache can occur in extreme cases.

Anxiety is perhaps the clearest indicator that someone is unable to cope. It affects the abilities to concentrate and relax, creates irritability and generates feelings of malaise and unease.

Perceptions are affected — stress-ridden individuals can become irrational, emotionally volatile and excessively suspicious. Employees who experience stress-created fatigue will be dull, clumsy, unable to think clearly or perform work for long periods.

Work performance typically deteriorates when individuals experience protracted exposure to high levels of stress. Some individuals become antagonistic, others withdraw into themselves. Tension, tiredness and anxiety often lead to outbursts of hostility and aggression. Workers become oversensitive to criticism, and increasingly unable to relate to friends and working colleagues. Sleep patterns alter, daytime tiredness ensues. The general run-down in a person's health can lead to frequent colds, upset stomachs and other minor illnesses. Routine errors become more frequent. Stress-prone individuals have more accidents than others. Many people respond by taking tranquillisers (or anti-depressants), smoking heavily (with consequent health problems), or by drinking excessive amounts of alcohol. Marital and other family difficulties are common among stress-ridden people.

4. Coping with stress

The first step in coping with stress is to recognise its inevitability in certain types of work: repression of anxiety only makes the situation worse. Thereafter, the following techniques and strategies might be useful for accommodating stress.

(a) Delegation of duties to subordinates to avoid work overload.

(b) Deciding in advance when to withdraw from particularly stressful activities, e.g. making a conscious predetermined decision to leave a meeting if certain contentious issues are discussed, or specifying a maximum personal workload and never exceeding this.

(c) Keeping a *stress diary* to record all stressful occurrences and hence identify common causes.

(d) Conscious relaxation.

(e) Training in personal assertion and/or psychological self-awareness methods such as transactional analysis.

(f) Restructuring jobs in order to remove exceptionally stressful elements (which should then be redistributed equally among all the staff).

5.   Fatigue and the design of jobs

It is in the interests of both employers and employees to reduce fatigue. Rest pauses have been shown to be very effective in this, ten minutes away from the job bringing large dividends in increased production. (It is strange that when the benefits of rest pauses are well-established they are so frequently used as bargaining counters; employees often agree to give up their rest pauses in exchange for a pay increase, as though management were buying back a troublesome concession.)

Besides introducing rest pauses managers may find it possible to adopt one of the measures described in 2:**20–22**, in the hope that it may increase motivation. Another approach is to apply ergonomics to the design of jobs (*see* **9, 10**); fatigue can be reduced by attention to illumination, noise, position of controls, avoidance of extreme temperatures or humidity, etc.

6.   Visual display units (VDUs)

Perhaps the most problematic working 'hazard' of recent times is the effect on workers of protracted exposure to computer visual display units. Critics suggest that heavy VDU users (especially those who operate wordprocessors) suffer eye strain, headaches, muscular disfunctions, and absorb excessive amounts of radiation. It may be that the heat and static electricity generated by VDUs engenders lethargy and general feelings of ill-health among long-term users, and this might cause persistent tiredness. Pregnant women, it is sometimes alleged, are especially vulnerable. Staring at a VDU hour after hour can make workers clumsy, drowsy, and unable to think clearly or to concentrate.

Such concerns have led to an EC Directive on VDU work. This is discussed fully in 24:**7**.

Accidents at work

7.   Definition

An accident at work is an unplanned event which occurs within a planned programme and is actually or potentially harmful to the worker.

8.   Accident proneness

During the 1914–18 war, studies in munitions factories produced the concept of accident proneness — that certain employees are inherently likely to be involved in accidents to a greater degree than others, irrespective of the job or working environment. The original research showed that a large proportion of the accidents suffered by a group of workers happened in fact to a very small minority; the members of this small minority were then called accident prone.

Later research has not always confirmed the findings. It has often been found, for example, that workers who appear to be accident prone during one period are safe workers during another period, their places being taken by workers who previously had low accident records. As an illustration of this, it was found in a study of nearly 30,000 bus drivers in America that the unsafe drivers in a three-year period became the safe drivers over the next three years. Conversely, the safe drivers in the first period, i.e. those who had one accident or none, became unsafe in the second, causing no less than 96.3 per cent of all accidents occurring in the whole group.

The explanation of this kind of result seems to be that the liability to become involved in accidents is due more to chance factors and the behaviour of others than to an inherent quality in the worker. On the other hand, accident statistics have sometimes shown that even in different periods the same workers have an above-average proneness to accidents, but only when their jobs have not changed. The generally accepted view at present is that accident proneness in the sense of a disadvantage that certain workers always take with them wherever they go is very rare; we must think instead of accident proneness as a result of the interaction between the worker and his or her job situation.

Thus insofar as accident proneness exists at all, it is due to:

(a)   unsuitability for the job, or lack of training in it;
(b)   temporary factors, e.g. frustration, worry or ill-health;
(c)   a very small number of inherently unsafe workers.

Other theoretical approaches to the explanation of differences in accident rates between organisations and workers are:

(a) *the domino theory* of accidents, which asserts that accidents typically occur following a predictable series of independent stages involving (*i*) an unsafe environment, (*ii*) individual fault, and (*iii*) a dangerous act.

(b) *the situational theory* of accidents, i.e. the hypothesis that accidents typically result from failures in working systems rather than individual behaviour or accident proneness.

Chapter 23 will deal with practical measures for reducing accidents and will outline the legal position. A great contribution to industrial safety may also be made by ergonomics, described in the next section.

Ergonomics

9. Definition

Ergonomics is concerned with the study of the mutual adjustment between people and their work. It draws contributions from both psychology and physiology in order to design equipment, the environment and working procedures which will promote both the well-being of employees and the effectiveness of work processes. It regards the worker not as an adjunct to the machine but as part of a human/machine production unit, behaving according to the following sequence.

(a) Stimulus, e.g. instruments, warning lights and buzzers, appearance, sound or smell of work in progress.

(b) Perception (through the appropriate senses) and decision making.

(c) Response, e.g. operating controls, using tools or hands, communicating with others.

(d) Result, i.e. a change in the work, which produces new stimuli, thus repeating the sequence.

> NOTE: In the USA the terms human factors engineering or human engineering are used instead of ergonomics.

10. Ergonomic design of equipment

Although designers of working equipment have always considered the human operator to some extent, there are many machines which are unnecessarily difficult for the human being, i.e. stimuli are hard to recognise and responses cannot be made easily or quickly. These problems were very important in the 1939–45 war when ergonomics was rapidly developed and applied to the design of tanks, guns and aircraft.

The ergonomist tries to fit the process to the person, rather than expect the individual to do the best with equipment which has been designed with engineering, rather than human, considerations in mind. The following approaches are adopted.

(a) *Displays* — are the things the operator looks at and listens to providing information quickly, easily and unambiguously? Should dials, gauges, warning lights, etc., be redesigned? Is perception difficult?

(b) *Controls* — can the operator change the state of the machine and materials, quickly, easily and naturally? Are levers, wheels, switches, etc., in the most convenient position?

(c) *Working environment* — is the operator's place of work well lit, heated to an appropriate temperature and free from excessive noise or humidity?

The working environment

11. Illumination

Research has established minimum standards of illumination necessary for many industrial tasks. Examples of these standards, expressed in lux, are:

Very fine assembly work	1,500
Medium assembly work	300
Weaving of light cloth	300
Weaving of dark cloth	700
Sheet metal work	200

A lux is the light given by a standard candle at a distance of one metre from the work; very approximately 10 lux are equivalent to the light given by one-fifth of a watt passing through a filament lamp, or by one-fifteenth of a watt passing through a fluorescent tube.

The minimum lighting for the areas surrounding the actual task — environmental or amenity lighting — should not be less than 150 lux. The degree of illumination can easily be measured with light-meters, and the installation of suitable lighting is not usually difficult or expensive. Expert advice is available from illumination engineers, but some of the most important rules are as follows.

(a) Task lighting should be focused on the task itself; focusing on an area adjacent to the task will cause fatigue and loss of attention.

(b) Too much contrast between the lighting of the task and the lighting of the environment causes eye fatigue, and may lead to accidents because the worker may find difficulty in adjusting his or her vision when moving from a bright to a relatively dark area.

(c) Glare can produce discomfort or poor vision. It can be minimised by ensuring that lights do not shine in workers' eyes and that working surfaces do not reflect light.

(d) Some variety in the visual environment should be provided by walls of different colours or the sight of some distant object, e.g. a view through a window.

(e) Even when workshops and offices appear to be well lit by daylight from windows and glass roofs, the illumination may have to be supplemented by artificial light because some areas may be in shadow. The colour of the supplementary lighting should then be a good match to daylight.

(f) Dirty windows, walls or light sources reduce the illumination available. They should be cleaned and maintained regularly.

12. Noise

Like illumination, noise can be measured by meters and its intensity expressed in numerical terms, the unit of measurement being the *decibel*.

Confusion can sometimes occur because the scale of decibels is logarithmic, i.e. an increase of x units in the scale means that sound intensity has increased by x *times* the previous amount, not *plus* x. Therefore an increase from 70 to 80 decibels means that the sound is ten times louder. The noise made by a hydraulic press (approximately 130 decibels at one metre) is 10,000,000,000,000 times the intensity of the faintest sound the average person can hear (one decibel).

There are four unfortunate effects of noise in industry.

(a) *Deafness* — exposure to loud and prolonged noise will in most people produce deafness, beginning with inability to hear high notes. Deafness may occur so slowly that the worker may not notice it; an enlightened employer will test the hearing of the firm's employees to see if their hearing is deteriorating in noisy conditions (very roughly an intensity of 80 decibels or more).

(b) *Efficiency* — research shows that repetitive work which is not mentally demanding does not suffer when carried out in noisy conditions. On the other hand, work which requires accuracy, concentration and alertness will deteriorate. For example, inspection and calculation become less efficient under noise, and scrap or spoiled work becomes more frequent. It is also probable, though not definitely proved, that noise increases the number of accidents.

(c) *Annoyance* — employees seem able to become accustomed to practically any level of noise in time, but they will complain about it when the noise is:

   (*i*) occasional (particularly when high pitched);
  (*ii*) apparently unnecessary;
 (*iii*) unexpected;
  (*iv*) unexplained.

Therefore the annoyance caused by noise can often be reduced by explanations or warnings.

(d) *Interference with communication* — oral messages may be unheard or misunderstood in noisy conditions.

Noise may be reduced by silencing the machine or enclosing it in insulating material, and by facing interior walls, floors and ceilings with sound-absorbent surfaces. If it is still above an acceptable level, employees should be given ear-defenders to wear, though quite often complaints are made that they are cumbersome. It may be necessary for supervisors to enforce their use.

13. Heating and ventilation

In this field three factors are important: temperature, humidity and air movement. All three can affect performance and comfort at work.

(a) *Temperature* — in factories the optimum air temperature for light work is 10°C (65°F) and the range in which most people feel comfortable is 15° to 20°C (60° to 70°F). Heavy work in factories is best carried out within a range of 12° to 15°C (55° to 60°F). In offices the comfort zone is 19° to 23°C (67° to 73°F).

(b) *Humidity* — this is only important when conditions are extremely damp or extremely dry. In the first case employees complain of stuffiness and in the second they feel uncomfortable because of dryness of the nose and throat.

(c) *Air movement* — it is generally agreed that an air movement of about ten metres per second should be aimed at; this level of movement is just perceptible. If temperatures are above or below the ideal, then air movement should be greater or less, respectively, than ten metres per minute. Air movement may be improved by the use of fans or by an air conditioning system.

Unlike illumination and noise, which can be fairly easily modified at any time, the heating and ventilation characteristics of the working environment are much less flexible and often depend on the way in which the building was designed. It can be very expensive to install air conditioning or improve the central heating after a building is complete; they should be fully considered at the time when the building is being planned.

14. The sick building syndrome

Deficiencies in some of the previously mentioned environmental factors can combine to create what has come to be known as the 'sick building syndrome' (a syndrome is a collection of several symptoms of a malaise). The term is commonly applied to certain types of recently constructed office premises that have air conditioning, sealed heating systems, sound-proofed rooms, uniform layout of sections, etc., which in unison tend to cause headaches, eye strain, lethargic depression, and other minor illnesses among the people who work in them.

Progress test 6

1. What are the two most important laws of physical fatigue? (2)

2. State the ways in which psychological fatigue can be reduced. (3, 4)

3. What are the major causes of stress at work? (3, 4)

4. Is there such a thing as accident proneness? (8)

5. Describe how ergonomic principles can be applied to the design of machines and equipment? (10)

6. How should a large workshop containing several machines used for high precision work be illuminated? (11)

7. In what ways does deafness detract from a worker's efficiency? (12)

8. Explain why heating and ventilation can be a more difficult problem than illumination or noise? (13)

7
Social psychology at work

The behaviour of working groups

1. The formation of a working group

So far in this book the employee has been studied mainly as an individual, responding in various ways to the psychological and physical conditions in which he or she works, without reference to fellow-employees. This assumption is very often quite unrealistic. Work is rarely an activity carried out in solitude; most of us have colleagues whose wishes and personalities we have to learn to understand because we work closely with them. When we work with others, merely understanding them is not enough; it is necessary for us to modify our behaviour to some extent, acting in ways which are acceptable to them rather than completely satisfying to ourselves.

After people have worked closely and continuously with each other for some time, the mutual adjustments of behaviour settles down into a fixed pattern, a set of mental attitudes becomes established which all share, and very often certain customs become so strongly entrenched that they are almost compulsory. A collection of individuals has now been transformed into a *working group*, which is a special type of *social group*.

2. The work of Elton Mayo

The importance of the working group was first shown clearly by Elton Mayo and his colleagues in a detailed study of worker behaviour at the Western Electric Company factory at Hawthorne, near Chicago, between 1924 and 1932.

Mayo had been called in by the management because production at the factory was thought to be too low. At first Mayo experimented with the illumination, following the current belief that if physical conditions were suitable and the pay adequate there was no reason why employees should not work hard. A puzzling result of the experiment was that output increased even when lighting was made worse. Because definite conclusions were difficult to draw from the behaviour of a large department when its working conditions were varied, he eventually segregated five female operators into a separate room so that their behaviour could more easily be controlled and observed.

3. The relay assembly test room

During the period 1927 to 1929 variations in rest pauses and working hours were made and compared with the output of the five women. Throughout the period, even during the times when working conditions had been made worse, output steadily increased. When the women were interviewed to find an explanation for this unexpected result they said:

(a) they enjoyed working in the test room, and worked harder there than in the factory because they felt special;
(b) they did not regard the observer who was present in the room with them as a normal supervisor because he explained things to them and reassured them;
(c) the experiment seemed to show that management was interested in them;
(d) they helped each other at work and had developed close friendships with each other away from work;
(e) they felt united and had a common purpose.

4. The bank wiring room

Between November 1931 and May 1932 a group of men were put into a special room but in other respects continued working under their usual conditions. The group, which was engaged in the assembly of banks for use in telephone exchanges, consisted of nine wiremen, three soldermen and two inspectors. An observer also sat in the room but did not participate in any way, the men sometimes being interviewed outside the room by another member of Mayo's staff. A supervisor was formally in charge of the men, but was present in the room only part of the time.

Payment was made according to a rather complicated piece-work scheme. The following observations were made.

(a) The men worked to an unofficial level of output; if anyone worked harder than this he was abused by the others.

(b) Reported figures for output and delay time(when stoppages occurred for reasons beyond a worker's control) were false; they showed a constant, instead of a variable, output week by week.

(c) The men often exchanged jobs, contrary to management instructions. They often helped each other.

(d) The supervisor knew about these practices, but did not try to stop them. He was not regarded by the group as their leader.

(e) One wireman, though conforming with the unofficial norms of production, used to tell the foreman about irregular practices. He was the outcast of the group, and was called 'squealer'.

(f) Unofficial leaders in the group were more influential than the official leader, the foreman.

5. Conclusions from the Hawthorne studies

The steadily increasing level of output in the relay assembly room was ascribed by Mayo to the beneficial effects of a united working group outweighing the deteriorating physical working conditions. The bank wiring room study had shown, however, that a united working group could oppose management interests by restricting its output. Thus the working group was shown to be powerful enough to override working conditions on the one hand and a payment-by-results scheme on the other.

When the Hawthorne results were published the relay assembly room received most attention, and the human relations movement which appeared soon afterwards emphasised the encouragement of united working groups because it was thought that good performance would follow. This advice did not always bring the hoped-for result, firstly because it is not always possible to manipulate employees into cohesive groups, and secondly because it is never certain that the groups, if formed, would agree that their own objectives coincided with those of management, i.e. they might resemble the bank wiring room rather than the relay assembly room.

6.   Working groups — benefits to the employee

An individual at work can derive certain benefits from becoming a member of a group:

(a) satisfaction of social needs;
(b) the benefits of shared experience, e.g. an experienced worker showing the ropes to a newcomer;
(c) mutual support, e.g. colleagues backing up someone who is having a dispute with management;
(d) a basis for self-expression, because the security afforded by the group often encourages creativity.

7.   Formation of working groups

A collection of individual employees does not automatically become a working group. The conditions which will cause a group to form and make it cohesive are as follows.

(a) The employees must be near enough to each other for easy face-to-face communication.
(b) The work they are doing must be related; e.g. they form parts of a chain (like a progressive assembly line), are doing similar jobs (as in the relay assembly room), or have the same purpose (like a committee organising a works outing).
(c) The individuals must be compatible, without great differences in status, skill or education.
(d) The total number should not exceed about twelve, though this depends on physical arrangements in the workplace.
(e) An external threat will often cause a collection of individuals to form themselves into a group.

8.   Behaviour of working groups

When a working group has come into existence it will behave in certain characteristic ways, very much as if it had a life of its own independent of the lives of the individuals included in it.

(a) The group will produce a settled system of personal relationships and customs.
(b) These customs sometimes include restrictions on output.
(c) Individuals will often behave more in the way the group expects than as they would if left to themselves.

(d) The group exerts great pressure on all its members to conform to its own standards of behaviour.

(e) Newcomers to the group are often made to feel unwelcome. Groups vary in this respect just as individuals vary in their ability to become easily accepted by a group.

(f) The group tends to resist change imposed on it, and will react to it slowly because of the threat to its existence, its security, its customs and its pattern of relationships.

(g) Unofficial leaders emerge in the group, changing according to the needs of the situation at the time. When the group is in open conflict to the management, for example, it may choose as its leader a person whom normally its members would describe as an agitator. When conditions settle down, a new leader might emerge who would be a more diplomatic person.

(h) A group often seems to follow the same motivation process as an individual — searching for and eventually perceiving satisfying goals. It can be frustrated and show the negative reactions of aggression, regression, resignation and fixation.

(i) The character of a group will not change because one person leaves it or joins it, unless that person is extremely influential.

(j) An external threat or the competition of another group will increase the cohesiveness of a group.

9. Group cohesiveness

The extent to which individuals feel that they are members of a group, and the strength of their attachment to the group is called cohesiveness or morale. It is shown by the frequent use of the word 'we' instead of 'I', the help group members give each other and the perseverance and enthusiasm they show. Cohesive working groups usually have low rates of labour turnover (*see* Chapter 17) and absence.

Many factors contribute to the creation of group cohesion, including the following.

(a) How often group members come into contact with each other.

(b) How enthusiastically members support group aims.

(c) The extent to which members feel they belong to an exclusive and special group.

(d) Whether members share common interests.

(e) Whether members have a common background, education, age, outlook, or ethnic or social origin.

(f) The existence of external threats to the group.

(g) How easily group members can communicate.

(h) Whether members are engaged on similar work.

A high degree of cohesiveness is not always linked with high productivity. Restriction of output by working groups is widespread, and is usually found in groups cohesive enough to be able to rely on the observance of limits of output by its members. On the other hand when organisation structure or work methods are rearranged to facilitate the formation of working groups, productivity is sometimes increased.

It is possible to find any combination of cohesiveness and productivity; no doubt many people have encountered happy united groups which do very little work, or sections composed of workers who dislike each other but nevertheless show above-average rates of output. The relationship between cohesiveness and productivity is similar to that between individual job satisfaction and productivity (*see* 2:28), that is, it depends on the group's perception of its own interests. However, although the effect of group cohesiveness on output is uncertain, an employer's costs will nearly always be reduced by the presence of cohesive working groups because labour turnover and absence will be comparatively low.

10. Working groups: implications for management

Research shows that working groups can be powerful forces within an organisation. Sometimes their presence is beneficial to management, e.g. the relay assembly room, and sometimes the reverse, e.g. the bank wiring room, because there is no reliable connection between the cohesiveness of a group and its rate of production.

The working group must also be considered in relation to the formal structure of the organisation; does the group coincide with an official section or department, or does it draw its membership from several of them? Frequently a company is organised by function, i.e. production workers belong to one department, maintenance workers to another and clerks to a third. An informal working group, consisting of people working near each other on the same task, could possibly include members of each of these three departments. A somewhat similar situation occurs when the unofficial leader of the group and the officially appointed foreperson or manager are rivals for the allegiance of the group, creating confusion and lack of control.

If management wishes to make constructive use of informal working groups, and minimise the difficulties they can sometimes bring, the following measures are often recommended.

(a) By ensuring that working conditions are good, that employment policies are fair and by taking a personal interest in the employees, encourage groups to perceive the company's interests as coinciding with their own, thus increasing productivity.

(b) In any case, making it easier for cohesive groups to form because labour turnover and absenteeism will be reduced.

(c) When making changes, remember the instinctive opposition of the working group.

(d) Arrange for competition between groups, so that cohesiveness will increase. Greater output may also occur.

(e) Examine incentive schemes to see if they can be based on the output of the group instead of the individual (*see* 22:**6**).

(f) If practicable, make the working group coincide with the official section or department. In some cases the functional division of authority may have to be abandoned.

(g) If it is not possible to give the unofficial leader an official post, give some sort of recognition perhaps by including that person in joint consultation procedures. Train forepeople and managers in human relations skills so that the group will be more satisfied with its official leadership.

11. Contemporary views about working groups

In recent years the human relations movement (*see* **5**) has become less influential; although the working group is still regarded as a very important factor in industrial behaviour it is no longer thought to be supreme. The reasons for this change of view are as follows.

(a) An increasing recognition of the importance of ego and self-actualisation needs (*see* 2:**2**), placing more emphasis on the content and meaning of the job. It is often thought more useful to make the work intrinsically interesting than to try to manipulate social groupings.

(b) Many human relations writers seem to adopt a paternalistic attitude, accepting the jobs as they are and merely advocating more attention to the social climate.

(c) It is difficult to predict the behaviour of working groups, except as regards labour turnover and absenteeism. Sometimes a cohesive group has high productivity, sometimes the reverse (*see* 9).

(d) Evidence that many workers expect to satisfy only their physiological and security needs at work, forming few friendships there and accepting uninteresting jobs providing a good wage is paid.

(e) Changes in technology which sometimes break up working groups, separating individuals from each other and making communication difficult because of noise or pressure to work at a certain pace.

The human relations movement has, however, been very valuable in opening up the study of non-economic incentives at work, though the emphasis has now changed from the rewards of social satisfaction to the rewards of job extension (*see* 2:20–21). It also stimulated research into leadership in commerce and industry, described in the next chapter.

Attitudes

12. Definition of attitude

An attitude is an individual's characteristic way of responding to an object or situation. It is based on experience and leads to certain behaviour or the expression of certain opinions.

In contrast to a need, which is short-lived and transitory, an attitude is long-lasting and exists even when all needs are for the moment satisfied. For example, a professional social worker will have taken up that occupation because he or she has a certain attitude towards the care of others, but within that occupation he or she will be motivated from time to time by the considerations discussed in Chapter 2. Attitudes provide a predetermined set of responses, so that a person's behaviour or opinions can often be forecast in certain situations. Knowing a person's attitude towards politics, for example, one can be fairly accurate in predicting what that person will say when asked to comment on a topical issue.

Attitudes may be held on any subject, though frequently it appears that attitudes held by a person may be grouped together under a general heading such as authoritarian or permissive. Someone having a certain attitude will hold corresponding beliefs, but a person having an opposite attitude will hold equally sincerely beliefs of a quite different kind. Perception is also strongly influenced by attitudes; thus some people will perceive a situation as favourable to them while others will perceive a situation as unfavourable. In extreme cases attitudes can prevent people from believing facts which a very large majority consider true and abundantly proved.

At work, attitudes towards management will strongly influence the reactions of the employees towards any management communication; in extreme cases practically any announcement will be greeted with complete scepticism.

13. How attitudes are formed and changed

Research shows that experience within a social group is the most important factor in determining attitudes, starting with experience in the family group and continuing in groups at school, among friends and at work. The process of attitude formation is somewhat mysterious but need not be examined in detail here.

Attitude change is more important at work, since it may explain why an employee's behaviour has altered and it may be necessary sometimes to attempt to bring about a change in a desired direction for training purposes (*see* 20:**1–3**) or to improve industrial relations. There are three main ways in which attitudes are changed.

(a) The pressure exerted by a social group on an individual member to conform with group standards, which include the accepted attitudes of the group. This may occur naturally when a newcomer joins a group, or may be contrived as a part of training. In the latter case the group is made to undergo an experience like discussing or acting out a real or imaginary situation which it is hoped will cause the attitudes of all the participants to change to some extent.

(b) Through the influence of a highly-respected individual.
(c) As a result of a severe shock or intense pressure, e.g. a wartime experience.

Process **(a)** is the most likely to occur in commerce and industry and it will be dealt with in 20:2.

14. The measurement of attitudes

It is useful for management to know the nature and strength of the attitudes of its employees as a guide to future policy and to show possible causes of poor industrial relations. For example, if a large number of employees were leaving the company an enquiry into attitudes might reveal the reasons and indicate what could be done to retain more employees. The chief ways in which attitudes may be detected or measured are as follows.

(a) A *searching interview* in which the employee is encouraged to express his or her attitudes. Because this method is so lengthy and costly it is usual to apply it to a random sample of employees rather than to all. To encourage frank speaking the interviewing is done by people independent of management, e.g. a firm of consultants.
(b) An *exit interview* given when an employee is leaving the company. The employee is asked to explain fully why he or she is leaving, the reply often revealing the attitudes of that person and his or her colleagues. Although it seems reasonable to expect that someone who is leaving a company will speak more freely than someone who is not, experience shows that often the leaver is guarded in his or her remarks, partly to protect colleagues and partly to be able to leave in a friendly and placid atmosphere.
(c) *Attitude surveys*, which ask employees to comment on a list of statements or questions, indicating those with which they agree. The two principal types are those devised by Thurstone and Likert; both enable an attitude to be given a numerical score which can be correlated by statistical methods with other measurable behaviour (*see Statistics* by W. M. Harper, in this series).

The attitudes of employees are shown, of course, in their everyday conversation and behaviour at work. A supervisor or manager whose communications with subordinates are good will from this evidence know many of their attitudes and how strongly they are held, though the difference in status will probably prevent his or her knowledge from being complete.

Roles

15. Roles

A 'role' is a self-contained pattern of behaviour considered typical of a person who occupies a certain social position, e.g. husband, mother, office boy, senior manager, etc. Role theory concerns how individuals behave, how they feel they ought to behave, and how they believe other people should respond to their actions. For example, a supervisor might be expected to behave (perhaps even dress and speak) in a particular manner — distinct standards and norms of conduct may be anticipated from those who occupy a supervisory role.

The term 'role category' describes a complete class of person belonging to a specific social division ('leader', 'old person', 'senior executive', etc.). Through experience, individuals eventually form role categories into which people of the various occupational classes they encounter may be placed. A company welfare officer, for instance, may be expected always to behave in a sympathetic manner — regardless of his or her personality, background or general approach to management affairs. Such generalisations simplify social interrelationships, since once stereotypes are established it is no longer necessary for the individual to analyse every situation he or she confronts.

A person's actual role behaviour may or may not conform to expectations; it might deviate significantly, or be quite irrelevant to the situation in hand. Thus, for example, a high-ranking executive might be an extremely bad organiser, despite the ability to organise being a major assumption of a senior manager's role. Ideally, an individual's perceptions of 'correct' behaviour in a job will correspond to senior management's interpretation of what the worker ought to be doing and thinking about his or her occupational role. Sometimes, however, these perceptions differ — possibly resulting in 'role strain', which occurs when the demands of a role overtax its occupant's ability to cope to the extent that he or she does not behave in accordance with the expectations attached to the role. Consider, for example, the supervisor whose subordinates expect him or her to represent them to senior management but whose own superiors insist on that person implementing all management decisions regardless of their industrial relations effects.

Individuals who cannot live up to role expectations may experience feelings of inadequacy, embarrassment and guilt. Interactions with others become difficult, and could eventually collapse.

A person might be unclear about the exact nature of his or her role. The more explicit and specific the expectations attached to a role the easier it is to conform to its requirements. Role ambiguity can cause stress, insecurity and loss of self-confidence. An example might be a newly-appointed head of department who is not entirely clear about how much authority he or she commands.

Serious problems occur when role occupants and others disagree fundamentally about the contents of a role, i.e. the duties it covers, ranges of acceptable behaviour, whether certain actions are voluntary or mandatory and (importantly) which of the role occupant's obligations should assume priority.

In setting role priorities, a person might select for priority those role behaviours which:

(a) correspond to his or her personal ethical standards and perceptions of moral worth;
(b) are expedient;
(c) bring the greatest personal reward and/or avoid personal cost;
(d) avoid controversy or unpleasant relationships with people the individual particularly respects.

16. Jobs and careers

A career is a related series of jobs in an ascending order of status and responsibility. Career development may occur within a single (usually large) organisation; through a person moving between organisations; or by a mixture of the two. Advantages to *organisations* of having employees who are pursuing careers (rather than holding *ad-hoc* jobs) are as follows.

(a) Individuals might be motivated to work hard in order to further their careers.
(b) Employees have definite career targets at which to aim.

(c) Workers' loyalties to their occupations and/or employing organisations might be enhanced.
(d) Employees' competence will increase systematically over time.
(e) Management succession schemes can be drafted more easily.
(f) Career planning can be directly related to the firm's performance appraisal and management by objectives systems.

Advantages to *individuals* of following a career include:

(a) feelings of security resulting from the likelihood that his or her job opportunities will increase as the person's career progresses;
(b) enhanced self-awareness resulting from being forced to analyse personal strengths and weaknesses and the career options available;
(c) acquisitions of useful experience as the employee selects jobs in organisations, departments, divisions, etc., that will best promote his or her career;
(d) having a tangible long term objective.

To plan a career a person needs to establish career priorities, closely observe the behaviour and attitudes of individuals who have already succeeded in the field, select jobs which build on personal strengths and minimise the effects of personal weaknesses, obtain the appropriate training, and if possible find a 'sponsor' who is an existing senior manager in the occupation or organisation concerned and who can assist and advise the junior person. Thereafter, the individual must regularly monitor his or her career achievements and carefully analyse the reasons for any shortcomings. Some organisations provide career counselling to assist employees in these respects.

Progress test 7

1. Summarise the results of the experiment in the relay assembly test room at Hawthorne. (3)

2. What were the main observations made in the bank wiring room at Hawthorne? (4)

3. What benefits does an employee obtain from membership of a working group?   **(6)**

4. Under what conditions is a working group likely to form?   **(7)**

5. Describe some of the main characteristics of a working group.   **(8)**

6. What is the relationship between group cohesiveness and productivity?   **(9)**

7. How can the existence of working groups affect management policy?   **(10)**

8. Define attitude. How can an attitude be changed?   **(12, 13)**

9. What is a role expectation?   **(15)**

10. What is a career?   **(16)**

8
Leadership and participation

Unofficial and official leaders

1. The unofficial leader

Leadership is the ability of a person to influence the thoughts and behaviour of others. In psychological studies, a leader is usually defined in terms of the group he or she leads; the leader is the person who directs and controls the group so that the purposes of the group are achieved. When a group forms spontaneously by a process of social interaction, it quite frequently has more than one leader at any one time. The leaders in such a situation may be rivals, but more frequently share between themselves the various leadership functions of planning, directing, reviewing, etc. Different circumstances may bring about a change in leadership, different leaders emerging who seem more capable of dealing with the new situation.

In commerce and industry the unofficial leader can be a very important person, particularly when the working group is strongly united. The leader is sometimes given the semi-official status of shop steward (*see* 26:**10**), which recognises his or her importance and that person's place in relations between management and employees. Even when they do not have this status, unofficial leaders are often given special and privileged treatment by management. However, the importance of the unofficial leader tends to be intermittent, becoming active at times of crisis and quiescent in more placid circumstances. On the other hand, the official leader, the person given formal authority over others, is always important because of his or her function of seeing that a certain area of the firm's business is effectively dealt with.

2. The official leader

Extending the definition in the preceding section, an official leader is a person who motivates and controls subordinates to work towards goals which are regarded by the organisation as desirable and possible. The subordinates must therefore be led in such a way that they value the rewards they are able to obtain from their work; these may be money, friendship, status, approval, a sense of achievement or a mixture of these.

The official leader, who may be called, for example, supervisor, section leader or manager, possesses *authority* partly because he or she has been appointed by the owners of the company (or their representatives) and partly because of his or her competence to hold the post. Subject to employment law, official leaders have *power* over subordinates, i.e. such leaders can get them to do things they would otherwise not do, through their right to punish or reward, control of resources, knowledge of the job, skills in handling people and the respect for authority they may have. The way they combine these factors is called their *management style*, and a great deal of research has been carried out to try to identify the style which a manager should adopt to bring the best results from subordinates.

Note that authority and power need not coincide. Authority is the *right* to control, as determined by a person's position in the official management hierarchy. It is associated with taking decisions, giving orders, allocating work, and assigning rewards (pay rises, for instance) and penalties (e.g., demotion, suspension) to subordinates. Nevertheless, a person does not have to occupy an official management position in order to exercise power. Individuals can be powerful in consequence of their charisma, ability to satisfy other group members' needs, or their control over information or resources. Other determinants of power include:

(a) the extent to which a person is known, liked, trusted and respected by the group;

(b) whether group members identify with that individual;

(c) group members' perceptions that the person has expert knowledge of the activities on which the group is engaged, and/or their feelings that the person's position is legitimate — say because of seniority within the group.

Leadership studies

3.   Research in leadership

Early writers on leadership took the view that the *personality* of the leader was all important; they said that leaders were born, not made, perhaps coming from a certain class of society. They compiled lists of the personal qualities (intelligence, integrity, steadfastness, etc.) that were needed in a successful leader. These lists reflected of course the writers' own prejudices and were not based on careful observation and research. It was not an approach which could lead to any ways of improving leadership behaviour.

Later work on leadership has been conducted from a *behavioural* point of view; leaders and their subordinates are studied in actual work situations in order to discover whether certain kinds of leadership behaviour are more effective than others. Research of this kind has obvious difficulties, e.g. the presence of observers may distort normal behaviour, effectiveness is often difficult to measure, leaders' behaviour may be influenced by the quality of their subordinates, and descriptions of different management styles easily become very subjective. However, quite consistent results have been obtained from many hundreds of studies, two of the most important being summarised below.

4.   Empirical studies

Systematic empirical research into leadership style began in the USA in the late 1940s. One of the first of the major studies occurred in the offices of the Prudential Life Insurance Company. Researchers divided the firm into relatively high-producing and relatively low-producing departments, using the available records of the clerical time taken to deal with a certain amount of work. The supervisors of all the departments were then interviewed to find out how they approached their jobs and their attitudes towards the company, their subordinates and their colleagues. As a result of these interviews it was possible to divide the supervisors into two classes.

(a) *Employee-centred*, in which emphasis was given to relationships within the department, and to the preferences, needs and capacities of individual subordinates. The supervisor believed in helping subordinates to get promotion and in giving them general rather than close supervision.

(b) *Production-centred*, in which the subordinates were closely supervised and controlled, both as to the pace and the method of work. The need to get the work done on time was continually emphasised.

When the productivity of the departments and the management styles of the supervisors were compared, it was found that there was a very strong tendency for the high-producing departments to be run by employee-centred supervisors and for the low-producing departments to be under production-centred supervisors, the efforts of the latter to push the work through being apparently self-defeating.

The lesson drawn from this study was that supervisors should be encouraged or trained to move away from a production-centred approach and adopt an employee-centred style of management to obtain the best results from their subordinates.

This pioneering study was followed by a wide-ranging investigation into management style conducted by researchers from Ohio State University, who collected a large amount of information about leadership approaches by means of interviews, observation and questionnaires. A preliminary examination of this material suggested that nine dimensions of management behaviour might exist. Statistical analysis was applied to the data, and two major factors emerged by which managerial style could be described.

(a) *Consideration* — including emphasis on mutual trust and respect between manager and subordinate, consideration for subordinates' feelings, and two-way communication.

(b) *Initiating structure* — the close definitions of the jobs of subordinates, great activity by the manager in planning, controlling, initiating new ideas and criticising subordinates.

It will be seen that these definitions of two independent dimensions of management behaviour are very similar to the definitions of employee-centredness and production-centredness which were assumed to be at the opposite ends of one dimension. For convenience and clarity, the two dimensions will be called emphasis on task and emphasis on the people.

In the first the manager regards subordinates as factors of production at his or her disposal for performing a certain task. The manager will direct and control them in precise terms, their reward for accepting this being monetary payment. It is improbable that they would obtain satisfaction of ego or self-actualisation needs in these circumstances.

Managers who put the emphasis on people regard subordinates almost as equals and do not exercise strict authority over them. The manager assumes that they have ideas to contribute and that it is part of the leadership function to draw out these ideas. Another assumption is that they will produce good work without close or detailed supervision, i.e. that the job itself provides part of the motivation, perhaps by the satisfaction of the higher needs.

Another part of the Ohio State University study was concerned with the relationship between management style and employee satisfaction, as expressed in the rate of labour turnover and the number of grievances. It was found that both turnover and grievances were highest when the management style showed low consideration, irrespective of the degree of initiating structure that was shown. The lowest rates of turnover and grievances were found when the management style showed medium to high consideration with low initiating structure. Thus the degree of consideration seems to be the dominant factor in determining this area of employee behaviour. The research did not, however, show a similar clear relationship between a particular management style and productivity.

5. Subsequent research

Subsequent research has confirmed the Ohio findings, though the dimensions are often given other names.

(a) The analysis of leadership behaviour worked out by Blake and Mouton (*see below*) and known as the managerial grid uses the terms concern for people and concern for production.

(b) Another approach, by W. J. Reddin, calls the dimensions relationships orientation and task orientation, but adds a third dimension, effectiveness.

(c) F. E. Fiedler, in his research into leadership, uses the terms permissive, non-directive and task-controlling, directive.

(d) Douglas McGregor's theory X and theory Y which are described in 12 are similar in that theory X has a resemblance to initiating structure and theory Y to consideration.

(e) R. Likert uses the terms co-operative-motivation system and job-organisation system.

Other important studies were those of:

(a) K. Lewin, R. Lippitt and R.K. White, who investigated the effects of autocratic, democratic and *'laissez-faire'* leadership styles in boys clubs in Iowa in the USA, concluding that democratic approaches were generally more effective. Use of autocratic styles caused test subjects to become aggressive, discontented, and to lack initiative and commitment when completing tasks.

(b) R. Tannenbaum and W.H. Schmidt, whose researches led them to argue that managers should consider three sets of factors when choosing a leadership style:

(*i*) the background, values and experiences of the leader (including his or her abilities and attitudes towards employee participation);

(*ii*) the characteristics of subordinates (their competence, experience, interests, etc.);

(*iii*) the nature of the situation (type of task, extent of group cohesion, time available for taking decisions, and so on).

(c) W.W. Soujanen, who suggested that organisations which regularly experienced crisis situations tended to adopt authoritarian management styles, whereas 'routine-orientated' firms (i.e. normal, conventional businesses) usually opted for participative approaches.

Recent research into leadership has drawn a distinction between *'transactional'* and *'transformational'* leaders. Transactional leaders organise work efficiently, provide subordinates with the assistance and resources necessary for them to complete their duties, but do not attempt to transform employees' attitudes in order to increase their commitment to the firm. Transformational leaders, conversely, possess charisma, vision, and the ability to inspire subordinates towards *transcending* their immediate goals. This and other aspects of leadership theory are discussed at length in *Organisational Behaviour* in this series.

Effective leadership

6. The managerial grid

Robert Blake and Jane Mouton devised a 'managerial grid' illustrating degrees of concern for human relations and for efficiency. The grid is a taxonomy of management styles classified according to the manager's interest in subordinates as people in comparison with his or her concern for production. Each concern is rated on a scale from one to nine so that a '9,9' manager, for example, is one who possesses both a very high concern for people and a high concern for production. A '1,9' manager, who has a low concern for production but who greatly emphasises human relations, will pay careful attention to subordinates' human needs, but will exert little effort to ensure that work is actually done. Such a manger is likeable, enjoys satisfactory relations with subordinates and generates a friendly atmosphere in his or her department. The '9,1' manager arranges work as efficiently as possible, with scant regard for subordinates' feelings. Other potential combinations are '1,1' managers, who make little effort to get work done or develop close personal relationships, and '5,5' managers who balance task performance with human relations considerations. Best of all is the '9,9' manager who achieves high production from committed, satisfied subordinates. The various positions on the grid are illustrated in Fig. 8.1.

7. Management style and effectiveness

Although reductions in labour turnover and grievances are very valuable, the principal aim of the research into management style is to establish its relation to effectiveness, that is the degree to which it facilitates adequate or high productivity.

The studies at the Prudential Life Insurance Company showed a clear relationship, i.e. that the effective manager emphasised people. Later studies, however, did not produce such clear-cut results, some in fact showing the reverse relationship. Various other factors were then examined, among them the size of the firm, the personalities of the subordinates, the nature of the production process, the liking the subordinates had for the manager and the power the manager held in the organisation. It appears from all this research that no managerial style can be identified which will be effective in every situation; different work situations require different styles if they are to be managed effectively.

It is sometimes said that a manager's main skill is *diagnostic*; he or she assesses all the relevant factors in the work situation and diagnoses what management style will be the most effective. Unfortunately diagnosis cannot always be followed by appropriate behaviour, since many managers find it difficult to change their style (*see* **10**).

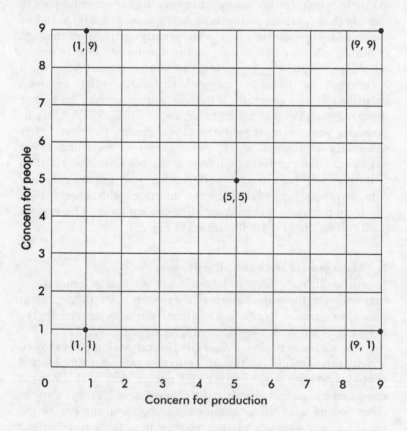

Figure 8.1 *Blake and Mouton's managerial grid*

8. The importance of the process

An important factor determining which particular management style is effective is the task structure — the extent to which the work is defined or programmed. Task structure in most cases depends on the technology, and is best illustrated by describing its two extremes.

(a) Structured or highly-programmed work, e.g. assembly-line work in a mass-production factory, is strictly defined as to method and time. Each individual job is specialised and must be carried out as defined in order that it may fit into a complex production system. There are few work decisions the subordinate can make.

(b) Unstructured or loosely-programmed work, e.g. as found in a research laboratory, is defined in very broad terms and gives the subordinate a large number of decisions regarding methods and sequence. Sometimes the task itself is rather vague, and there may be many possible ways of accomplishing it. The subordinate is often given the freedom to choose the way he or she prefers.

In highly-programmed work the manager will almost inevitably emphasise the *task*, for it is his or her responsibility to ensure that jobs are done according to their precise specification. There is little purpose in asking employees for their suggestions about the way the work should be done, and it is impracticable to allow them to work at their own pace; such deviations would certainly upset the efficiency of the process, and might indeed be dangerous.

In contrast, the manager of unstructured work will as a rule obtain the best results by emphasising *people*, because most employees prefer to control and arrange their own work rather than be closely supervised, and they often welcome the opportunity to contribute suggestions and ideas. When the work is loosely-programmed, close supervision is unnecessary and tends to be resented. The manager's job should be to see that subordinates are self-motivating and self-directing. The success of the employee-centred managers at the Prudential Insurance Co., where the work was comparatively unstructured, is an example.

In this analysis, individual differences among subordinates should not be overlooked; some do not expect or wish to contribute suggestions or take responsibility, while others (probably an increasing proportion) expect management to emphasise the people dimension and arrange jobs so that they will be less structured. The manager must therefore use his or her judgment to decide whether the attitudes of subordinates must override the requirements of the process.

9. Fiedler's theory of leadership effectiveness

The American psychologist F. E. Fiedler has put forward a theory, based on several studies, which modifies the simple relationship which has just been described. Fiedler suggests that although in general the task-centred approach is best for structured work, it may also be effective when the work is unstructured, relations between the manager and subordinates are poor and the manager's formal powers, e.g. of dismissal or promotion, are weak. In other words, when conditions are unfavourable for the manager the best plan is to take firm control of subordinates.

The theory goes on to confirm that in general the people-centred approach is best for unstructured work, but adds that this approach may also be effective when the work is structured and the manager powerful but not well-liked. Fiedler's analysis thus uses four variables:

(a) emphasis on task or people;
(b) task structure;
(c) manager-subordinate relationships;
(d) powers of the manager.

It shows that management style, to be effective, should take account of technology, social relationships and the place of the manager in the organisation.

Fiedler's work together with that of Tannenbaum and Schmidt and W.W. Soujanen formed the basis for the *contingency approach* to leadership, which asserts that there is no single management style that can be relied on to be completely effective in *all* situations. Rather, a leader's style should be varied to meet the needs of the particular situation to hand. Thus, leaders must be prepared to adjust their behaviour as circumstances change. This enables leaders to adopt management styles appropriate for specific groups and situations (e.g. using an autocratic approach when quick and unpopular decisions are needed). However, it could also lead to unpredictable and inconsistent behaviour on the leader's part. Moreover, managers require leadership training and experience to enable them to apply the contingency approach.

Further contingency approaches are those of P. Hersey and K.H. Blanchard, and J. Adair. Hersey and Blanchard developed a 'situational' model of leadership based on the 'maturity' of subordinates. Maturity is taken to mean an employee's work experience, technical competence, ability to assume responsibility, self-confidence and self-respect. According to the model, directive leadership is necessary for the control of freshly-recruited workers. Gradually, however, subordinates 'learn the ropes' and a participative management style becomes appropriate. Eventually, workers are able to act independently so that the need for close direction ends. A *laissez-faire* approach can now be applied.

John Adair suggests that, to be more effective, a leader must simultaneously satisfy three sets of interconnecting needs: task, group and individual. Task needs relate to the job being completed and involve planning, setting objectives, performance appraisal (*see* Chapter 18), work scheduling, etc. Group needs refer to the maintenance of team spirit, group cohesion, discipline, and other means for ensuring the group does not disintegrate. Individual needs concern the personal requirements of each group member and how these can be satisfied. Examples of measures for meeting individual needs are counselling (*see* 5:**16–18**), coaching (*see* 20:**8**), motivating and staff development (*see* Chapter 2).

10. Changing managers
It may sometimes be quite obvious that a manager's style is quite unsuitable for the work he or she is responsible for, and that the manager would be more effective if his or her style were to change.

The most usual example is the authoritarian, task-centred manager, in charge of relatively unstructured work. Because attitudes of this kind are deeply rooted in the manager's personality, they are very difficult to change, except superficially and temporarily. The techniques most often attempted are role-play and group discussions of various kinds (*see* 20:**2**), but there is no guarantee of their success. It is much easier to improve a manager's knowledge, both of the immediate job and of new techniques which might be useful. Possibly the added self-confidence this knowledge brings may modify the individual's management style.

When a manager's style is reasonably appropriate, but not quite suitable, knowledge of leadership theory and discussion with other managers may well bring about an improvement. This change will not be maintained, however, unless the company where he or she works is sympathetic to the change and has a work pattern which is compatible with the changed management style. For example, in a company which from top to bottom is run on very authoritarian lines, with rigid rules and procedures, it is impossible for one manager to maintain a people-centred style; he or she must conform to the prevailing code of managerial conduct in the company.

Since the style of many managers cannot be changed, it may be necessary in order to make the best use of their abilities to transfer them to work more appropriate to their style. Another possibility might be to change the degree to which the work is structured, but this would have great difficulties in practice.

Participation

11. Definition

Worker participation is the inclusion of the employees in the decision-making process of the organisation. It implies also that the employees have access to sufficient information on which to base their share in decisions. Sometimes the power of the employee in making decisions is complete because he or she is also regarded as a co-owner, as in co-operative enterprises, for example. On the other hand, in many companies in Great Britain participation may merely consist of the management informing employee representatives of decisions that have already been made, and asking for their comments.

12. Theory X and Y

The American writer Douglas McGregor described two contrasting assumptions about the behaviour of employees, called theory X and theory Y.

(a) Theory X takes the view that the average employee dislikes work, will try to avoid responsibility, and will only be made to work by a mixture of close control and threats.

(b) Theory Y assumes that work is a natural and welcome activity which need not be externally controlled if the employee is adequately motivated, that employees will seek responsibility and that they can give valuable help in solving work problems.

McGregor took the view that theory Y was the correct assumption to make, and that firms should be organised on that basis. He said that theory X gave employees the opportunity to satisfy only basic and security needs at work, but a theory Y management attitude would enable them to satisfy Maslow's higher needs, in particular ego and self-actualisation needs. A person's job should be so constructed that it gave the opportunity for full self-development.

There are similarities between theory X and task-centred management on the one hand, and theory Y and people-centred management on the other, and the comments made in the previous section about styles of management apply to a large extent to theories X and Y. Most employees would no doubt welcome the opportunity to have more control over their work and to put into practice their own ideas. There is undoubtedly a large fund of valuable expertise, experience and originality among employees that is often untapped by management.

Unfortunately some jobs are so closely limited, defined and integrated into a complex production process that opportunities to satisfy the higher needs at work are completely absent. Workers in jobs like these must quite often be treated in a theory X manner, i.e. coerced and controlled, if adequate effort is to be obtained. Moreover, there are many employees who do not expect to take responsibility at work and avoid it if they can. Therefore, management is sometimes justified in making theory X assumptions about employees.

13. Quality and acceptance in decisions
The previous discussion of management style was concerned with the general tone of the manager's behaviour and his or her typical ways of dealing with work situations, but of course the manager will have decisions of many kinds to make and should deal with them in different ways.

The psychologist N. R. F. Maier has suggested a way of analysing the various decisions which have to be made by a manager which should help to decide how they should be handled. According to Maier, decisions may be described according to their *quality* and their *acceptance*.

(a) *The quality of a decision* is the extent to which it uses objective facts, particularly as regards technical knowledge or financial resources. A high-quality decision would involve the consideration of complex technical data or the expenditure (or saving) of large sums of money.

(b) *The acceptance of a decision* is the extent to which it affects the personal feelings of subordinates, how much their emotions and need-satisfactions are involved.

14. The four types of decision

This analysis is illustrated in Fig. 8.2, in which four types of decision are shown, involving various proportions of quality and acceptance.

	Low QUALITY	High QUALITY
High ACCEPTANCE	EXAMPLES: Canteen questions tea breaks. *a*	EXAMPLES: Pay, working hours and other conditions of employment. *b*
Low ACCEPTANCE	EXAMPLES: Arrangements for cleaning premises. *c*	EXAMPLES: Purchase of raw materials. *d*

Figure 8.2 *Quality and acceptance in decisions*

(a) *High-acceptance, low-quality decisions* do not need expert technical knowledge or incur large financial outlay, but they matter a great deal to the subordinates. Canteen questions are an obvious example, others being holiday rotas and arrangement of desks in an office.

(b) *High-acceptance and high-quality decisions* not only affect subordinates' personal lives to a great extent but also have important technical and financial implications for management. Wages and salaries are the obvious example, others being changes in hours or working methods.

(c) *Low-acceptance and low-quality decisions* are trivial and unimportant; they arouse little interest among subordinates and do not require very much money or technical knowledge.

(d) *Low-acceptance and high-quality decisions* do not affect subordinates very much personally, but have a high technical or financial content. The purchase of raw materials, the design of products, and the prices charged for products are examples of this type of decision.

15. How to deal with decisions

This analysis is useful because it can guide a manager in the way he or she should deal with the different decisions which come along. The manager can assume that if a decision matters a great deal to subordinates they will want some part in making the decision, but if it does not affect their interests the decision can be made without involving them.

A decision which has to be based on complex technical and financial considerations, perhaps affecting the long-term interests of the company, needs the expertise of qualified managers, who must keep in mind the requirements to maximise profits or comply with the law. In many cases the subordinates do not have the knowledge necessary to make decisions of this type, nor are they interested in them. Obviously, the most difficult decisions to make are those which are not only of high quality but also affect the subordinates personally.

A manager may therefore deal with the four main types of decision as follows.

(a) *High acceptance, low quality* — by consultation with subordinates, sometimes allowing them to play the major part in making the decisions. In many companies canteen committees have been formed, consisting almost entirely of rank-and-file employees, to supervise the running of the canteen.

(b) *High acceptance, high quality* — by negotiation with the subordinates. Management and employees both have interests they wish to protect, which in many ways are incompatible. The usual way of resolving the conflict is by bargaining and compromise, neither side being completely satisfied with the decision but both accepting it as fairly reasonable.

(c) *Low acceptance, low quality* — either by the manager without reference to subordinates, or by delegation to a lower level of supervision. Maier suggests that in many cases they may be decided by tossing a coin.

(d) *Low acceptance, high quality* — by the manager alone, or with the advice of experts. The employees would not expect to be consulted, nor would they have the knowledge to make a useful contribution.

Maier's method of describing decisions is therefore very useful in identifying the extent to which employees should participate in decisions affecting themselves or their work. It guides a manager in his or her day-to-day work, but does not claim to deal with participation on the larger scale, i.e. at the level of the organisation as a whole.

16. Participation in company-level decisions

McGregor and Maier were concerned above all with employees' participation in decisions affecting them directly and in the short term. There is plenty of evidence that most, though not all, employees are more than willing to take part in decisions of this type, but not very much evidence about their willingness to be involved in decisions at the highest level, e.g. manufacturing or investment policy.

In the great majority of organisations there is very little participation by employees in policy decisions; sometimes there are varying degrees of *consultation*.

(a) Employees are consulted before a decision is made, but the management is not bound by their views, though it usually tries to take them into account.

(b) Employees are informed of decisions and are consulted about their effects. The decisions may be modified in detail.

(c) Employees are informed of decisions, and negotiations take place between them and the management about implementation. The detailed application of a redundancy decision is an example.

(d) There is a company suggestion scheme.

In many companies there is neither participation nor consultation, but merely information to employees about the decisions that have been made.

17. Quality circles

A quality circle is a departmental workers' discussion group that meets regularly to consider, analyse, investigate and resolve production and quality problems. The group is trained in problem-solving techniques and, importantly, is given resources and (limited) authority to implement decisions. Circle leadership might be assumed by an existing departmental supervisor or by someone directly elected from the group. In their Western form, circles meet during working hours and participation may or may not be compulsory. If membership is voluntary, management might encourage participation *via* group bonuses, generous payments for expenses, hints of promotion for enthusiastic members, etc. Circles normally concentrate on mundane practical (rather than organisational) problems, and solve them using ideas and methods developed by circle members. Typically, circle activities are initiated by the circle, although management might occasionally refer problems to it for analysis and resolution. The advantages of quality circles are:

(a) improved morale as workers become involved in departmental decision-taking;
(b) workers apply their skill, personal knowledge and experience to quality and productivity issues;
(c) circle decisions are taken by the people who must implement them so there is a high probability they will be carried out.

The problems with quality circles are:

(a) apathy may arise among circle members who might feel they are undertaking (unpaid) extra duties the benefits of which will accrue entirely to the firm and not to circle members;
(b) frustrations may result from the circle's inability to solve problems the sources of which are beyond its control;
(c) antagonisms might develop between circle leaders and other managers about how particular difficulties should be overcome

and over the extent of the resources and executive authority the circle should command;

(d) within the group, friction may occur as low-status, low-paid employees offer more and better solutions to problems than do appointed supervisors and other higher-paid departmental superiors;

(e) the circle acquires experience of participative decision making, and may wish to apply this to other areas of the organisation's work (industrial relations or welfare, for example) — even though management might oppose employee participation apart from in quality circles.

18. Participation — a summing up

In such a controversial subject, influenced so much by individual attitudes, it is impossible to come to a clear conclusion. Readers might like to make their own judgments, based on the following arguments, firstly in favour of participation and secondly against it.

In favour

(a) It makes use of the knowledge and experience of employees, which are usually at least as valuable as a manager's.

(b) Employees are more motivated in their work if they can take part in decisions affecting their work. If they think that decisions are unfair to them, they will be less motivated.

(c) The greater the number of people involved in a decision, the less the possibility of important factors being overlooked.

(d) Unworkable impracticable decisions are avoided.

(e) Many decisions impinge directly on employees' lives; it is only right that they should help to make them.

(f) Employees by their efforts contribute to the prosperity of the company; it is right that their voice should be heard.

(g) Modern educational methods and policies encourage independent, informed thinking. Employees should be encouraged to apply this to their work.

Against

(a) Involving the employees in decisions is time-consuming; many decisions have to be made urgently.

(b) Most employees do not have the technical knowledge on which to base the majority of decisions.

(c) Employees have no responsibility for making the best use of the company's assets and maximising profits; the managers of the company have this responsibility and their decisions must recognise it.

(d) Employees tend to take the short-term view, and may oppose decisions which may benefit the company in the long run but do not offer many rewards to employees in the immediate future. Innovation and enterprise may be discouraged.

(e) Employee participation at company policy level needs such cumbersome machinery that it is only possible and genuine in small companies.

(f) Many employees take the view that they are not paid to make decisions, and will only become involved in decisions which affect them directly.

(g) There is a fundamental conflict of interests between employers and employees; negotiation is more realistic than participation.

The arguments against participation are much weaker, some would say non-existent, when the employees are also the owners of the company. There are a few companies, usually rather small, of this type in the UK; they seem to be both commercially successful and stable. Most have been created and built up by a single owner who has then given them away to the firm's employees. Possibly the number of such companies is too small for reliable conclusions to be drawn.

19. Company reporting procedures

Participation has been encouraged by a law passed in 1982 and now embodied in the Companies Act 1985 which requires companies with 250 employees or more to make an annual statement of the action they have taken to:

(a) provide employees with relevant information;

(b) consult employees or their representatives on a regular basis;

(c) encourage the involvement of the employees in the company's performance, e.g. through an employees' share scheme;

(d) make the employees aware of the financial and economic factors affecting the performance of the company.

Progress test 8

1. What is the difference between an unofficial and an official leader? **(1, 2)**

2. Define employee-centred and production-centred leadership. **(4)**

3. What is the relationship between management style and labour turnover? **(4)**

4. What is the managerial grid? **(6)**

5. Define unstructured work and describe the most appropriate management for it. **(8, 9)**

6. What is worker participation? **(11)**

7. Summarise theories X and Y. Is theory Y always preferable to theory X? **(12)**

8. Describe the different types of decision which confront a manager. **(13, 15)**

9. Describe the problems attached to quality circles. **(17)**

10. Summarise the arguments for and against worker participation. **(18)**

9
Communications and change

Communications

1. Definition

Communications consist of all the processes by which information is transmitted and received. The subject matter may include facts, intentions, attitudes, etc., and the chief purpose of communications is to make the receiver of a communication understand what is in the mind of the sender. Therefore a communication is incomplete unless it is received and understood. As the usual result of the understanding is a change in behaviour, effective communications can be regarded as part of a learning process (*see* Chapter 3). A general model of the communication process is offered by Claude Shannon and Warren Weaver who characterise communication systems as relations between inputs and outputs of data. The Shannon and Weaver model is sketched in Fig. 9.1.

Figure 9.1 *Shannon and Weaver's model of the communication process*

Within the system there will exist separate mechanisms for:

(a) encoding messages (e.g. choosing an appropriate form of words prior to transmission); and

(b) decoding (interpreting) the information sent. The recipient may or may not provide feedback to the sender of a message. Noise is any form of interference with messages that has the effect of producing extra and distracting information. Examples of noise are technical jargon, unclear sentences and flowery language.

2. The importance of communications

An organisation may consist of management, employees, premises, equipment, materials, etc. but will not come to life unless communications effectively link all these parts together and co-ordinate their activities. The decisions of management must be made known to employees, and some kind of control system arranged to ensure that these decisions are acted on; the decisions themselves should be based on a flow of information reaching management from all parts of the organisation. Communications in a large, complex organisation with many departments and locations are obviously more difficult than those in a small single organisation; in a large company errors and inefficiency can easily occur because an individual or a department has not informed another of its actions, or has not been informed.

From the psychological point of view, communications have an importance which goes beyond the transmission and reception of information. The form which a communication takes (or, of course, whether communication takes place at all) can profoundly affect the attitudes of the employees and the degree to which they understand and support management policies. Many industrial disputes originate in a failure of communications — a misunderstanding by the employees of the intentions of management (or vice versa) or a misinterpretation of company policy.

3. Types of communications

It is useful to divide communications within an organisation into two kinds: *formal*, meaning arranged or approved by the management; and *informal*, meaning unofficial and unplanned methods of communication.

Another distinction that can be made is between *one-way* communication, in which the sender makes no provision for a reaction from the receiver, and *two-way* communication, which is framed in such a way that a response from the receiver is provided for and encouraged. One-way communication is quick and preserves management authority; two-way communication is much slower and indicates a more participative approach to decision making.

The written or spoken word dominates formal communications, but informal communications also include for example gestures, facial expressions, what is *not* said, or who is present or not present at a meeting. Many rumours begin because someone has drawn conclusions from several non-verbal indications. A glimpse of a senior manager studying a plan of the offices, accompanied by a stranger who holds a large tape-measure, would no doubt start a rumour that the office accomodation is to be changed.

Communications may be analysed yet again according to their *direction.* They may be:

(a) *downwards* — from a higher level in the organisation to a lower;
(b) *upwards* — from a lower level to a higher;
(c) *lateral* or *sideways* — from one level to another of approximately the same level.

Most formal communications are downwards, while informal communications are mostly upwards or lateral. It seems that many organisations have communications problems because they do not make formal arrangements for communications to flow upwards or laterally, thus cutting management off from employees' ideas and opinions and making co-ordination between departments unnecessarily difficult.

4. Barriers to communication

Both vertical and horizontal communication systems sometimes experience obstacles that prevent information from flowing smoothly around the organisation. Examples of such barriers are listed below.

(a) *Distortion of messages* as they are passed from one person to another through long channels of communication.

(b) *Communication overload* occurring when individuals receive so much information that most of it is disregarded.

(c) *Transmitting messages that are not suitable for the audience* for which they are intended (e.g. sending complex, closely argued memoranda containing long words and sentences to people who possess only a low level of literacy).

(d) *Using vague, meaningless words* and sentences that fail to convey the meaning of a message effectively.

(e) *Inability to listen.* Communication involves receiving as well as issuing information. Some managers are good talkers but poor listeners, hearing only what they want to hear and disregarding any critical comment.

5. Formal methods of communication

The various formal methods of communication may be summarised as follows.

(a) Written instructions and announcements by notices on boards, internal memoranda, notices in pay-packets, company magazines, letters to each employee. One-way, downwwards and permanent.

(b) Broadcast messages over a public address system. One-way, downwards and not permanent, i.e. misunderstandings cannot be checked.

(c) Large meetings of employees addressed by a senior manager. One-way (because response is inhibited in a large meeting), downwards, and not permanent unless the information given is confirmed later in writing.

(d) Small meetings of no more than about twenty employees. Two-way (because comments and questions are easy). Mainly downwards, but with some provision for upwards communication. Not permanent.

(e) Inter-departmental committees. Two-way and lateral. Not permanent in themselves, but usually followed by a written summary of the discussion and decisions reached.

(f) Interviews to give instructions or information or to review a subordinate's performance, i.e. appraisal (*see* Chapter 18). One-way or two-way according to the manner in which the interview is conducted. Downwards and not permanent. If this method is used to transmit instructions through several layers of the organisation by a series of interviews, distortion is possible because the original instructions may be reworded or misunderstood on their way down.

(g) Joint committees of management and employee representatives. Two-way, downwards, upwards and lateral, usually followed by published minutes of proceedings and therefore permanent. These committees may meet regularly, or meet only when required, e.g. to hear appeals against dismissal.

(h) Suggestion schemes. Mainly one-way and upwards, but to some extent, two-way and downwards (*see* 23:**23–25**). Permanent, because suggestions are submitted in writing.

(i) Attitude and other questionnaires (*see* 7:**14**). One-way, upwards and permanent.

6. Briefing sessions

In a briefing session the manager is concerned not only with imparting information but also with inculcating in employees feelings of participation, security and involvement with the firm. Briefing sessions give managers the opportunity to explain their decisions and remind subordinates of current company procedures. Unfortunately, managers frequently err in calling these meetings only when crises arise. Rather, they should occur regularly (preferably at predetermined intervals) and not just as things go wrong. Sessions should be short and offer:

(a) brief reviews of progress to date;
(b) the manager's opinions on contemporary problems;
(c) outline proposals (with justifications) for future activities.

Suitable topics for briefing sessions include suggested changes in working arrangements, staff transfers and promotion, results of implementation of new methods, details of available welfare and recreational facilities, and examples of how efficiency has been improved in other departments. Briefing sessions, however, are not an appropriate medium for collective bargaining on significant issues such as pay or terms and conditions of employment. Their fundamental purpose is to transmit decisions that have already been taken. Decision making itself requires separate procedures.

7. Informal methods of communication

(a) The normal casual conversations which occur between employees at all levels. Two-way, multi-directional, not permanent.

(b) A private network of telephone or personal contacts in other parts of the organisation, to help in getting the work done more quickly than by using the official methods of communication. This network, often based on mutual favours or personal friendships, is extremely active in most organisations. It is two-way, multi-directional and not permanent.

(c) Surreptitious written material circulating within the organisation, e.g. caricatures, satirical poems. One-way, multi-directional, permanent.

(d) Secret signs and gestures, e.g. warning others of the approach of a manager. One-way, lateral, not permanent.

(e) Rumour, or the grapevine, spread by a combination of the four methods above, and based on miscellaneous sources of information and guesswork. It is rarely entirely false but concentrates on the more sensational aspects of a situation.

It is probably true to say that when the formal communication systems of an organisation are comparatively inefficient, the informal systems become more active.

8. The psychology of communications

It is possible to improve the effectiveness of communications by applying the psychology of attention, perception and motivation. The subjective and objective factors of attention (*see* 1:7) are important in the following ways.

(a) The wording of a message should show that it is directed towards the receiver personally, e.g. 'You will be pleased to hear that . . .', not 'It has been decided that . . .'.

(b) Rumours spread rapidly because they emphasise the subjective factors of attention.

(c) A crowded untidy notice board carrying many out-of-date notices will not be looked at; it should only carry relevant material, arranged in such a way that it is easily read, and that new notices are immediately obvious.

(d) An urgent or important notice should be very large, printed on coloured paper, have a title printed in unusual type or appear more than once on the same notice board.

9. The importance of perception
Communication is also affected by perception (*see* 1:**9–10**).

(a) A communication, written or spoken, which uses words which appear long and unfamiliar to the receiver may be perceived as condescending and may therefore arouse resentment. The meaning of the words may be misinterpreted. Short words in clearly constructed sentences should be used where possible.

(b) The intention of the communication may not be understood, sometimes because the sender of the message is not clear in his or her own mind as to what he or she wants to say and why, but more often because the perceptions of the sender and the receiver regarding the subject of the communication are different. The attitudes of management and employees regarding a change in working arrangements may well be diametrically opposed; a well-meant communication about them from management will probably then be perceived by the employees as a threat of some kind. A statement by a manager to a subordinate that he or she wishes to discuss the previous year's work may be made in a helpful, problem-solving spirit but perceived by the subordinate as some kind of accusation against which a defence must be presented.

10. One-way and two-way communication
The sender of a communication should always try to motivate the receiver to understand the message and put it into practice. People can become frustrated quite easily when they try to understand a difficult communication, especially when it is unexpected (*see* 2:8). When they hear an announcement about important matters concerning their personal welfare, or about topics on which they could express useful opinions, frustration is again likely to occur because it is obvious that decisions have been made without consultation. The conclusions that may be drawn are as follows.

(a) *One-way communication*, which is easy and quick, is quite adequate for subjects which are straightforward, expected or urgent. Methods which can be used are notices, letters, public address announcements, and talks to large meetings.

(b) *Two-way communication*, which can be quite time-consuming and demands some patience and personal skill, should be used for subjects which are complicated, unexpected, of personal concern to the receivers or about which they could make a worthwhile contribution. A better decision may be reached, and it will be accepted more readily. Methods which can be used are small meetings, interviews and committees.

11. Communication and participation

The subject of communication has much in common with leadership and participation, discussed in the previous chapter. Whatever style a manager uses, he or she must communicate effectively. Even if an extremely task-centred approach is adopted, the manager will obtain a better response if instructions are communicated clearly, if possible explaining the reasons for them. A manager whose style is to work through his or her subordinates must obviously foster effective and frequent two-way communication with them.

Participation, which by definition involves a sharing of decision making by the employees, can only be successful if communications are two-way and efficient. The decisions must be based on adequate information reaching the employees or their representatives, and management and employees must both be assured of the other's good faith. This again implies efficient and frequent two-way communication.

Dealing with change

12. The effects of change

During recent years radical changes have been occurring in all parts of commerce, industry and the public services. A very rapid rate of technical innovation has produced new materials, new methods and new products. Some companies have ceased to exist, some have been taken over by larger and more successful competitors, while others have grown very quickly and changed their character completely.

The consequences of change include the following.

(a) Increased complexity of methods of production.
(b) Job changes or redundancy for many workers.
(c) The need for employees to acquire new skills or to modify existing competencies.
(d) Geographical relocation of industries and workers.
(e) Extensive reliance on computers, information technology and decision-support systems.

13. Resistance to change

Research and experience show that there is a widespread tendency among employees to resist change, even though it might appear to outside observers that working conditions would be improved. The resistance may, of course, disappear eventually, the employees then saying that they prefer the new arrangements to the old, but before this happens opposition from employees, accompanied sometimes by industrial action, can make the introduction of change very difficult.

The main reasons for resistance to change are as follows.

(a) Important and permanent decisions about an employee's working life are made by people who are often unknown and remote.
(b) The employee may lose his or her job or be transferred to a lower-paid job.
(c) The skill and experience he or she has acquired over the years may suddenly become valueless.
(d) The worker's status in the firm may be lower.
(e) Cohesive social groups may be broken up, together with established relationships, roles, and customs.
(f) New relationships must be established, new customs learned.
(g) Familiar things represent security: unfamiliar things insecurity.
(h) Personal life may be upset by new working times or a move to a new district.
(i) Workers may feel personally inadequate vis-à-vis new technologies, fearing they will not be able to understand new methods and systems.
(j) An individual may resent not having been consulted about a proposed change.

There are individual differences in employees' attitudes to

change. Some people welcome change, enjoying the excitement and the disturbance of familiar routine. Others dislike change of any kind, even in their private lives. The great majority lie between these two extremes, their reaction to change at work being influenced partly by the nature of the change and partly by the way it is handled. Again, some companies have a tradition of frequent change and tend to attract employees who like uncertainty and variety. In these companies changes are not likely to be resisted by the employees unless they are obviously unreasonable.

14. Reducing resistance to change

Investments in technological or organisational innovations will not bring the benefits that management expect if the employees show resistance to change. The costs of dealing with disputes and the low level of productivity that is often found can be so great that some managers, particularly in companies where industrial relations are poor, prefer to retain an out-of-date technology rather than face the turmoil that the introduction of new methods would bring. A manager should therefore realise that resistance to change is likely to occur, is not based on stupidity or obstinacy, and can be reduced, if not overcome, by some forethought.

Managements intending to introduce changes in working methods or company organisation should consider carefully the effects of the changes on the firm's human resources. The following should be taken into account when implementing change.

(a) Details of proposed changes and their effects on groups and individuals must be precisely defined. Current attitudes and perspectives on working methods must be identified, as must the attitudes and perspectives necessary for affected employees to adapt successfully to new environments.

(b) Where it is practicable, there should be some participation by the employees in decisions which affect their daily work. If the decision cannot be changed in principle then there should be participation about the way it is put into effect.

(c) The threat to security which many employees feel may be reduced by telling employees individually, and at the earliest possible moment, what their new jobs will be and their position in the new organisation structure.

(d) The loss of valuable skill and experience can be counter-balanced by a programme of retraining, emphasising that no one will be expected to do work he or she is unfitted for, and that an opportunity to learn a new skill is being offered.

(e) It is occasionally possible to preserve existing social groups, transferring them to new work as a unit instead of dispersing them.

(f) The employees who will suffer financially should be at least partially compensated, e.g. by removal and settling-in expenses if they are required to move house, by guaranteeing their previous income for a period if they are transferred to a lower-paid job, and by giving generous *ex gratia* payments if they are made redundant.

(g) Even when the change is comparatively small, perhaps affecting only a few people, resistance will be reduced if the top management of the company show that they know about the change and understand its effects on the employees.

(h) The change should be made known by a two-way communication process (*see* 10), and two-way communication should be encouraged while the change is proceeding.

(i) Organisations can prepare 'skills inventories' listing all their employees' qualifications, work experiences and competencies. This information can assist management when assessing employees' suitabilities for alternative types of work and perhaps thereby avoid compulsory redundancies.

(j) Bonus schemes might be introduced to encourage the acceptance of new methods.

In some companies it must be admitted that the procedures described above would not be practicable. Employees in a company which has very bad industrial relations may not respond favourably to participation and may not believe statements made to them by management. In such cases, the advice often given is to plan the change in all its aspects very carefully, but secretly, and then implement it very suddenly and without warning. Drastic action of this kind is rarely justified, however, and managers usually have to make their own diagnosis of the situation and decide what position to take up between participation and two-way communication on the one hand and complete authoritarianism on the other.

15. New technology agreements

A new technology agreement is an accord whereby management and unions jointly consider, negotiate and agree procedures for the introduction of major technological innovations. Such an agreement will (hopefully) encourage acceptance of change, reduce uncertainty and involve unions directly at the time a significant change is contemplated. Bargaining then ensues over the amendments to job specifications, working practices and employee reward structures implied by new methods and systems.

Altering technologies by introducing new equipment, materials, etc., is one way of implementing change. Other possible measures are the alteration of *structures* (by changing authority and accountability systems, by centralisation or decentralisation of functions, etc.); the alteration of *tasks* through changing the contents of workers' duties; or the alteration of the *people who* do the work.

Progress test 9

1. Why are communications important in an organisation? (2)

2. What is the difference between these types of communication:
   (a) formal and informal;
   (b) one-way and two-way;
   (c) downwards, upwards and lateral? (3)

3. Describe three methods of formal communication. (5)

4. Describe three methods of informal communication. (6)

5. What is the connection between perception and communication? (9)

6. When should two-way communication be used in preference to one-way? (10)

7.   Why do most employees resist change?   **(12)**

8.   How can resistance to change be reduced?   **(14)**

10
Other influences on employee behaviour

1. The importance of the work situation

In the preceding chapters various influences on the behaviour of people at work have been discussed. These can be summarised under the following headings.

(a) *Physique*, making the individual more suitable for some jobs than for others.

(b) *Intelligence*, which also affects suitability for jobs and the capacity for learning.

(c) *Personality*, which includes the important factors of perception, motivation, and social adjustment.

(d) *Physical working conditions*, which should make the immediate job environment suitable to the employee and minimise fatigue and accidents.

(e) *The working group*, imposing its own standards of conduct and output on the individual but offering some advantage in return.

(f) *Style of leadership*, which to be effective should take account of the nature of the process and the type of employee.

(g) *Participation*, the degree to which employees can share in decision making.

(h) *Communications*, the spread of knowledge about policies, intentions and attitudes within the company. Particular reference was made to the connection between communication and the handling of change.

It has been shown, for example in the discussion on job satisfaction and leadership, that the type of production process is an important factor in behaviour at work. It is logical to assume, therefore, that the actions of an employee depend not only on his or her individual qualities and the influence of the working group but also on the type of job he or she is doing and the type of company in which the worker is employed. The same individual in a different job, or in a different company, could behave in quite a different way.

2. Effects of unemployment and new technology

The level of unemployment in the local community can affect employee behaviour. For example, workers may deliberately work slowly and restrict their outputs in the belief that this will stretch out the periods their present jobs will last. Also, the absence of alternative job opportunities could cause employees to be less inclined towards striking, working-to-rule, withdrawing co-operation, etc., when seeking to secure pay increases. Further consequences could include:

(a) less solidarity among workers;
(b) increased resistance to change (*see* 9:**13**)
(c) fewer confrontations with management over petty issues;
(d) fewer invocations of grievance procedures.

Technology affects behaviour through its effects on working conditions, e.g. the extent of the division of labour, employee involvement in management decision making, the amount of discretion exercised by the individual worker, etc. New technologies require new work patterns, incentive systems, occupational mobility and fresh attitudes towards change. They alter employee training needs, organisation structures, and possibly employee job satisfaction and perspectives on work. A further factor influencing behaviour is the novel work patterns which are being gradually introduced.

3. New work patterns

There are two ways in which an employer can organise his employees to deal with new technology.

(a) Two main classes of employee: one is skilled at programming and setting the equipment, the other carries out routine, unskilled work.
(b) One class of employee, carrying out the complete range of tasks associated with the process.

In **(a)** the work force is clearly divided; there are, for example, two separate pay structures and recruits are drawn from two separate pools of labour. One class will require careful selection and training while the other can be selected against less stringent standards and will need little training.

In **(b)** the employees will be asked to carry out a wide range of tasks from the unskilled to the skilled, and all will need careful training. A split of the employees into two classes is avoided. Because the company has invested heavily in training it will try to promote job security, promotion prospects and good rates of pay and conditions in order to hold on to its employees.

4. Fluctuations in work

Most companies experience variable demands for work. When demand is high the usual response is overtime working (*see* 23:**10**), sometimes augmented by the recruitment of temporary employees. When it is low the employees are under-employed and some may eventually be made redundant (*see* 16:**11**). In either case the traditional remedies are expensive.

Alternative methods, believed to be more cost-effective, are as follows.

(a) Defining the period of work by reference to a year instead of to a week. This allows extra hours worked in a busy time to be compensated during a slack time either by a shorter working day or by whole days off. There are similarities with the system of flexible working hours (*see* 23:**12**).
(b) Removing the distinctions between jobs, so that, for example, during a slack time a production operative can overhaul his or her machine instead of calling in a maintenance worker.
(c) Reducing the permanent employees of the company to a core group who have secure employment, supported by peripheral groups who may be temporary employees (sometimes part-time) or workers supplied by sub-contractors. The number and type of the peripheral groups will vary according to the current demand for work (*see* **9**).

5. Flexibility (multi-skilling)

Faced with the problems caused by a rapid rate of economic and technological change, managers have produced solutions such as those described in **3** and **4** above. It is certain that in all cases the employees will be expected to show more flexibility than before, for example in the following ways.

(a) Undertaking a wider range of tasks, from manual unskilled to skilled/technician level.

(b) Crossing traditional boundaries between skills; for example, a mechanical craftsman also carrying out electrical work.

(c) Willingness to work an irregular pattern of hours.

(d) For many workers, being employed temporarily, or as a member of a sub-contracting firm, instead of having a fixed relationship with an employer.

(e) Accepting throughout working life retraining in new skills.

6. Effects on employees

Flexibility requires employees to accept drastic changes affecting their personal lives, security and status. They will therefore expect its introduction to be handled with the utmost care, following the principles described in Chapter 9. Employee participation and frequent two-way communication are extremely important. Some of the changes affecting the employee are as follows.

(a) Flexibility of task is difficult to reconcile with strict supervision; employees will work with a loose control only. Fewer supervisors may be needed, and they will behave more as co-ordinators and advisors than as disciplinarians. Job satisfaction will almost certainly be increased.

(b) Some changes in trade union organisation will be necessary to accommodate the multi-skilled worker.

(c) The employee's leisure time will be affected by irregular hours or temporary employment. Leisure may become more important if he or she is a temporary worker doing a monotonous job.

(d) Those employees who are engaged temporarily or as members of a sub-contracting firm must accept insecurity of employment. They will be difficult to organise in trade unions and there is a danger that hostility will grow between them and the permanent unionised employees who will seem to be in a privileged position and members of closely-knit working groups.

(e) Employees of all kinds must be ready to accept retraining and be capable of benefiting from it. They must be willing to recognise that old skills sometimes have to be discarded for the new.

7. Effects on management

The flexibility which is advocated for manual and clerical workers is necessary also for managers. They too will find it necessary to work irregular hours, accept retraining and cross traditional job boundaries. They may need to devise new methods of management and work out their implications. For example, the changes described in **3** and **4** have the following effects on management practices.

(a) The multi-skilled worker will require very careful selection (*see* Chapter 14).

(b) Job specifications (*see* Chapter 13) can no longer be detailed.

(c) Job evaluation systems (*see* Chapter 21) must be changed in order to cope with flexibility.

(d) Pay structures based on output may be impossible and systems based on merit difficult to operate (*see* Chapter 22).

(e) The training function of the company will become very important and probably expensive.

(f) New working arrangements will be resisted unless through some kind of consultative machinery they are discussed and possibly amended before they become effective (*see* Chapters 8 and 9).

(g) Contracts of employment (*see* 14:21) must be revised on the one hand to encourage stability among the core group of workers and on the other to provide fair conditions for those who work temporarily.

8. The influence of occupations on behaviour

The changes described in this chapter so far affect only a minority of employees; in most companies job structures and occupations continue in their well-established ways and produce typical behaviour as follows.

(a) *Professional workers*, e.g. lawyers, teachers and doctors, who have undergone a long course of training carefully controlled by a professional body which usually has statutory recognition. There is a strict code of ethics, and often some restriction on the numbers entering the profession. Most professional workers seem to have high job satisfaction, their working life often extending into their leisure time. When they are employed by a company their loyalties appear to be divided between their profession and their employer.

(b) *Craftspeople*, e.g. skilled manual workers in engineering, building, printing, etc., who have served an apprenticeship which is controlled jointly by the employer and the trade union, the latter frequently restricting the numbers entering the craft. They enjoy high status among other manual workers, have an independent outlook because they can use their skills fairly easily with another employer, and become more valuable as they get older because of their increased experience and skill. There are many similarities between the craftsperson and the professional.

(c) *Machine minders and assembly workers*, who apply a moderate level of skill to a very restricted range of operations. Training is short, the work has little interest or variety and generally is part of a tightly controlled process. These workers often become less valuable as they get older because their stamina and speed of reaction decrease. When they change employers they frequently change their occupation also. They tend to have a detached attitude to the job and company.

(d) *Process workers*, who monitor processes which are almost entirely automatic, e.g. chemical manufacture and oil refining. They have to be intelligent enough to understand the science and technology on which the process is based so that they may deal with emergencies and breakdowns. A fairly long training period is necessary, emphasising theory and procedures rather than physical skills. Their job satisfaction is often high because of the responsibility they feel for the safety of the process, the lack of human pressures to increase production and the special training they have received. On the other hand, the need to do shift work to keep the process continuously operating may cause some job dissatisfaction.

(e) *White collar workers*, who traditionally are expected by employers to share management attitudes rather than associate themselves with manual workers. They enjoy greater fringe benefits, shorter hours and less discipline than manual workers, and are on progressive salaries. They are usually treated by managers as individuals rather than as categories; differences in salaries usually reflect this. Their job satisfaction can be quite high when they are able to control their own work and see its results, but low when they do routine and apparently meaningless clerical operations. Their experience is often valuable to one employer only, and is difficult to transfer.

There appears to be a trend towards the merging of types (b), (c) and (d) as processes become more automatic and computer controlled.

Use of casual and part-time employees

9. Changes in the workforce

A large increase in casual and/or part-time work has occurred in the UK during recent decades, creating several new problems of human resources planning, control, and the appraisal of employees. In many firms there now exists an important distinction between 'core' workers (who are permanent and full time) and 'peripherals' engaged part time or casually and laid on or off as market conditions change. Core workers plan, take decisions and supervise peripherals. Typically, they are superannuated, receive training and staff development, and qualify for a variety of fringe benefits. Peripherals, conversely, exercise little discretion over their work and undertake routine duties organised by core workers. This arrangement enables the size of the workforce to be changed quickly and with few legal consequences (frequently, casuals and part-timers are not covered by employment protection legislation). Also the wage cost of a casual/part-time workforce may be lower than for full-time workers (who might not be fully occupied throughout the year).

The special problems attached to the management of a 'flexible' workforce include:

(a) possible low morale among peripherals (who are denied permanent status and benefits) possibly resulting in high labour turnover;

(b) communication difficulties including communication overload on core workers (each of whom must deal with very many peripherals) and the need to arrange peripheral employees' representation on health and safety and other important employee relations committees;

(c) control problems attached to day-to-day operations

(peripherals are not normally capable of handling crises without the help of core staff), performance appraisal (*see* Chapter 18), and ensuring the quality of recruitment of fresh peripheral employees (which by definition occurs on a regular basis);
(d) interpersonal relations difficulties emerging from permanent employees possibly regarding low-cost peripherals as a threat to their jobs, and from peripherals' resentments against higher paid full-time workers.

Some of these problems might be overcome through job extension (*see* 2:20) among peripheral workers, through explicit recognition of peripherals' contributions to the firm (*via* the provision of fringe benefits, guarantees of re-employment following breaks in continuity of service, etc.), and through incorporating grievance procedures, right of appeal against dismissal and so on into peripherals' contracts of employment. Other possibilities are the introduction of job-sharing arrangements (although the 'two Monday mornings' syndrome might result from this); making peripherals responsible for the quality of their work; homeworking (*see* below); and having peripherals attend training and staff development courses.

10. Homeworkers
The rapid development of computerised networking systems has made it possible for many employees to work from home; communicating with head office though a computer terminal, telephone calls, and occasional face-to-face meetings. Homeworkers save much (productive) time through not having to travel to and from work (which can be fitted around the transportation of children to and from school); there are fewer interruptions to the working day; the individual may complete duties when he or she wishes; and the completion of work in a relaxed environment might lead to a higher output, increased effort and greater job satisfaction. Also there are savings on premises costs for the employing organisation. However, a number of significant problems attach to the management of home-based workers, including the following.

(a) Control problems and the need to employ head office staff to liaise with outside employees, provide them with input materials and information, etc. Such difficulties are especially severe when project completion depends on several outworkers meeting deadlines simultaneously. Note, moreover, that homeworkers who are constantly on the phone or meeting supervisors and colleagues would be more conveniently employed in a central head office.

(b) Appraisal problems. Management needs to know how energetically each outworker is working, how much time is actually spent on particular assignments, whether certain jobs might be deskilled and completed elsewhere at lower cost, how efficiency can be improved, and so on.

(c) Security problems. Ambiguities could arise over the ownership of intellectual property (patents, designs, computer programmes and other copyright materials) developed by outworkers. Also, head office will want to ensure that a homeworker is not simultaneously working for competitors using equipment and knowledge provided by the parent organisation.

(d) Morale problems possibly caused by homeworkers feeling isolated and not really part of the firm. Usually, homeworkers are not able to progress through the career ladder available to head office staff.

To deal with these problems head office will set targets, conduct inspections, possibly pay homeworkers through a piecework system (*see* 22:3) or perhaps treat outworkers as self-employed sub-contract labour paid *ad-hoc* sums for specific assignments. In the latter case, the head office cannot directly control the homeworker's working methods (otherwise the Inland Revenue will not allow the homeworker self-employed status) and the homeworker is free to work for other employers.

11. Culture of the workplace

A firm's culture evolves gradually, and employees may not even be aware that it exists. Organisational culture is important, however, because it helps define how workers feel about their jobs. Culture involves common assumptions about how work should be performed and about appropriate objectives for the organisation, for departments within it and for individual employees. It consists of the organisation's customary ways of doing things and its members' shared perceptions of issues affecting the organisation's work. Culture helps define how workers *feel* about their jobs and about what is and is not correct. It affects individual perceptions of colleagues and situations, and the leadership style (*see* Chapter 8) applied within the organisation.

Determinants of a firm's culture include senior management's core values and goals, employee selection methods, induction systems (*see* 14:**22**), training techniques applied, and procedures for bonding the worker to the firm (e.g. company uniforms, housing loans, superannuation schemes, provision of fringe benefits, etc.).

Charles Handy distinguishes four types of culture: power, role, task and person. One of these might dominate the entire organisation, or different cultures may exist in various parts of the firm. The *power culture* stems from a single central source, as in a small business that has begun to expand. Here, there are few rules and procedures, and few committees. All important decisions are taken by a handful of people, and precedents are followed.

A *role culture*, in contrast, is highly bureaucratic. It operates through formal roles and procedures, and there are clearly defined rules for settling disputes. Organisations dominated by role culture offer security and predictability but, since they are rigidly structured, cannot adapt quickly to accommodate change (as can a power culture organisation). The *task culture* is job or project orientated. There is no single dominant leader; all group members concentrate on completing the collective task. A task culture will encourage flexibility in approach, and is ideal for an environment of change. Job satisfaction is high and there is much group cohesion. However, relationships are complex and control is difficult. A *person culture* might arise in an organisation which exists only to serve the people within it. Examples are partnerships, consultancy firms and professional organisations.

According to Handy, none of these cultures is 'better' than the others. A culture arises, he argues, from historical circumstances, the existing environment, technology, and the human needs of people within the organisation. The problem, of course, is that whereas an organisation's needs will alter over time, its culture may remain constant. Alteration of a culture might require extensive external recruitment of new staff, the implementation of incentive schemes designed to alter workers' attitudes, or the conspicuous promotion of individuals who display flexible and appropriate cultural values.

12. Total influences on employee behaviour

It has been shown that an employee's attitudes and behaviour are influenced not only by personal qualities but also by the technology and work arrangements at the place of employment and the constraints and opportunities of his or her occupation. In addition, the working group, the style of leadership and the extent of participation are important.

Many interdependent factors, forming a system which is not only complex but rapidly changing, influence the behaviour of people at work. It is the task of personnel management to formulate and administer policies, methods and institutions which take account of these factors, are consistent with our culture and conform to the law.

Progress test 10

1. What do you understand by flexibility? **(5)**

2. Define the difference between core workers and peripheral workers. **(9)**

3. Name three ways in which flexibility can effect management practices. **(7)**

4. Define the differences between task culture and role culture. **(11)**

Part two

Personnel
management

11
What is personnel management?

1. Definition

The Institute of Personnel Management has published the following definition.

'Personnel management is that part of management concerned with people at work and with their relationships within an enterprise. Its aim is to bring together and develop into an effective organisation the men and women who make up an enterprise and, having regard for the well-being of the individual and of working groups, to enable them to make their best contribution to its success.

In particular, personnel management is concerned with the development and application of policies governing:

Human resources planning, recruitment, selection, placement and termination;

Education and training; career development;

Terms of employment, methods and standards of remuneration;

Working conditions and employee services;

Formal and informal communication and consultation both through the representatives of employers and employees and at all levels throughout the enterprise;

Negotiation and application of agreements on wages and working conditions; procedures for the avoidance and settlement of disputes.

Personnel management is also concerned with the human and social implications of change in internal organisation and methods of working, and of economic and social changes in the community.'

Further personnel management responsibilities are as follows:

(a) Conducting research into local wage levels to ensure that the firm's reward system is competitive with those in other companies.

(b) 'Incentivating', i.e. devising remuneration systems to stimulate workers into enhanced effort and efficiency.

(c) Administration of superannuation schemes (in conjunction with finance department) and advising employees about their pension and other entitlements.

(d) Maintenance of personnel records and statistics.

(e) Preparation of accurate job descriptions and other recruitment aids.

(f) Implementation of health and safety regulations, accident prevention and the provision of first-aid facilities.

(g) Management training, development and succession planning.

(h) Employee communications, transmitting information of interest to employees *via* newsletters, notice boards, briefing sessions, etc.

2. The application of industrial psychology

Another way of defining personnel management is to regard it as a range of policies, institutions and procedures which enable the principles of industrial psychology to be put into practice. Its purpose is not only to make effective use of people at work and develop satisfactory relationships among them but to motivate them both by providing them with jobs which are satisfying in themselves (if this is practically possible) and by offering them financial and other rewards.

To emphasise the psychological basis of personnel management, it may be re-defined as that part of management which deals with people at work as regards:

(a) *utilisation* — recruitment, selection, transfer, promotion, separation, appraisal, training and development;

(b) *motivation* — job design, remuneration, fringe benefits, consultation, participation, negotiation and justice;

(c) *protection* — working conditions, welfare services, safety, implementing appropriate legislation.

These three divisions are not separate and self-contained. For example, an employee who has been well selected and trained for his or her job will be more motivated in it than someone who has been carelessly selected and untrained. The use of consultation and participation, besides motivating employees, will often show how they can be better utilised. A well-designed and safe working environment will enable better use to be made of people's abilities and will in most cases help to provide satisfaction of human needs.

3. Personnel management and human resources management

Personnel management is an important element of the broader subject of human resources management, although in practice the two terms are frequently used interchangeably — emphasising the fact that the people employed in a company are resources which are at least as important as financial or material resources and must be given careful and expert attention.

Employees will not submit passively to manipulation or dictatorial control by management but more and more expect and demand some influence in the way they are employed. Research in the behavioural sciences shows that an appropriate response by management will benefit the company (*see* Chapter 2, 8:8–18 and 9:14).

Personnel management techniques in, for example, appraisal, training and job evaluation can only be successfully applied with the consent and support of the employees.

The following relationships and differences between human resources management (HRM) and personnel management may be distinguished.

(a) Personnel management is practical, utilitarian and instrumental, and mostly concerned with administration and the *implementation* of policies. Human resources management, conversely, has *strategic* dimensions and involves the total deployment of human resources within the firm. Thus, for example, HRM will consider such matters as:

(*i*) the aggregate size of the organisation's labour force in the context of an overall corporate plan (how many divisions and subsidiaries the company is to have, design of the organisation, etc.);

(*ii*) how much to spend on training the workforce, given strategic decisions on target quality levels, product prices, volume of production and so on;

(*iii*) the desirability of establishing relations with trade unions from the viewpoint of the effective management control of the entire organisation;

(*iv*) human asset accounting, i.e. the systematic measurement and analysis of the costs and *financial* benefits of alternative personnel policies (e.g. the monetary consequences of staff development exercises, the effects of various salary structures, etc.) and the valuation of the human worth of the enterprise's employees.

(b) HRM is concerned with the wider implications of the management of change (*see* 9:**12**) and not just with the effects of change on working practices. It seeks proactively to encourage flexible attitudes and the acceptance of new methods.

(c) Aspects of HRM constitute major inputs into organisational development exercises (*see* 20:**14**).

(d) Personnel management is (necessarily) reactive and diagnostic. It *responds* to changes in employment law, labour market conditions, trade union actions, government Codes of Practice and other environmental influences. HRM, on the other hand, is *prescriptive* and concerned with strategies, the initiation of new activities and the development of fresh ideas.

(e) HRM determines general policies for employment relationships within the enterprise. Thus, it needs to establish within the organisation a *culture* that is conducive to employee commitment and co-operation. Personnel management, on the other hand, has been criticised for being primarily concerned with imposing *compliance* with company rules and procedures among employees, rather than with loyalty and commitment to the firm.

(f) Personnel management has short-term perspectives; HRM has long-term perspectives, seeking to *integrate* all the human aspects of the organisation into a coherent whole and to establish high-level employee goals.

A contentious view of the difference between HRM and personnel management is the proposition that whereas the latter is 'pluralistic' in orientation, HRM has a 'unitaristic' approach (*see* below).

4. Pluralistic and unitary frames of reference

A frame of reference is the totality of all the attitudes, preassumptions and psychological influences that determine how a person perceives and interprets issues and events. In the industrial relations context, people with 'unitary' frames of reference regard both sides of industry (management and employees) as having identical interests and, in consequence, believe that workers should naturally co-operate with management, should work together as a team, and actively seek to assist management achieve its objectives. Human resources management, therefore, needs to involve (*i*) the unification of effort, (*ii*) the implementation of measures designed to inspire and motivate the workforce, (*iii*) the communication to workers of details of the organisation's wider goals, and (*iv*) the construction of policies for securing employees' loyalty and commitment to the firm.

The problems with unitarism are that:

(a) it cannot comprehend the motives of individuals who do not regard everyone in the organisation as 'being in the same boat';
(b) arguably, it fails to recognise the *inevitability* of conflicts of interest in certain management/employee situations;
(c) it can impair the efficient resolution of disputes.

Hence, 'pluralism' has been suggested as a more effective approach. A pluralistic frame of reference is one which sees conflicts of interest and disagreements between managers and workers over the distribution of the firm's profits as the normal and inescapable state of affairs. Realistically, therefore, management should accept that conflicts will *necessarily* occur, and thus should seek to resolve them by establishing sound procedures for settling disputes. Pluralism assumes that the best way to achieve consensus and long-term stability in management/worker relations is for management to recognise conflicting interests, to negotiate compromises, and to balance the demands of various groups. This implies the need for grievance procedures, joint-negotiation committees, union-recognition agreements, arbitration arrangements, and so on, i.e. all the mundane, practical and utilitarian devices traditionally associated with *personnel management*.

5. Differences in personnel management

In the same way as behaviour at work is influenced by technology and organisation (*see* Chapter 10), the practice of personnel management varies in different types of company.

In a large progressive company the full range of personnel procedures is found, the personnel department is active and influential, and quite often there are well-established arrangements by which employees can participate in decisions, or at least be consulted about them.

In a smaller company a specialist personnel department may not exist, and personnel management functions may be carried out by the various managers as part of their normal duties. The emphasis here may be on recruitment, selection, wage structures, compliance with employment law and perhaps industrial relations; other matters such as training, appraisal, job evaluation and participation are probably dealt with in an unplanned, informal and almost intuitive way. Organised and thoroughly documented personnel procedures are instinctively felt to be inappropriate in a small company.

6. Roles of the personnel manager

The mundane tasks of writing copy for job advertisements, organising training courses, personnel records, operating wages systems, looking after the firm's health and safety at work arrangements, etc., are known collectively as the *service* function of the personnel role. Other major personnel management functions are as follows.

(a) The *control* function, comprising:
- (*i*) analysis of key operational indices in the personnel field: labour turnover, wage costs, absenteeism and so on;
- (*ii*) monitoring labour performance (staff appraisal, for example);
- (*iii*) recommending appropriate remedial action to line managers.

(b) The *advisory* function, whereby the personnel department offers expert advice on personnel policies and procedures, for example:
- (*i*) which employees are ready for promotion;
- (*ii*) who should attend a certain training course;

(*iii*) how a grievance procedure should be operated;

(*iv*) interpretation of contracts of employment, health and safety regulations etc.

So wide-ranging are the many tasks that personnel managers may be called upon to undertake that special problems are attached to personnel work, including the following.

(a) Line managers may interpret personnel department initiatives as unwarranted challenges to their authority.

(b) It is difficult to define the boundaries of the personnel role. To what extent should personnel considerations figure in normal operational decisions?

(c) Personnel department represents management; yet individual personnel managers — who through their duties communicate directly with the firm's employees — may sympathise more with labour than with management on certain issues. Consequently, a personnel manager may be called upon to implement policies with which he or she does not wholeheartedly agree.

It follows that the personnel officer has to be a *diplomat*; mediating between management and worker, between manager and manager, and among various groups of employee. He or she must gather and assess facts, *diagnose* situations and prescribe solutions. Thus a personnel manager has to be an effective planner, analyst, team worker and communicator, capable of presenting proposals and arguing a case at all levels within the organisation — from the board room to the employees' workplaces.

7. Organisation of the personnel department

The personnel officer is necessarily a generalist, since the variety of issues typically dealt with in a personnel department is so diverse that no one person could master all aspects of the job. Thus, a personnel manager requires a working rather than a detailed knowledge of:

(a) the firm, its products and the industry in which the business operates;

(b) production methods and company organisation structure;

(c) pension schemes, wage and bonus arrangements;

(d) law relating to employment;

(e) the fundamentals of management theory and practice.

Consequently, the personnel manager requires wide-ranging knowledge and skills, in contrast to the highly specialised qualifications and experiences of many of the line managers whom the personnel manager will advise. This might cause reluctance among line managers to accept advice from a personnel manager who does not possess their detailed knowledge of specific functions.

The structure of a personnel department should depend on the relative importance of the various tasks it performs, which in turn depends on the organisation of the firm — its size and complexity, production technology, degree of bureaucracy and historical tradition. Some personnel departments employ a number of personnel officers who share work equally, operating a 'single-door' policy whereby any problem that arises (no matter how serious or complex) is assigned to the first officer who becomes free. This recognises the generic nature of personnel work, and it ensures that personnel department staff acquire experience of all personnel tasks. Alternatively, a personnel department might be segmented according to particular functions, with separate staff and sections responsible for recruitment, industrial relations, welfare services, personnel records, etc. Such 'functional' organisation enables staff to specialise in a certain area and hence develop great expertise in that field, but it has the disadvantage of encouraging narrow and introspective attitudes among personnel department staff.

8. Personnel policies

Well-constructed personnel policies are essential for the well-being and long-term survival of the firm. Conflicts between management and labour can be minimised through:

(a) giving workers security of employment;

(b) offering promotion to suitably qualified staff;

(c) consultation and negotiation with employees' representatives on all issues affecting terms and conditions of employment and working environments;

(d) avoidance of discrimination in recruitment and/or promotion on the grounds of sex, ethnic origin, religion, marital status, age or physical disability;

(e) providing opportunities for retraining and the acquisition of new skills;

(f) establishing codes of practice for dealing with redundancies and dismissals, and grievance procedures for complaints against management by staff.

Personnel management is difficult because human relations problems are complex and difficult to solve, and there are many constraints that restrict the personnel manager's capacity to improve conditions at work. For instance, physical working conditions in some jobs (routine assembly-line work, for example) are unavoidably unpleasant, causing boredom and ill temper; or current economic conditions may be so poor that the firm is unable to pay workers the wage increases they feel they deserve.

9. Ethical issues in personnel management

Ethics concerns moral principles and how people should conduct themselves in social affairs. Personnel officers are perhaps more likely to confront ethical dilemmas in the course of their duties than most other executives, since in many respects the personnel manager occupies a 'mediative' role between management and the workforce — balancing the interest of employees against the needs of the overall organisation. Examples of ethical problems that might arise in the course of a personnel officer's work include the following.

(a) Conflicts between a personnel manager's desire to improve the quality of employees' working lives (*via* job extension (*see* 2:20), improvement of conditions, increased participation, etc.) and the insistence of other managers that the division of labour be applied as extensively as possible, and/or that pay and conditions be kept constant.

(b) Senior management demanding that the personnel officer deliberately misrepresent unsound personnel policies in order to promote them to workers.

(c) Awareness that certain employees are not receiving fair rewards for their efforts; that equal opportunities legislation is not being obeyed; that there is unfair discrimination preventing the promotion of certain individuals, etc.

(d) Having to decide whether to report to the police illegal acts of employees (e.g. theft) or of the employing firm (e.g. serious and deliberate contravention of health and safety legislation).

There are two basic approaches to the resolution of such moral dilemmas.

Either

The personnel manager predetermines for him or herself a strict code of behaviour and adheres to this always — regardless of extenuating circumstances. Advantages to this approach include consistency in behaviour (the people with whom the personnel officer deals with always know what to expect) and the fact that the individual does not have to wrestle with his or her conscience every time an ethical problem arises. The difficulties with the approach are that it can lead to obstinacy and intolerance of human weaknesses, and that the manager's credibility will be totally destroyed if that person is seen to break his or her self-imposed moral principles.

Alternatively

The individual consciously chooses to vary his behaviour according to the requirements of each and every situation. Here the manager changes his or her moral outlook as circumstances alter. This creates scope for flexibility in decision making and could lead to fairer decisions but might also result in inconsistency and in the person never being entirely sure whether he or she behaved correctly. Also those affected by a manager's ethical inconsistency might resent and retaliate against decisions.

10. Use of consultants

Human resources management consultants are increasingly engaged by organisations to undertake specialist personnel assignments and/or to advise on personnel policies. Typically, consultants are used when an unusual human resources problem arises within the firm and the existing management has little idea of its nature and implications. An outsider can analyse the issue objectively and explain how similar difficulties have been dealt with in other organisations. Advantages to using an HRM consultant include the following.

(a) It can be cheaper than employing a full-time personnel specialist; no overheads need be incurred; and there are no costs of training and staff development. Internal staff might not be fully employed throughout the year.

(b) Consultants should possess detailed and expert knowledge of the latest specialist techniques and of complex personnel matters (the legal aspects of job evaluation, for instance).

(c) The independence of the consultant, who can question *anyone* within the organisation without concern for internal politics.

(d) Senior management may prefer to discuss sensitive HRM issues with an outside consultant than with its own subordinate staff.

(e) The consultant's wide experience should enable him or her quickly to identify the critical factors affecting a situation and to analyse all the available options.

(f) In-house staff may lack the specialist skills needed to complete unusual or difficult HRM projects. Also, in-house employees are not subject to penetrating expert criticism, and security of tenure could lead to lack of effort and innovation.

(g) Outside consultants should have numerous contacts with other external specialists in the personnel field.

(h) Managements can learn a lot simply through observing a high-calibre consultant at work.

The disadvantages to using external consultants are that:

(a) they lack intimate knowledge of the firm's day-to-day operations;

(b) vital information might be concealed from them by employees suspicious of their work;

(c) consultants are not accountable in the long term for the consequences of their recommendations (they usually move on to another organisation immediately an assignment is completed);

(d) their careers do not depend on achieving success on a particular *ad-hoc* project undertaken for a specific client firm;

(e) consultants might not be instantly available (as are in-house staff).

Effective control of a consultant requires the detailed specification of the assignment, clear objectives (accompanied by concrete criteria for determining whether they have been achieved), and the predetermination of how much information the consultant must gather independently and how much will be collected by the client's own staff.

Consultancy costs should not normally be assigned to the budget of any one department (especially not the personnel department) because the benefits of the consultant's efforts should eventually be felt throughout the firm. Rather, consultancy costs should be absorbed generally, as happens with the salary of a managing director or company secretary.

11. The future of personnel management

A number of issues seem likely to be increasingly important for UK personnel management in the future, notably:

(a) EC interventions in matters affecting employee protection and employee relations (*see* Chapter 24) and the need for personnel (and other) managers to adopt international orientations towards their work;

(b) growing concern for the application of ethical approaches to personnel management;

(c) implementation of equal opportunities policies (*see* 14:**24**);

(d) the human resources management implications of flexible workforces (*see* 10:**9**);

(e) heightened awareness (following the example of successes achieved by Japanese companies in Britain) of the need for effective employee participation in company production systems (*see* 8:**11**)

(f) the consequences for personnel management of the demographic time bomb (*see* below);

(g) changing attitudes among trade union leaders and members (partly due to the higher levels of unemployment experienced over the last 15 years) which give managements a wider range of policy options in industrial relations matters;

(h) greater involvement of the law in personnel issues, including laws on hiring, firing, equal opportunities, and the conduct of industrial relations.

12. The demographic time bomb

This refers to the fact that the average age of the workforce is increasing, creating thereby a shortage of younger workers. The latter are often preferred by employers for a number of reasons.

(a) Young workers have completed their educations more recently and are thus more up to date than older colleagues.

(b) On the whole, younger employees tend to be more flexible in their attitudes and less resistant to change than older workers, who might have a vested interest in maintaining the *status quo*.

(c) The family commitments of older employees are typically more extensive than for young people, so that older workers usually expect higher levels of remuneration.

(d) Since young recruits have recent experience of the learning process (attending lessons, taking notes, concentrating on the key points of lectures, reading and absorbing instructional materials, etc.), they can usually be trained faster than older workers, who may have forgotten the basic techniques of 'how to learn'.

The demographic time bomb will cause recruitment difficulties for firms wishing to engage young workers, and will create skills shortages in certain areas and occupations. Another consequence will be an oversupply of people in middle management and hence the need for more extensive outplacement procedures (*see* 12:9). Further effects of the demographic time bomb could involve the following.

(a) Greater female participation in the labour force with employers offering women:

    (*i*)   financial assistance towards childcare;

    (*ii*) flexible benefits packages that allow them to trade off, e.g. pension rights against increased maternity leave and payments;

    (*iii*) guaranteed re-entry to jobs following time out from the labour force for child raising, etc.

(b) Retraining of older workers in new technologies.

(c) Greater equality of opportunity for young people from disadvantaged ethnic minorities.

(d) A higher level of immigration of young people from other countries.

(e) Higher wages and benefits for young workers, with employers competing for their services by offering training schemes, career development packages, large bonuses for remaining with a firm for a certain number of years, etc.

(f) A reduction in age discrimination ('agism') by employers. Currently there is no UK law forbidding agism, which is frequently criticised as unfair on the grounds that older employees may in fact make extremely good workers. Older employees have lower-than-average absenteeism, lateness and labour turnover, and it has been demonstrated that older employees tend to be more satisfied with their jobs (possibly because their expectations are lower and because they are better adjusted to work routines than younger workers). Note, however, that companies which recruit large numbers of older employees might become unattractive to young people because of the consequential loss of immediate short-term promotion prospects for young workers. Also, since older employees are less likely to quit their jobs, reduction of the size of a firm's labour force through natural wastage can become extremely difficult. This is because a freeze on recruitment means that younger people (who tend to leave their employers more frequently) are not replaced, thus increasing the average age of remaining workers. Consequently staffing crises arise when older cohorts simultaneously retire.

13. Outline of the following chapters

In order that personnel management may be seen as a whole, an outline will now be given of the following chapters, under the three main headings of utilisation, motivation and protection.

(a) *Utilisation* begins with a description of human resources planning, followed by the analysis and description of jobs. The next group of topics together form what is sometimes called the employment process, which in many large personnel departments is the responsibility of a specialist officer. It comprises recruitment, selection, transfer, promotion, demotion and separation, together with the relevant legislation. Appraisal, training and development, which together are sometimes called the development process, complete the subject of utilisation.

(b) *Motivation* is implicit in many of the topics dealt with under utilisation, because to make the best use of human resources a manager must try to motivate employees. Job satisfaction is also increased by being employed in suitable work. The areas of personnel management which are particularly concerned with motivation are job evaluation, methods of payment, fringe benefits, participation and justice.

(c) *Protection* includes the study of working conditions, e.g. hours of work, overtime and shift working, and safety, together with the relevant statutory and common law provisions.

Progress test 11

1. Define personnel management. **(1, 2)**

2. What is the meaning of the term human resources management? **(3)**

3. What is a pluralistic frame of reference? **(4)**

4. Define the service role of the personnel department. **(6)**

5. What are the implications of the demographic time bomb? **(12)**

Human resources planning

1. Definition

Human resources planning (HRP) may be defined as an attempt to forecast how many and what kind of employees will be required in the future, and to what extent this demand is likely to be met. It involves the comparison of an organisation's current human resources with likely future needs and, consequently, the establishment of programmes for hiring, training, redeploying and possibly discarding employees. Effective HRP should result in the right people doing the right things in the right place at precisely the right time.

2. Purpose

Human resources planning can help management in making decisions in the following areas:

(a) recruitment;
(b) avoidance of redundancies;
(c) training — numbers and categories;
(d) management development;
(e) estimates of labour costs;
(f) productivity bargaining;
(g) accommodation requirements.

Company HRP needs continuous readjustment because the goals of an organisation are unstable and its environment uncertain. It is also complex because it involves so many independent variables — invention, population changes, resistance to change, consumer demand, government intervention, foreign competition and above all domestic competition. It must include feedback because if the plan cannot be fulfilled the objectives of the company may have to be modified so that they are feasible in human resources terms.

3. The importance of company objectives

Figure 12.1 shows that the essential first step in company HRP is a statement of company objectives which covers products, methods, markets, etc. From this is derived the demand for labour, which is then related to the supply of labour to produce the human resources plan.

Figure 12.1 *The human resources planning process*

The implications of the human resources plan must then be considered by the top management of the company in case company objectives need amendment — for example, it may not be possible to increase production by the planned amount because labour of the kind required is either impossible to train in the time available, or does not exist in the quantity needed.

4. Steps in long-term company HRP

A long-term company human resources plan is usually regarded as one which attempts to forecast for about five years ahead.

As shown in Fig. 12.1, the company must consider the demand for labour, its potential supply (with corrections for its present misuse, over-use or under-use) and the external environment. By studying the interaction of all these factors it can then produce a plan showing how many and what kind of employees are expected to be required in the future. The main points to be considered are as follows.

(a) *The creation of a company HRP group*, including the managers in charge of the main functions within the company.

(b) *The statement of human resources objectives* in the light of company objectives by considering:

  (*i*) capital equipment plans;
  (*ii*) reorganisation, e.g. centralisation or decentralisation;
  (*iii*) changes in products or in output;
  (*iv*) marketing plans;
  (*v*) financial limitations.

(c) *The present utilisation of human resources*, in particular:

  (*i*) numbers of employees in various categories;
  (*ii*) estimation of labour turnover (*see* Chapter 17) for each grade of employee and the analysis of the effects of high or low turnover rates on the organisation's performance;
  (*iii*) amount of overtime worked;
  (*iv*) amount of short time;
  (*v*) appraisal of performance and potential of present employees;
  (*vi*) general level of payment compared with that in other firms.

Note that for all the above, accurate and complete personnel records are essential.

(d) *The external environment of the company:*

    (*i*) recruitment position;

    (*ii*) population trends;

    (*iii*) local housing and transport plans;

    (*iv*) national agreements dealing with conditions of work;

    (*v*) government policies in education, retirement, regional subsidies, etc.

(e) *The potential supply of labour, in particular:*

    (*i*) effects of local emigration and immigration;

    (*ii*) effects of recruitment or redundancy by local firms;

    (*iii*) possibility of employing categories not now employed, e.g. part-time workers;

    (*iv*) changes in productivity, working hours and/or practices.

5. The final company HRP

After considering and co-ordinating these factors a human resources plan may then be made, showing in detail, by function, occupation and locations, how many employees it is *practicable* to employ at various stages in the future. The following should appear in it:

(a) jobs which will appear, disappear, or change;

(b) to what extent redeployment or retraining is possible;

(c) necessary changes at supervisory and management levels;

(d) training needs;

(e) recruitment, redundancy or retirement programmes;

(f) industrial relations implications;

(g) arrangements for feedback in case modifications in the plan or company objectives are necessary;

(h) details of arrangements for handling any human problems arising from labour deficits or surpluses (e.g. early retirement or other natural wastage procedures).

The advantages of HRP include the following.

(a) The organisation should be better equipped to cope with the human resourcing consequences of changed circumstances.

(b) Careful consideration of likely future human resource requirements could lead the firm to discover new and improved ways of managing human resources.

(c) Labour shortfalls and surpluses might be avoided.

(d) It helps the firm create and develop employee training and management succession programmes.

(e) Some of the problems of managing change (*see* 9:12) may be foreseen and their consequences mitigated. Consultations with affected groups and individuals can occur at an early stage in the change process: decisions can be taken unhurriedly and by considering all relevant options, rather than being taken in crisis situations.

(f) Management is compelled to assess critically the strengths and weaknesses of its labour force and personnel policies.

(g) Duplication of effort among employees can be avoided; co-ordination and integration of workers' efforts is improved.

When agreed, the plan must be communicated to all levels of employees, but particularly to managers and unions or employee representatives; it is often necessary and advisable to negotiate with the trade unions on the detailed implementation of the plan.

6. Short-term company HRP

This type of plan, which usually covers a period up to one year ahead, is much more common than a long-term plan. Many firms do not have the quality of management to forecast long-term objectives, or they feel that the nature of their business makes it impossible to look ahead for more than one year.

A short-term manpower plan is comparatively easy because a firm will usually make a production or marketing plan for a year ahead involving budgets, orders for new materials and components, and sales quotas. From this can be derived the amount of *direct labour* in terms of labour-hours required in future, and then, by dividing into this figure the number of available working hours, the number of workers can be obtained. Overtime and the average level of sickness absence and machine breakdowns must be taken into account when available working hours are calculated.

The amount of *indirect labour* may be estimated partly by fixed commitments and partly as a rule of thumb percentage of indirect to direct labour. From the total labour requirements a recruitment or redundancy plan can be derived, but the period is usually too short for any worthwhile training plan to be made.

An advantage of the short-term plan is the ease with which the forecast can be compared with the labour that was actually required, and any discrepancies analysed.

7. Limiting factors

In practice, human resources planning can be difficult and often inaccurate. The chief reasons are as follows.

(a) The type of industry: some depend on new product development in an extremely competitive environment; others may depend on political decisions which are impossible to forecast; while others work on a tendering basis, so that plans can only be short term because it is never known whether a tender will be accepted.

(b) Opposition or scepticism among members of management; all must be convinced of the value of human resources planning if it is to be a success.

(c) Resistance to the changes expressed in the plan. The forecasts of labour structure, with their effects on skills and status, may be regarded as a threat.

(d) The difficulty of forecasting social and economic changes accurately, particularly in an era of high unemployment.

(e) The need to have very complete and accurate employee records, maintained for at least the last five years, which it is hoped can be used to detect trends in employee movements. These trends may, however, be very unreliable in times of high unemployment.

(f) The rapid growth of new technologies (*see* Chapter 10).

(g) The plan may indicate recruitment and training programmes which, although desirable, may be impossible to put into practice because the money to pay for them may not be available now. Because of its financial position the company may find long-term plans useless.

In general, the longer the period over which the plan is made, the greater the effect of these limiting factors. Nevertheless, long-term HRP is a growing practice, particularly in large companies which have to plan their expenditure on capital equipment several years ahead in any case. Even when unemployment is high, the difficulties of recruiting, selecting and training some types of employee are so great and the cost of redundancy so expensive that HRP is amply justified, even though its results may be somewhat inaccurate. Plans may be made more easily when the personnel records are held on a computer (*see* Chapter 25). It is possible to purchase ready-made HRP programmes for use with mini- or microcomputers.

8. Relocation
The physical relocation of a business's premises creates a number of human resource management problems, including the needs:

(a) for staff and union consultation;
(b) possibly, for redundancy planning and the application of outplacement procedures (*see* below);
(c) to assist relocated employees find suitable accommodation, schools for children, new jobs for spouses, etc;
(d) to recruit fresh workers locally.

There exist personnel management consultants (*see* 11:**10**) who specialise in relocation. As well as handling the human aspects of the situation they will also locate suitable premises, liaise with local authorities, arrange for the transport of files and equipment, etc. Their objective is to ensure the business runs smoothly immediately before the move, during it and in the subsequent settling-in period.

9. Outplacement
Outplacement is the practice of employers actively helping workers threatened with redundancy to obtain other jobs. Examples of outplacement procedures include:

(a) counselling to assist affected employees cope with the psychological effects of being declared redundant;
(b) psychometric testing to discover employees' aptitudes for alternative types of work;
(c) providing retraining facilities within the firm;
(d) contacting supplying and client company to ascertain whether they have any vacancies;
(e) circularising local firms advising on the availability of labour in the company in question and inviting them to conduct recruitment interviews on its premises;

(f) helping employees draft and wordprocess their CVs;
(g) giving workers time off to look for other jobs over and above minimum statutory requirements.

Progress test 12

1. Define human resources planning. What is its purpose? **(1, 2)**

2. What are the main points to be considered in formulating a long-term human resources plan? **(4)**

3. What is a short-term human resources plan, and what are its advantages? **(6)**

4. What factors reduce the accuracy or the benefits of human resources planning? **(7)**

5. Define outplacement and explain how it operates. **(9)**

13

Job analysis and job specifications

Job analysis

1. Purpose of job analysis

In personnel management it is very often necessary to obtain and record a description of a job (*see* 5). The description must then be kept up to date to take account of changes in organisation or technology. Job analysis is the process by which a description of a job is compiled.

2. Methods and difficulties

There are many difficulties in job analysis, some practical, some concerned with the attitudes of employees. The following are the most important methods which may be used.

(a) *Direct observation* — this is always necessary but has several drawbacks:

  (*i*) a skilled worker can make a job look easy;
  (*ii*) an experienced worker can make a job look difficult;
  (*iii*) mental processes are not revealed;
  (*iv*) some manual work is too fast or intricate to be observed accurately, unless film or video is used.

(b) *Interview with the job-holder* — this is nearly always necessary but difficulties often occur, largely because the worker may be suspicious of the job analysis. The employee may decide to exaggerate the importance of the job or occasionally try to make it seem unimportant. The main problems with these interview are as follows:

(*i*) the worker's attitude may influence his or her account of the job;

(*ii*) the employee may, even if co-operative, forget some details of the job, and emphasise the most recent events;

(*iii*) the employee may not be able to express him or herself clearly.

(c) *Interview with the supervisor* — this again is an inevitable occurrence, though its value varies for the following reasons:

(*i*) supervisors are surprisingly often out of touch with the details of the job;

(*ii*) they frequently have never done the job themselves;

(*iii*) they sometimes allow their description of the job to be influenced by their opinion of the job-holder;

(*iv*) they may exaggerate the duties and responsibilities of the job in order to increase their own importance.

(d) *Materials of work* — a study of the tools, working materials, machines, documents, communication media, etc., frequently provides a useful check on information obtained in other ways, and may suggest questions to be asked.

(e) *Previous studies*, e.g. work study records, training manuals and accident reports, are sometimes available and can be brought up to date or added to other information.

(f) *Do-it-yourself* — in some jobs it is feasible for the analyst to spend some time actually performing the work personally. The analyst should then be careful not to form too subjective an impression, e.g. if he or she is not good at figures the analyst may tend to over-estimate the difficulty of an accounting job.

(g) *Questionnaires* are sometimes used, but are highly unreliable. The job-holder is asked to fill in answers to written questions about the job, but may be suspicious of the questionnaire (*see* (b) above), may not understand questions, and feel unduly restricted by them.

(h) *Work diaries* are sometimes used, chiefly for managers and clerical workers. The job-holder records his or her activities in detail throughout the day over a period of about a month. The diary is then analysed to obtain a list of duties and their frequency. If kept conscientiously and accurately, a work diary can be very helpful, but often the job-holder forgets to complete it until the end of the afternoon when recollection of the day's work may not be reliable.

In order to analyse a job with some degree of accuracy it is obviously necessary to use a combination of several of the above methods, each checking the other.

Job specifications

3. Definitions
The Department of Employment has published a glossary of training terms from which the following definitions have been taken.

(a) Job description — a broad statement of the purpose, scope, duties and responsibilities of a particular job.
(b) Job specification — a detailed statement of the physical and mental activities involved in the job and, when relevant, of social and physical environmental matters. The specification is usually expressed in terms of behaviour — i.e. what the worker does, what knowledge he or she uses in doing it, the judgments he or she makes and the factors taken into account when making them.

4. Use of job descriptions
For general discussions of jobs, a broad description is all that is necessary. For example, when examining the staffing of a department for human resources planning purposes a detailed statement of activities is not required.

A job description can be written under these headings:

(a) title of job;
(b) scope of job (in broad terms);
(c) reporting to . . . ;
(d) responsible for . . . .

5. Use of job specifications
For several personnel functions a detailed account of the job is necessary. The most important of these are:

(a) selection;
(b) promotion;
(c) appraisal;

(d) setting performance standards;

(e) job evaluation;

(f) training.

The job specification is therefore of fundamental importance in personnel management, though it should be used with discretion. When relations are poor between manager and subordinates, the latter may use their job specifications (if they have been issued) as self-defensive weapons, refusing tasks or responsibilities because they do not appear in the specifications.

There are few companies where job specifications can genuinely remain unchanged for any length of time, since they are partly the result of the organisational needs (which frequently change) and partly the result of the way in which successive employees have carried out the job. Many companies therefore prefer to keep job specifications confidential, giving employees copies of their job descriptions only.

6. Drawing up a job specification

There is no standard layout or set of headings for a job specification; it is found that variations are necessary according to the type of work, e.g. manual or non-manual, and to the organisation.

The statement in the definition (*see* **3**) that a job specification should emphasise activities and behaviour is most important. A specification written in terms of responsibilities, for example, can be very misleading. To say that someone is responsible for obtaining and collating information from the company's branches may sound very important but in fact that person may simply receive straightforward sales statistics on standard forms and copy them onto an analysis sheet.

Whenever possible the job specification should show *what* the person does, and by *what means*. It is also desirable to indicate approximately what proportion of working time is spent on each activity, or group of activities, and how frequently any occasional duties occur.

The job specification should begin with the job description (*see* **4**) and then continue with a more detailed account of the job, perhaps using these headings:

(a) major responsibilities and results expected;
(b) routine duties under the headings in (a);
(c) non-routine or infrequent duties under the same headings;
(d) working conditions;
(e) equipment and materials used;
(f) personal contacts.

For appraisal and training purposes, performance standards should also be included; these are dealt with below. An example of a job specification for a manual job appears in Appendix 1.

Performance standards

7. Purpose

It is sometimes necessary to specify the quantity or quality of work which should be attained by the holder of a certain job. As stated above, the most frequent use of performance standards is found in appraisal and training; to assess an employee either in his or her normal work or after training it is essential to have a criterion against which to compare actual performance. Performance standards are also used in some wage systems (*see* 22:3).

8. Setting standards

Performance standards are most easy to set when some kind of physical activity takes place. They can state how many articles should be produced, how many documents completed or how many selling calls made in a day. When the task becomes varied, e.g. when articles of several different types are made during a working day or the calls are scattered over a large area, standards expressed in such simple terms become misleading. A performance standard should also contain some reference to the quality of work.

In many cases, therefore, they are less easy to set than may appear at first sight; the standard of output may have to refer to a period considerably longer than one day in order to include a typical range of tasks, or subjective judgments introduced, e.g. 'performs work satisfactorily'. To reduce these difficulties it may sometimes be possible to select from the range of tasks the employee performs a very small number which must be done satisfactorily if the complete job is to be accomplished well. Careful analysis of the job may reveal these key points or critical incidents for which it may be possible to set performance standards expressed in measurable behaviour.

9.   Standards for managers and supervisors
It is a very difficult problem to set performance standards for managers and supervisors because their work is extremely varied and emphasises mental rather than physical activity.

In some cases there may be obvious targets, e.g. a sales manager may be expected to maintain sales at a certain minimum level, or a supervisor to keep waiting time in his or her section below a certain level. Criteria such as these, which are similar to the key points or critical incidents mentioned in **8**, are particularly valuable when they can be measured objectively and are within the control of the person concerned. A target for a supervisor to 'maintain satisfactory industrial relations within the section' would be valueless, first because of the subjective interpretation of the word satisfactory and secondly because the quality of industrial relations would depend on many factors outside the supervisor's control.

It is often claimed that careful analysis aided by ingenuity will show that any job contains elements for which performance standards can be expressed in terms of measurable behaviour, and some approaches to appraisal (*see* 18:8–) and training (*see* 19:3) are based on this assumption.

Personnel specifications

10. Definition
According to the Department of Employment's glossary of training terms a personnel specification (sometimes called a person specification) is an interpretation of the job specification in terms of the kind of person suitable for the job.

11. Purpose
A personnel specification is used above all in recruitment,

selection and promotion as part of the process of utilisation, i.e. finding the most suitable person to fill a job. It contains a series of desired attributes against which candidates for a job are judged; in some cases it may be possible to set an achievement or aptitude test (*see* 4:**16–17**) to obtain a more exact measure of their suitability.

12. Method

For convenience, and to ensure that no important points are overlooked, it is common practice to use a standard set of headings in a personnel specification. These headings often correspond with those used in recording the interview (*see* 5:**7**), e.g. the seven-point plan or the five-fold grading, so that the candidate can be matched more easily against the requirements of the job.

The personnel specification must always be based on the job specification; every statement in it must be justified by evidence obtained from the analysis of the job. Phrases like 'possessing outstanding initiative', which are sometimes found in personnel specifications, are not only vague but often have no relation to the actual demands of the job. The specification is intended to describe the person who is capable of doing the job adequately, not an impossible ideal.

13. Adapting the job to the employee

It is unrealistic and somewhat inhuman to suppose that a candidate will be found who fits the personnel specification exactly or can be precisely moulded into it by training. Quite often the job is changed after it has been analysed, sometimes deliberately, sometimes gradually and unconsciously by the job-holder to suit his or her abilities, personality and experience. In any case job analysis can never produce a completely reliable result (*see* **2**) and job and personnel specifications based on it must always be interpreted flexibly.

Progress test 13

1. Describe, with comments, the chief methods of analysing a job. (2)

2.   What is the difference between a job description, a job specification and a personnel specification?   **(4, 5, 10)**

3.   For what purposes is a job specification used?   **(5)**

4.   Define performance standards.   **(8)**

5.   For what purposes is a personnel specification used?   **(11)**

14
Recruitment and selection

Recruitment

1. Definitions

It is useful to make a distinction between recruitment and selection.

(a) *Recruitment* is the first part of the process of filling a vacancy; it includes the examination of the vacancy, the consideration of sources of suitable candidates, making contact with those candidates and attracting applications from them.

(b) *Selection* is the next stage, i.e. assessing the candidates by various means, and making a choice followed by an offer of employment.

2. Examining the vacancy

If the vacancy is additional to the present workforce, i.e. it has occurred because of some new or increased activity, then in all probability the need for the new employee has been established and a job specification compiled. The majority of vacancies, however, occur as replacements for people who have left the company or as the final event in a chain of transfers and promotions following on a reorganisation. In these cases consideration may be given to the following points.

(a) It may be possible to fill the vacancy from within the company.

(b) It may be filled by a different kind of employee, e.g. a school-leaver or a part-timer.

(c) The job and personnel specifications may need to be revised.

3. Internal sources

The advantages of filling the vacancy internally rather than externally are:

(a) better motivation of employees because their capabilities are considered and opportunities offered for promotion;
(b) better utilisation of employees, because the company can often make better use of their abilities in a different job;
(c) it is more reliable than external recruitment because a present employee is known more thoroughly than an external candidate;
(d) a present employee is more likely to stay with the company than an external candidate;
(e) internal recruitment is quicker and cheaper than external.

4. External sources

Very many vacancies are filled from external sources; even when an internal candidate is transferred or promoted the final result is usually a vacancy elsewhere in the company which has to be filled from outside. External recruitment can be time-consuming, expensive and uncertain, though it is possible to reduce these disadvantages to some extent by forethought and planning.

External sources may be divided into two classes: those which are comparatively inexpensive but offer a limited choice, i.e. (a) to (f) below, and those which are comparatively expensive but give the employer access to a wider range of candidates, i.e. (g) and (h) below.

Even when unemployment is high certain categories of employee who possess scarce skills are difficult to find and the employer may have to use the more expensive means of recruitment. Other types, for example unskilled workers, can be found very easily using inexpensive means; the problem then lies in selecting the suitable candidate from among a very large number of applicants. Means for finding suitable candidates include the following.

(a) Recommendations by present employees.
(b) Unsolicited applications.
(c) Direct links with universities, colleges and schools.
(d) Jobcentre or careers office.

(e) Professional bodies' appointments services.
(f) Private agencies.
(g) Advertising.

5. Recommendations by present employees

This is sometimes encouraged by rewards to employees who introduce successful candidates. It gives a limited field of choice, but it costs very little and, as a rule, the candidates are of good quality.

6. Unsolicited

Applications are sometimes received from candidates who either call personally at the place of work or write letters of enquiry. This is another inexpensive source which provides a limited choice, but the candidates are of variable quality.

7. Direct links with educational establishments

Many employers maintain connections with universities, colleges and schools. Candidates are usually available from these sources only at one time of the year, but this difficulty can often be overcome if companies begin their internal training courses in the autumn, or fill junior vacancies with temporary staff until school-leavers are available.

8. Trade unions

Some companies recruit certain kinds of employees through the appropriate trade unions. The choice is limited, but there is some certainty that the candidate has the skill or knowledge the job requires.

9. Government agencies

The Careers Service and the various services of the Department of Employment provide a means of recruitment which is either free of charge or costs very little. The choice offered by these services is limited, however, because many types of employee prefer to seek jobs by other methods and do not register with the appropriate government agency.

10. Professional bodies

Many professional bodies have an employment service with

which their members can register, supplying details of their experience and the kind of job they are looking for. An employer who uses this service can be sure that all candidates submitted will be professionally qualified, and if the vacancy requires a certain qualification the limited choice offered is not a disadvantage.

Instead of running an employment service, which needs careful administration, some bodies prefer to encourage employers to advertise in their journal.

11. Private agencies

Organisations which are run as commercial enterprises for supplying employers with candidates for jobs are of two main types.

(a) *Office staff employment agencies*, which mainly deal with clerical, typing and office machine operator vacancies. The employer informs the agency of the vacancy, and the agency submits any suitable candidates on its register. When a candidate is engaged the employer pays a fee to the agency, part of which is usually refunded if the employee leaves within a specified time. There is no charge to the candidate, who of course is at liberty to register with several agencies if he or she likes. Unless the agency takes care to submit only reasonable candidates for the vacancy its services can be expensive because of the time taken up in interviewing, testing and processing applications.

(b) *Selection agencies for senior staff*, which usually undertake the complete recruitment process and the first stages of selection for managerial and professional vacancies. The agency analyses the job, prepares job and personnel specifications, advertises, sends out application forms and interviews selected candidates, sometimes testing them also. The employer is then presented with a short list of candidates, the career and qualifications of each being described, so that the employer may make the final choice. This method of recruitment is expensive because it is usual for the employer to pay a substantial fee whether or not a suitable candidate is found. Agencies have two disadvantages:

(*i*) in many cases it is impossible for an outside body to understand in a short time what kind of a person will fit in with the present management of the company;

(*ii*) it is very difficult for the agency to follow up and validate its recommendation (*see* **23**).

12. Headhunting

Very senior managers are sometimes recruited by a process known as 'executive search' or 'headhunting'. Its advocates believe that the best candidates are not those who reply to advertisements or look for new jobs in other ways, but those who are successful in their present jobs and are not thinking of moving elsewhere.

On receipt of a commission from a client the headhunter will search for potential candidates (*i*) in competing businesses (possibly obtaining their names from company reports, brochures, etc.), (*ii*) in the membership lists of professional bodies, trade association yearbooks, newspaper and magazine reports that mention successful managers in the relevant industry, and (*iii*) through confidential headhunting networks. Selected individuals are then approached discreetly and, following a discussion regarding the job and its remuneration, one or two of them are introduced to the client firm. Advantages to headhunting are as follows.

(a) Headhunters should possess expert knowledge of the salary levels and fringe benefits necessary to attract good calibre candidates. Also, they will analyse the vacancy and offer an opinion about the type of person required, will conduct initial screening, administer psychometric tests (*see* **4:4–14**), etc. This saves the client many administrative costs and advertising expenses.
(b) Possibly, top managers already in employment will not bother to read job advertisements, newspapers and other conventional media and hence cannot be reached by these means.
(c) Senior managers prepared to consider a move sometimes make this known to leading headhunters, even though they would not openly apply to competing companies.
(d) If a targeted candidate does not want the job, he or she may suggest someone else who is equally suitable and who may in fact be interested.
(e) Recruiting firms are assured that candidates presented to them will almost certainly be well equipped for the vacant position.
(f) The anonymity of the recruiting organisation is preserved until the final stages in the procedure.

Criticisms of executive search include the following.

(a) Headhunting is highly disruptive to successful businesses, which stand to lose expensively-trained senior managers.

(b) It can be used to avoid equal opportunities laws on recruitment and selection.

(c) A headhunted individual might subsequently be enticed by other headhunters to leave his or her new firm after a short period. To avoid this some companies attach 'golden handcuffs' to senior management positions, i.e. they pay large cash bonuses which are only available to executives who stay with the firm a certain number of years.

(d) Arguably, headhunters rely too heavily on existing networks and trade contacts, creating thereby a glorified 'old boy system' which ignores good people from other sources.

(e) Headhunters' fees are far higher than for conventional employment agencies (up to 50 per cent of the recruited individual's initial salary in some instances).

(f) An unsuitable candidate might bribe the headhunter to recommend that person for the vacant job.

(g) The headhunter might acquire confidential information about the client company which could then be passed on to competing firms.

(h) Headhunters are not subject to the same long-term accountability as personnel managers employed within the business. Also they lack detailed knowledge of the client organisation's culture (*see* 10:11) and operations.

(g) A headhunter might misleadingly suggest to potential candidates that a job carries a high level of salary when this is not actually the case. The salary quoted may in fact depend on meeting unrealistic targets. Equally, a recruiting firm might expect a headhunter to find a candidate capable of solving all its difficulties, when in reality the business is so weak it is bound to fail.

13. Advertising

The most popular method of recruitment is to advertise the vacancy and invite candidates to apply to the company. It has been estimated that about 10 per cent of all press advertising expenditure is devoted to situations vacant advertising; there is not doubt that much of this huge sum is wasted, chiefly because so little research has been carried out compared with research in the field of product advertising.

Many employers have been able to reduce their job advertising costs with no adverse effect on the quality or quantity of candidate response by experimenting with styles of advertisements, media and wording, and keeping careful records of the number of replies received to each advertisement and the candidate who was eventually selected. The only reliable guidance about advertising comes from the person who receives and analyses the replies, i.e. the employer. Newspapers and advertising agencies, which often claim to advise on the style and size of advertisements, are not usually in a position to know and evaluate the response.

Job advertisements should aim at procuring a small number of well-qualified candidates quickly and as cheaply as possible. Note the high cost of placing job advertisements in newspapers. A single advertisement covering 140mm x 2 columns (approximately one-eighth of a page) in one issue of a quality daily newspaper will cost between £1750 and £3100, depending on the newspaper's circulation and the page position of the advertisement. Even a small advertisement in a regional newspaper can cost in excess of £200. An advertisement which produces hundreds of replies is bad; the employer will then be faced with the lengthy and expensive task of sorting out a few candidates for interview. The advertisement can become the first stage in selection by describing the job and qualifications required so comprehensively that borderline candidates will be deterred from applying and good candidates encouraged.

The small amount of research that has been done in this field shows that information about the job contributes much more to the effectiveness of an advertisement than its style or size. There is also general agreement that including the word training in an advertisement increases the response.

Advertising may be made more effective and less expensive if the following principles are observed.

(a) The advertisement should contain a job specification and a personnel specification in miniature, including the following:
    (*i*) job title;
    (*ii*) description of job and employer (including location);

(*iii*) experience, skills and qualifications required;

(*iv*) age range;

(*v*) working conditions, e.g. wage or salary, fringe benefits;

(*vi*) training given (if relevant);

(*vii*) what action the candidate should take, e.g. write a letter, telephone for an application form, etc.

(b) It should appear in the appropriate publication, e.g. local press for manual and routine clerical jobs, national press for senior jobs, professional journals for specialists.

(c) Experiments should be made to test the response for different sizes, headings, wording, page position, day of the week, etc.

(d) Careful records should be kept showing:

(*i*) which publication was used;

(*ii*) which date and day of the week;

(*iii*) which position on the page;

(*iv*) which style and size, e.g. display, semi-display, run-on;

(*v*) names of the candidates replying to each advertisement;

(*vi*) names of the candidates who are selected for interview;

(*vii*) name of the candidate who is successful.

(e) The response should be analysed so that advertising expenditure can be directed towards the publication and the style of advertisement which give the best result for a particular type of vacancy.

(f) Rejected candidates should be sent a prompt and courteous letter; inconsiderate treatment will eventually detract from a company's reputation and adversely affect the response to future advertisements.

Sometimes other considerations besides cost and response must be kept in mind. For example, suppose that evidence has been collected which shows that small advertisements are just as effective as large, providing the information given is the same (a not uncommon finding). The company may decide that small advertisements are not consistent with its prestige and that large advertisements must be used even though they can be shown to be wasteful. In this case part of the cost of the advertisement should logically be paid out of the company's general advertising account as it is concerned as much with public relations as with recruitment.

On the other hand, the prestige of the company can sometimes be made use of; a recruitment campaign is very often more successful if it follows a national advertising campaign for a new product which has brought the company into the public eye.

14. Box numbers
Occasionally a company decides to use a box number in a job advertisement instead of its own name and address. The reasons for this decision are usually:

(a) the company is beginning a new venture which at present it wishes to keep secret; *or*
(b) the present holder of the job is to be transferred or dismissed and has not yet been told; *or*
(c) the company wishes to state a salary in the advertisement but its salary policy is secret (*see* 22:14).

Only the first of these three reasons is entirely creditable. The response to box number advertisements is usually poor in quality and quantity partly because of the mystery incorporated in them and partly because they inevitably contain less information than a normal advertisement which specifies the company's name, address and business.

Some large companies who wish to preserve their anonymity ask a selection agency for senior staff to advertise on their behalf; the prestige of the agency may to some extent counterbalance the disadvantages of the use of a box number.

Selection

15. The application form
Whatever method of recruitment is used, the candidate should be asked to fill in an application form, firstly to ensure that no important details are omitted and secondly to provide information about the candidate in a logical and uniform order.

The layout of application forms varies, but most of them contain the following headings, usually in this order:

(a) job applied for;
(b) name, address, telephone number;
(c) date and place of birth, marital status, nationality;

(d) education;

(e) training and qualifications;

(f) medical history, e.g. any serious illnesses, whether disabled;

(g) employment history (names of previous employers, description of jobs held, dates of employments, reasons for leaving);

(h) any other information the candidate wishes to provide;

(i) a signature under the words 'This information is correct to the best of my knowledge';

(j) date.

The application form is not only the basis of selection, but is the fundamental document in an employee's personnel record (*see* 25:2) and has legal importance in the contract of employment (*see* 16:1).

16. Selection method

The manager's next step is to compare the application form with the personnel specification, looking for attributes which show the candidate to be apparently suitable for the job and shortcomings which may either rule out the candidate from consideration or necessitate special training if he or she were engaged. From this comparison the manager can make a list of candidates for interview and a list of those to be rejected. The latter should be written to at once regretting their lack of success.

When, because of high unemployment, a large number of applications is received the task of compiling a list of candidates to be interviewed becomes very difficult and time-consuming. Various suggestions have been made for dealing with this problem. When managerial, supervisory or specialist vacancies are being dealt with an enlarged application form can be used asking for precise details of past employment. Candidates are then rejected or not following a ruthless comparison of their experience with the demands of the post as shown by job analysis. A few companies ask candidates to complete a biographical questionnaire which has been carefully designed in respect of the job to be filled, though the process of compiling and validating the questionnaire is itself a lengthy and expensive undertaking. The majority of vacancies, however, are not suitable for such additional procedures, which assume that candidates have above-average powers of self-expression and are willing to complete complicated forms. Perhaps the usual method in such cases is first to reject some candidates on the application form and then give quick interviews to the remainder (often a very large number) concentrating on relevant experience. This will produce a short list who will go through a more searching selection procedure.

After the short list has been drawn up the manager will decide what type of interview should be given — individual, successive or panel (*see* 5:**10–12**), and what tests should be used, e.g. an intelligence test (*see* 4:**5**), an aptitude test (*see* 4:**16**) or an achievement test (*see* 4:**17**). The manager may also decide to use leaderless group discussion if the vacancy is appropriate (*see* 4:**13**). The interview, which is the main and indispensable part of the selection process, is described in 5:**3–9**. Notes are made, and filed for a reasonable period, of each candidate's performance in the interview and tests in case an unsuccessful candidate questions the decision, e.g. under the Race Relations Act or the Sex Discrimination Act.

17. Offer of the job

Assuming that a suitable candidate has emerged from the selection process, he or she must now receive an offer. It is usual for the person to be made an oral offer, and if he or she accepts it (perhaps after an interval for consideration) the individual is given a written offer. The initial offer of a job needs special care, particularly as regards the following points.

(a) The wage or salary offered must not only be appropriate to the job and attractive to the candidate but consistent with the earnings of present employees.

(b) The job must be named and any special conditions stated, e.g. 'for the first six months you would be under training at our Birmingham branch'.

(c) The candidate must know the essential conditions of employment, e.g. hours, holidays, bonuses and fringe benefits.

(d) Any provisos must be clearly stated, e.g. 'subject to satisfactory references and medical examination'.

(e) The next stage must be clearly defined; if the candidate asks for time for consideration, it must be agreed when he or she will get in touch. If the candidate accepts the oral offer, that manager must say what will happen next, and when.

18. References

A clear, unbiased and comprehensive description of a candidate's abilities and behaviour by his or her previous employer would be of enormous value in selection, particularly if the employer also supplied a job specification. Unfortunately this ideal is never realised, for several reasons.

(a) Most candidates are employed at the time of their application, and do not wish their employers to know they are looking elsewhere.

(b) Because of (a) a prospective employer would be breaking a confidence if he or she asked for a reference before an offer of a job had been made and accepted.

(c) By the time an offer has been accepted, selection is over and the reference is too late to affect it.

(d) An offer may be made 'subject to satisfactory references', but as most references are received after the candidate has started work they can only be used to warn managers of possible faults in the candidate which in serious cases may eventually lead to warnings followed by dismissal.

(e) Employers giving references are usually extremely cautious; many references merely state the job title, the dates of employment, and the reason for leaving.

(f) References are occasionally biased, giving a good reference to hasten an employee's departure or a poor one because of a grudge.

Most references do not give rise to second thoughts about the selection of a candidate, but in a few cases information is given (usually by a telephone call) which shows the request for a reference to have been worth while.

19. Medical examinations

Preferably, every candidate should have a medical examination before the offer of a job is confirmed (*see* 4:**3**). It will show whether he or she is physically suitable for the job and what risk there is likely to be of sickness absence or injury — though some doctors maintain that a very thorough medical examination indeed is necessary to fulfil these requirements.

Many employers, perhaps the majority, dispense completely with medical examinations because of their cost, the delay they cause in allowing the candidate to start work, and the very large number of jobs in which physique is not important (*see* 4:**3**). Others require candidates to be interviewed by a nurse who will refer them to a doctor if any serious disability is suspected.

Medical examinations should always be given:

(a) when the candidate is applying for a particularly arduous job, or when he or she will work alone, e.g. a security officer;

(b) when the job demands high standards of hygiene, e.g. catering and food manufacture;

(c) when the interview or other source reveals a doubtful medical history;

(d) to any employee whose health may be in danger because of the nature of the work — this decision is made by the Employment Medical Adviser, who has the statutory power (if the employee consents) to carry out the examination;

(e) to candidates who are known to be disabled, e.g. registered disabled persons (*see* **19**).

It is wise to include in the application form, above the space for the signature, a statement to the effect that the candidate agrees, if engaged, to be medically examined at any time.

20. Employment of disabled persons

Many employers believe they have a social duty to employ disabled people where possible adapting production lines or telephone exchanges, for example, to allow this. There is also statutory backing for the employment of the disabled in the Disabled Persons (Employment) Acts 1944 and 1958, which provide for the following.

(a) A register of disabled persons, open to all who are substantially handicapped in getting or keeping suitable employment.

(b) A requirement that every employer with 20 or more workers should employ at least 3 per cent registered disabled workers.

(c) An employer may not dismiss a registered disabled person without reasonable cause if the firm is below its quota or if the dismissal would bring its numbers below it.

(d) The designation of two jobs, passenger lift attendant and car park attendant, which may only be filled by registered disabled persons.

The Acts have helped many disabled persons to find work, but in some areas employers find the quota difficult to fulfil, although they employ a reasonable number of disabled people. The reason for the difficulty is that although there is a legal requirement for employers to maintain a three per cent quota there is no legal requirement for disabled persons to register. Indeed, many disabled people maintain that being registered may be a drawback in their careers and that they prefer not to indicate that they regard themselves as in a category from other people. Employers who are not able to meet the quota of registered disabled persons must approach their local Jobcentre to explain their difficulties.

The 'designated employments' in the Acts are another problem, because both the occupations (*see* (**d**)) can be quite arduous and require regular attendance. It is often difficult to find candidates who are registered as disabled but yet are fit enough to meet the physical requirements of these jobs.

21. The written offer of employment

Assuming that the oral offer has been accepted (*see* **16**) the employer must now confirm in writing. The employer will repeat in this letter the conditions already stated, taking great care that they are accurate because they will be on permanent record as the basis of the contract of employment. In many companies it is the rule that written offers may only be sent by the personnel manager or company secretary to ensure their accuracy.

The Employment Protection (Consolidation) Act 1978 requires that employees must be given a statement of their conditions of service within the first 13 weeks of employment. Some employers combine the written offer of employment with the statutory statement which must contain:

(**a**) names of employer and employee;
(**b**) date when employment began;
(**c**) pay, or method of calculating pay;
(**d**) intervals at which payment is made, i.e. weekly, monthly, etc.;
(**e**) terms and conditions relating to:
    (*i*) hours of work;

(*ii*) holiday pay, including the pay due on termination of employment;

(*iii*) sick pay;

(*iv*) pension scheme;

(f) the length of notice of termination the employee is obliged to give and entitled to receive;

(g) a note indicating the employee's right to join, or not to join a trade union;

(h) a description of the manner in which an employee can seek redress of any grievance relating to his or her employment;

(i) the title of the job;

(j) a note showing whether any period of employment with another employer counts as part of the period of employment for notice purposes (*see* 16:2);

(k) reference to a document stating the disciplinary rules, and naming a person to whom the employee can apply (and by what method) if he or she is dissatisfied with a disciplinary decision.

It is not necessary for the written statement to cover all these points in detail; the employee may be directed to documents which are easily accessible for the full particulars. These documents could include, for example, pension scheme handbooks or copies of the works rules.

Employees must be informed in writing of any changes in conditions not more than one month after the change has been made.

22. Induction

The process of receiving employees when they begin work, introducing them to the company and to their colleagues, and informing them of the activities, customs and traditions of the company is called induction. It may be regarded as the beginning of training or the final stage of the selection process. It has also been shown to have a close relationship with labour turnover (*see* Chapter 17).

Induction may be divided into two stages.

(a) Introduction to the working group (*see* 7:8(e)) is important psychologically and best done by the employee's immediate supervisor, who should introduce the recruit to colleagues and show him or her round the department.

(b) Company background (in a large company), which may be described by lectures, films or visits. Probably this should not be done in the first day or week of employment because the employee is at that time more concerned with his or her immediate surroundings and his or her own job. The worker will become interested in the wider scene two or three months after joining the company and can then take part in a second-stage induction course at some central point in the firm, if the company is a large one, or a supervisor may talk to the worker informally if the company is small.

23. Follow-up

All selection should be validated by follow-up. The employee is asked how he or she feels about progress to date and the worker's immediate superior is asked for comments, which are compared with the notes taken at the selection interview. If a follow-up is unfavourable it is probable that selection has been at fault; the whole process from job specification to interview is then reviewed to see if a better choice can be made next time.

An employee can be followed-up about three months after starting if the job is fairly straightforward, and after a longer period if the job is more complex and responsible.

Discrimination in employment

24. Equal opportunity in employment

An equal opportunity employment situation exists when there is no unfair discrimination against either of the sexes or against any ethnic or legally constituted social group in terms of access to jobs, terms and conditions of employment, promotion, training remuneration, or termination of employment. Today, many organisations have 'equal opportunities policies' in which they formally state their commitment to equal opportunity ideals. The advantages to having such a policy are that:

(a) top management is seen to endorse equal opportunity measures creating an example to be followed at lower levels;
(b) as part of its policy the firm might critically examine the sex and ethnic compositions of all its departments, divisions, occupational categories and levels of worker, exposing any unfair employment practices currently operating;

(c) the best candidates for jobs will (or should) be recruited or promoted regardless of their sex or ethnic origin;

(d) discontent among existing minority group employees may be avoided.

Problems attached to equal opportunity policies are as follows.

(a) Organisations sometimes publish extensive equal opportunity policy documents in order to placate existing minority group workers and/or external bodies (local authorities, government purchasing agencies, the EOC or CRE (*see* 28), etc.) but in fact have no commitment to equal opportunities whatsoever. They have no procedures for *implementing* their equal opportunity policy documents. This creates disillusion and cynicism among all concerned.

(b) Recruitment costs increase substantially. Job advertisements have to be placed (expensively) in magazines and newspapers read by each of the sexes and by various ethnic minorities. All applications have to be examined carefully from an equal-opportunities viewpoint, interview panels need to be larger, more candidates most be interviewed and more time has to be spent in interviewing.

(c) An organisation might apply an equal opportunities policy to operatives and low-grade managers, but not to middle managers or senior executives. Hence the representation of minority groups collapses at higher levels, so that corporate strategy cannot be influenced by individuals from minority groups.

Implementation of equal opportunity policies can proceed through the following devices.

(a) Strict adherence to the terms and recommendations of government Codes of Practice on equal opportunities.

(b) Active encouragement of *both* sexes and people from minority groups to apply for jobs and for promotion at all levels within the organisation.

(c) For gender equal opportunities, application of flexitime and job sharing arrangements.

(d) Provision of special training for disadvantaged groups.

(e) Fast tracking, i.e. putting individuals from an underrepresented sex or ethnic group on to separate training and promotion systems where advancement occurs automatically—as of right — provided certain training and other targets are attained. A series of 'milestones of progress' towards senior management positions are identified and the precise requirements for reaching them are laid down. Any trainee satisfying these requirements is routinely promoted to the next level of the hierarchy.

25. Legal provisions

Three Acts, the Sex Discrimination Acts of 1975 and 1986 and the Race Relations Act 1976, make it illegal to discriminate in all aspects of employment, e.g. job advertising, selection, terms of employment, promotion, training, dismissal and retirement. Discrimination means the less favourable treatment of a person by reason of sex, colour, race or ethnic or national origins.

Employers are liable if their subordinates discriminate unlawfully. Indirect discrimination is also unlawful, i.e. applying a condition or requirement which, although applied to both sexes or to all racial groups, is such that a considerably smaller proportion of one sex or of one racial group can comply with it, unless the employer can show the condition to be justified. An example would be a requirement for applicants for a senior clerical post to be at least six feet tall. The Sex Discrimination Act also covers unfair discrimination against people who are married.

26. Exceptions

Employers may lawfully discriminate in the following cases.

(a) For sex discrimination:
   (*i*) where the job requires a person of a particular sex for reasons of physiology, e.g. modelling, authenticity (e.g. acting), or decency (e.g. lavatory attendant);
   (*ii*) jobs in a single-sex establishment;
   (*iii*) jobs which provide individuals with personal welfare or education services and those services can be most effectively provided by a person of a particular sex, e.g. a female counsellor for female offenders;
   (*iv*) jobs where there are legal restrictions on the employment of one sex;
   (*v*) employment in a private household, where the degree of physical or social contact or knowledge of intimate details

might reasonably cause objection to the employment of a particular sex;

  (*vi*) employment carried out wholly or mainly outside the UK.

(b) For racial discrimination:

  (*i*) where the job requires a person of a particular race for reasons of physiology, authenticity or the provision of food or drink for consumption by the public in a special ambience, e.g. a Chinese restaurant;

  (*ii*) jobs which provide persons of a certain racial group with personal services promoting their welfare and those services can most effectively be provided by a person of that racial group;

  (*iii*) employment in a private household (note, however, that this exemption probably falls foul of EC law and is unlikely to survive much longer);

  (*iv*) partnerships with less than six partners (but note the above-mentioned point on EC law;

  (*v*) employment carried out wholly or mainly outside the UK.

All these provisions apply to contract labour, employment agencies, partnerships, trade unions and to professional and training associations. Note, however, that it is lawful to recruit predominantly one sex or race on to a training scheme that seeks to redress an imbalance in employment of the races or sexes in a department or organisation where the imbalance has existed during the previous twelve months. People who give orders to discriminate are covered by the Acts as well as those who implement the unfair discrimination.

27. Complaints by individuals

A complaint of sex or racial discrimination in employment is made to an industrial tribunal within three months of the Act complained of. A conciliation officer may be asked by both parties at this stage to settle the matter without a tribunal hearing, or may intervene on his or her own initiative. If a settlement cannot be reached in this way a tribunal will hear the case and if it decides in favour of the complainant it may award the following:

(a) an order declaring the rights of both parties;

(b) an order requiring the respondent, i.e. the employer, to pay the complainant damages;

(c) a recommendation that the respondent should take a particular course of action within a specified time.

28. Enforcement through statutory bodies

The two Acts set up the Equal Opportunities Commission and the Commission for Racial Equality respectively. These bodies have a general duty to work towards the elimination of discrimination and promote equal opportunity between sexes and between racial groups. They may also investigate relevant matters, institute legal proceedings in cases of persistent discrimination and in exceptional cases help individual complainants.

If they find that an employer has contravened one of the legal provisions they may serve discrimination notices requiring the employer not to commit further unlawful acts. An employer may appeal against such notices to an industrial tribunal.

29. Codes of Practice

Both the EOC and CRE publish Codes of Practice setting out the steps to be taken to eliminate unfair discrimination in recruitment and other employment matters. The Codes offer practical guidance on how personnel policies and procedures should be constructed in order to avoid discrimination, and how existing employees must be instructed about preventing contravention of the Act when interviewing, dealing with subordinates, selecting staff for promotion, etc.

30. Implications for personnel management

Although discrimination in many areas of personnel management takes place constantly on the basis of personal qualities, experience, age and length of service, a company should be able to show that there has been no intention to discriminate unlawfully and that such discrimination has not taken place.

Job advertisements must not therefore state or imply that applicants of a particular race or sex will be favoured, and communications within a company regarding promotion, training or dismissal should obey the same rule. An employer should be able to show that the criteria for selection, promotion, etc., are fair, appropriate and without bias, and that candidates or employees are judged fairly against these criteria. As far as possible objective rather than subjective assessments should be made. Documentary evidence should be kept in case a candidate or employee makes a complaint.

Efficiency in recruitment and selection

31. Costs

As in other management processes, careful control should be exercised over recruitment and selection to ensure that money is not being spent unnecessarily. The recording of advertisements and response (*see* 13) is one control that may be used. Others include the following.

(a) Can new sources of candidates be found which are less expensive?
(b) Could a less expensive selection procedure be used?
(c) Is the application form too complicated, containing unnecessary information, or is it too simple, omitting important information?
(d) Are internal candidates being considered sufficiently?
(e) Are selection standards too high or too low?

32. Efficiency ratios

A manager who recruits and selects on a large scale can check the efficiency of recruiting procedures by calculating some of the following ratios.

(a) Average time during which a vacancy remains unfilled.

(b) $\dfrac{\text{Number of candidates replying to an advertisement}}{\text{Number of candidates called for interview}}$

(c) $\dfrac{\text{Number of interviews}}{\text{Number of offers made}}$

(d) $\dfrac{\text{Number of offers made}}{\text{Number accepted}}$

(e) $$\frac{\text{Number starting work}}{\text{Number judged satisfactory in follow-up}}$$

(f) $$\frac{\text{Number starting work}}{\text{Number still employed after one year}}$$

(g) $$\frac{\text{Cost of recruitment and selection}}{\text{Number starting work}}$$

(h) $$\frac{\text{Number of vacancies}}{\text{Number filled internally}}$$

(i) $$\frac{\text{Total value of wages and salaries offered}}{\text{Cost of recruitment and selection for those vacancies}}$$

A downward trend in any of these ratios, except (i), will show that an improvement is taking place in the efficiency of recruitment and selection.

Progress test 14

1. What is the difference between recruitment and selection? (1)

2. What are the advantages of filling a vacancy internally? (3)

3. Describe, with comments, three inexpensive external sources of recruitment. (4–10)

4. What are the advantages of using a headhunter? (12)

5. Are there any circumstances in which an employer is justified in advertising over a box number? (14)

6. Outline the steps in selection which occur before the candidate is called for interview. (15, 16)

7.   What should the initial job offer contain?   **(17)**

8.   Outline the law regarding employment of disabled persons.   **(20)**

9.   What information must be given to an employee under the Employment Protection (Consolidation) Act 1978?   **(21)**

10. What is induction?   **(22)**

11. In what circumstances is racial discrimination in the recruitment of employees lawful?   **(26)**

15
Promotion, transfer, demotion and retirement

Promotion

1. Definition

A promotion is a move of an employee to a job within the company which has greater importance and, usually, higher pay. Frequently the job has higher status and carries improved fringe benefits and more privileges. Its purpose is to improve both the utilisation and motivation of employees.

2. Methods

There are two main ways in which a company may promote its employees.

(a) *By management decision,* in which an employee is selected for promotion on the basis of information already known to the management. This method is quick and inexpensive and obviously suitable for a small company or for jobs for which the field of possible candidates is small and well known. In large companies it may cause discontent because the decision is arrived at in secret, possible candidates not having the opportunity to state their qualifications for the post. In all cases, this method depends for its success on complete and up-to-date employee records which can be used to identify all possible candidates for any job.

(b) *By internal advertisement;* employees are told by notices or circulars that a post is vacant and they are then invited to apply. Some or all of the candidates are interviewed and one finally selected. It is a comparatively expensive and time-consuming method, but is particularly suitable to a large organisation in which management cannot be expected to have personal knowledge of possible candidates. It does not rely on accurate employee records, and, being open rather than secret, appears fairer to the candidates than the management decision method. In the public sector promotions are made almost entirely through internal advertisements.

3. Promotion and motivation

Normally, employees derive satisfaction from a company policy of promotion from within, but badly handled promotions can cause dissatisfaction. The important points to note are:

(a) the criteria for promotion must be fair — usually a combination of ability, relevant experience and length of service;
(b) the method must be fair;
(c) selection for promotion must be based on appraisals by present and past managers (*see* Chapter 18);
(d) the wage or salary offered to the promoted employee must be what the job deserves rather than what the management thinks he or she will accept;
(e) unsuccessful candidates must be sympathetically treated;
(f) there must be no discrimination.

Transfer

4. Definition

A transfer is a move to a job within the company which has approximately equal importance, status and pay.

5. Selection for transfer

To manage human resources in a constructive way it is sometimes necessary to transfer employees to other jobs, sometimes because of changed work requirements and sometimes because an employee is unhappy or dissatisfied in his or her present job.

In some companies it is the custom for the least satisfactory employees to be transferred from one department to another with the result that a transfer is regarded as discreditable, particularly if it occurs at short notice and without explanation. An unhappy employee may therefore prefer to leave the company rather than seek a transfer.

In other companies transfers are used as a means of developing promising employees by giving them experience in several departments. A few companies advertise all vacancies internally and consider applicants for whom the new job would be a transfer rather than a promotion.

6. Transfer policy
Transfers can increase job satisfaction and improve utilisation under the following circumstances.

(a) A transfer is regarded as a re-selection.

(b) The need for a transfer is explained.

(c) Unsatisfactory employees are not dealt with by transferring them to other departments.

(d) Requests by employees for transfers are fully investigated.

(e) No employee is transferred to another district against his or her will.

(f) An employee transferred to another district is given financial assistance from the company to cover removal costs, legal fees, re-furnishing, etc.

Demotion

7. Definition
A demotion is a move to a job within the company which is lower in importance. It is usually, though not always, accompanied by a reduction in pay.

8. Reasons for demotion
An employee may be demoted for these reasons.

(a) His or her job may disappear or become less important through a company reorganisation.

(b) The worker may no longer be thought capable of carrying out his or her present responsibilities efficiently.

9. Effects of demotion
Unless the employee has requested it, demotion will probably have adverse effects.

(a) There will be less satisfaction of esteem and self-actualisation needs. The employee may show negative reactions to frustration (*see* 2:8–9).

(b) He or she may become a centre of discontent in the company.

(c) Other employees may lose confidence in the company.

An employee who resigns in consequence of a demotion may complain of unfair dismissal under a special category known as 'constructive dismissal' (*see* 16:5).

Retirement

10. Age of retirement

State retirement pensions are at present paid at age 65 for men and age 60 for women, providing retirement from work takes place. In the past, retirement policies were usually based on those ages, though in some kinds of public employment men normally retired at 60. Under the Sex Discrimination Act 1986 it is now unlawful for an employer to stipulate different retirement ages for men and women.

There are two schools of thought about the age of retirement; one maintains that the age is a minimum only and suitable and fit employees should be allowed to work on after this age. The other believes in a fixed retirement age.

11. Flexible retirement

(a) *Advantages:*

    (i) many employees are fit and active well beyond the official retirement age. By working on, they benefit financially and the employer profits from their knowledge and experience;

    (ii) the financial burden on the pension scheme may be relieved.

(b) *Disadvantages:*

    (i) eventually the employer must decide that an employee is no longer fit to work; the decision may not be accepted by the employee, who may make accusations of favouritism if others older than him or her are still working;

    (ii) promotion may be held up if a senior employee does not

retire, causing promising employees to leave the company;

(*iii*) the employee, not knowing when he or she will be asked to leave, cannot easily plan for retirement;

(*iv*) the company cannot prepare human resources plans (*see* Chapter 12) when retirement ages are uncertain.

12. Fixed retirement

A company which adopts a fixed retirement age policy insists on all its employees retiring from their present jobs at a certain age, although sometimes they are offered re-employment in a junior capacity for a limited period.

(a) *Advantages:*

(*i*) employees can plan for retirement more easily;

(*ii*) no invidious judgments about efficiency have to be made;

(*iii*) the company can plan ahead more precisely.

(*iv*) promotion is not held up.

(b) *Disadvantages:*

(*i*) the services of experienced and fit employees may be lost, though sometimes retired employees are used as consultants;

(*ii*) it is unfair to employees with a small company pension, e.g. those with short service.

Progress test 15

1. Describe two methods which a company may use to promote its employees. **(2)**

2. What is the connection between promotion and motivation? **(3)**

3. In what ways can transfers increase job satisfaction? **(6)**

4. Summarise the relative merits of a flexible or fixed age of retirement policy. **(11, 12)**

16
Resignation and dismissal

The contract of employment

1. Legal aspects

A contract of employment exists when, in return for a wage or salary, an employee undertakes to put him or herself at the disposal of an employer during the agreed hours of work. The employer has the legal right to supervise the employee's actions and decide the manner in which the work should be done, and the employee has the duty to put the employer's interests before those of him or herself. The employee also guarantees, by statements, written or spoken at the time of engagement, that he or she is competent to do the work in question.

Under the Employment Protection (Consolidation) Act 1978, the employer must state certain of the terms of employment in writing (*see* 14:21); other terms may be either written, spoken or implied by customary practice in that particular occupation or industry.

2. Termination of the contract

The contract of employment may be terminated by either side, i.e. employer or employee, giving notice making clear the date on which the contract will end. If the contract does not expressly state what period of notice must be given, the period can be deduced by reference either to accepted custom in the occupation or to previous case law. In many instances it has been held that the interval at which wage or salary is paid should be the notice period, e.g. an employee who is paid monthly is entitled to one month's notice.

The many difficulties which occur when the period of notice has not been clearly stated are removed to a large extent by the

Employment Protection (Consolidation) Act 1978. This Act lays
down minimum periods of notice which apply after an employee
has completed four weeks' continuous service with the employer.
Until that time has elapsed the period of notice, if not expressly
stated, depends on custom or case law. The Act states that after
four weeks' continuous employment an employee must give the
employer at least one week's notice. The employer must give the
employee minimum notice which increases with length of service
as follows:

After one month's service	one week
After two years' service	two weeks
After three years' service	three weeks

and so on, up to a maximum of:

After twelve years' service	twelve weeks

These are only minimum periods of notice, and if the contract
clearly or by custom provides for longer periods then the latter
will prevail. The Act does not affect the right of the employer to
dismiss an employee without notice under certain circumstances
(*see* **6**) or for the employer and employee to terminate the contract
without notice if they both agree to do so.

Resignation

3. Definition
A resignation occurs when an employee gives his or her
employer notice to terminate the contract of employment. The
minimum period of notice may be whatever is customary, the
period laid down in the Employment Protection (Consolidation)
Act 1978, i.e. one week, or the period expressly stated in the
contract. There is no legal requirement that a resigning employee
should tell the employer why he or she is leaving. During the
period of notice the employee remains, as before, under the
control of the employer.

4. Treatment of resignations
Some resignations are disguised dismissals, the employee

being allowed to resign as a face-saving measure. There is no objection to this if the employee has another job to go to, but if this is not the case, the employee may find difficulty in obtaining unemployment benefit. The worker should be warned of this possibility before agreeing to resign.

When an employee resigns it is not only courteous but necessary for a manager to interview him or her to find out the reason for leaving — the exit interview (*see* 7:**14**). Although many employees are not entirely frank about their reasons for leaving they may give information which throws light on employee attitudes and may thus lead to a reduction in labour turnover (*see* Chapter 17).

Dismissal

5. Definition

Dismissal is the termination of employment by **(a)** the employer, with or without notice, **(b)** the employee's resignation, with or without notice, when the employer behaves in a manner that demonstrates refusal to be bound by the contract of employment (this is termed 'constructive dismissal', meaning that the employer is behaving so unreasonably that the worker has no alternative but to quit), and **(c)** the failure of the employer to renew a fixed-term contract.

6. Dismissal without notice

This is termed 'summary dismissal'. In most circumstances the employer must give the employee the notice due under the contract (*see* **2**), but in rare cases the conduct of the employee is such that the employer is legally entitled to dismiss the employee without notice. Examples of misconduct which justify instant dismissal are as follows.

(a) Refusal to obey a reasonable instruction, providing the refusal is serious enough to indicate that the employee is repudiating the contract; a refusal in a fit of temper would not justify instant dismissal unless it was maintained afterwards.
(b) Serious neglect of duties.
(c) Absence from work without permission or good cause.

(d) Activities in private life which might adversely affect the employer's business, e.g. running a business in competition with the employer or discreditable behaviour which might drive customers or clients away from the company.

(e) Dishonesty towards the employer.

(f) Violence towards the employer or other employees.

It will be seen from these examples that there is considerable room for argument about the degree of misconduct in any particular case and whether it is sufficient to justify dismissal without notice. Unless the employer is sure that the necessary degree of misconduct has occurred, the employer will often prefer to dismiss with notice, or with money in lieu of notice.

7. Dismissal with notice

The Employment Protection (Consolidation) Act 1978 requires that one week's notice of dismissal be given to workers employed for one month or more; two weeks' notice to workers employed for two years, plus an additional week's notice for each further year of service up to a maximum of twelve weeks' notice. Employees with at least two years' service are legally entitled to a written statement of the reasons for their dismissal.

Because dismissal is such a serious matter, the employer must be careful to ensure not only that it is done for good reason but that the manner in which the employee is dismissed is fair. Capricious dismissals carried out in an unjust way adversely affect the motivation of employees, lower the reputation of the company, create an industrial relations problem and expose the employer to legal action (*see* **9**).

8. Model disciplinary procedure

The Code of Practice prepared by the Advisory, Conciliation and Arbitration Service contains a model disciplinary procedure which may be summarised as follows.

(a) A disciplinary procedure which is fair, full and quick should be agreed between management and employee representatives.

(b) Each employee should know what the procedure consists of, its rules and the offences which can lead to dismissal.

(c) The procedure should state who has power to dismiss, provide that senior management should be consulted, give the employee an opportunity to state his or her case and be accompanied by an employee representative, and provide for a right of appeal.

(d) Before dismissal takes place two written warnings should have been issued, setting out details of the alleged offence and the consequences of continued errant behaviour.

The Code of Practice is not legally binding but it may be taken into account in any proceedings before an industrial tribunal or the Employment Appeals Tribunal. The procedure it suggests is in any case good personnel management practice.

9. Unfair dismissal

Wrongful dismissal occurs when insufficient notice is given; *unfair* dismissal, in contrast, is defined under the Employment Protection (Consolidation) Act 1978 as dismissal which has occurred for reasons other than (a) genuine redundancy, (b) gross misconduct, (c) inadequate performance, or (d) some other *substantial* reason. The term 'misconduct' has no legal definition — each case must be considered on its merits. Gross misconduct (theft, violence, etc.) justifies summary dismissal in certain circumstances; but the law insists that the employer 'act reasonably' at all times. The employer must be able to specify where and when the misconduct took place, how it affected the worker's job and/or workmates, and how in consequence the organisation was harmed. And the firm has to demonstrate that any extenuating circumstances and the worker's past record were taken into account prior to the decision to dismiss.

The dismissed person must not have been selected unfairly from others who were equally guilty, and the firm must be able to show that (a) dismissal rather than some lesser action was required, (b) formal warnings were issued, (c) proper investigations were carried out, and (d) that a fair dismissal procedure was followed, which included the right of appeal.

Inadequate performance (incapability) means that the employee cannot satisfactorily complete his or her work, or does not have the qualifications for the job. Note that a sick employee may be 'fairly' dismissed on these grounds although tribunals expect the employer to discuss the position with the worker concerned to ensure that the illness will in fact prevent effective performance, and also to seek less demanding work for the sick worker. Nevertheless, employers are entitled to dismiss any worker whose skill, aptitude, health or physical or mental qualities are not up to the demands of the job (though the employing firm must show that it acted reasonably at all times).

Other reasons for fair dismissal include disruption of staff relations, 'organisational inefficiency' (the meaning of this must be established in each individual case), or a temporary job coming to an end provided the impermanent nature of the work was fully explained to the worker when the employment started. A business may also dismiss a worker if the continuation of that person's employment would cause the firm to break a law (for instance, if a driver lost his or her driving licence); and any worker who goes on strike may be 'fairly' dismissed. Note, however, that *all* striking workers must be sacked and not just some of them unless there are extenuating circumstances (e.g. certain strikers have been convicted for violence on picket lines).

Tribunals will hold that some dismissals are automatically unfair, and the victims of these sackings do not always have to satisfy the same eligibility criteria in order to be able to claim unfair dismissal in a tribunal. Three circumstances give rise to unquestionably unfair dismissal:

(a) sacking a pregnant woman simply because she is pregnant;
(b) dismissal for union membership or activity, or for refusing to join a union;
(c) dismissal of workers when a business changes hands — unless significant technical, economic or organisational changes warranting the dismissal of staff also occur simultaneously.

Certain categories of employee are excluded from the unfair dismissal provisions, the most important being those with less than two years' service, those who work for less than 16 hours a week (eight hours a week, if the worker has been with the firm for at least five years), and those over normal retirement age.

An employee who considers he or she has been unfairly dismissed may, not later than three months afterwards, present a complaint to an industrial tribunal. The employer will then be required to state the reason for dismissal and justify it as being fair in accordance with the Act. An attempt is then made to settle the dispute by conciliation, but if this is unsuccessful the tribunal will hear the case, when the employer will try to show not only that the dismissal was fair but that it was reasonable in all the circumstances, for example that warnings had been given and that the employee had been given the opportunity to present a defence.

If the tribunal finds that the dismissal was unfair it will first, if the employee agrees, make an order for the worker to be reinstated, i.e. restore that person in the job as though the dismissal had never happened, or re-engaged, i.e. return to his or her previous employer but in a different job. If the employee does not wish to return to the former employer, if reinstatement or re-engagement is judged by the tribunal to be impracticable or if the employer refuses to comply with an order for reinstatement or re-engagement, then monetary compensation must be paid by the employer. It consists of:

(a) a basic award calculated in the same way as redundancy pay (*see* 11); and

(b) a compensatory award assessed by the tribunal as being just in the circumstances, taking into account what the employee has suffered in hardship or in company benefits lost;

(c) a special additional award, usually of between 13 and 26 weeks' pay, which is given when the employer refuses to comply with an order for reinstatement or re-engagement.

Under the Employment Act 1980, if an employing firm claims that it was induced to dismiss an employee who was not a union member because of pressure from a union or person, an industrial tribunal, if it agrees, may require the union or person to pay part of the compensation.

10. Management action

In addition to complying with the Code of Practice summarised in 8, a company should take the following steps to ensure that no one is dismissed unfairly and that there is a defence if a dismissed employee complains to a tribunal.

(a) Managers and supervisors must know whether or not they have the powers to dismiss.

(b) Records of performance, attendance, timekeeping, etc., must be maintained and preserved.

(c) Job specifications must wherever possible include performance standards.

Redundancy

11. Legal definition

Under the Employment Protection (Consolidation) Act 1978 a dismissed employee is redundant when the whole or main reason for his or her dismissal is that the employer's needs for employees to do work of a particular kind in the place where he or she was employed have diminished or ceased. If an employee is no longer required in one section but instead of being made redundant is transferred to another section of the firm and displaces another employee who is dismissed, that employee is then redundant.

Acceptance by an employee of another job in the firm will prevent the employee from claiming he or she is redundant, even if that job has inferior conditions, prospects and pay to the previous job. If the worker refuses the offer of another job in the firm, that person will only be regarded as redundant if the alternative job is inferior to the previous job, unsuitable to his or her skill and training, or an unreasonable distance from his or her home.

An industrial tribunal hears disputed cases of redundancy; it requires the employer to prove that the employee was not redundant or that the alternative job that may have been offered was reasonable. The working of the Act is described in diagrammatic form in Fig. 16.1.

A redundant employee, providing he or she has had at least two years' service and has worked for at least 16 hours per week (8 hours if the worker has completed five years with the firm), is entitled to redundancy pay at the following rates:

(a) for each year of employment between ages 18 and 21, half a week's pay;

(b) for each year of employment between ages 22 and 40, one week's pay;

(c) for each year of employment between ages 41 and 65 one-and-a-half weeks' pay.

Figure 16.1 *The redundancy process*

12. Dealing with redundancy

The legal provisions for redundancy payments are reasonably clear and simple and are often supplemented by *ex-gratia* payments from the employer. The human problems of redundancy are much more difficult and if badly handled can have most unfortunate effects. A perfect human resources plan (*see* Chapter 12) would avoid redundancy completely because all changes in a company's activities would have been foreseen and their effects on employees provided for. Even a rudimentary plan can reduce redundancy or give some warning of it.

A company may try to avoid redundancy by encouraging early retirements and by ceasing to recruit until the number of its employees has fallen to the desired level. This method is often slow, but it avoids the personal disasters that redundancy can bring. The recruitment 'freeze', if continued for too long, creates a gap in the age structure of the work-force which can be very serious in later years. To some extent the employer loses control over the situation because the firm is never sure which employees will leave and at what rate. Doubts about their future may cause many of the most valuable employees to resign, lowering the general quality of the staff.

If redundancy is going to occur the company should, where possible, deal with it according to the method described in 9:**14**. It must also observe the relevant provisions of the Employment Protection Act 1975.

(a) The employer must consult the appropriate independent trade union so that discussions may be held with a view to reducing the number of redundancies or mitigating their effect. The consultation must take place at the earliest opportunity, but not later than the following times:

   (*i*) if 10–99 employees are to be dismissed over a period of 30 days or less at one establishment, at least 30 days before the first dismissal;

   (*ii*) if 100 or more employees are to be dismissed over a period of 90 days or less, at least 90 days before the first dismissal.

The trade unions must be told in writing the reasons for the redundancy, the numbers and descriptions of the employees affected, the present number of employees of those descriptions, the proposed method of selection for redundancy and the proposed method of carrying out the dismissals. The employer must reply to any representations made by the unions, giving reasons if any of them are rejected.

(b) If a union believes any of these requirements have not been met it may complain to an industrial tribunal. A conciliation officer of the Advisory, Conciliation and Arbitration Service will then be given the opportunity to try to bring about a settlement, but if this is not possible the tribunal will hear the complaint. The employer may offer the defence that consultation as required by the Act did in fact take place or that in the circumstances it was not reasonably practicable. If the tribunal finds the union's complaint justified it may either require the employer to postpone dismissal to enable consultation to take place or it may take a 'protective award', i.e. an award of pay to employees for a period regarded by the tribunal as 'just and equitable'. The length of the protected period will be determined by the tribunal but will not be more than:

(i) 90 days where 100 or more employees are to be made redundant over a period of 90 days or less;

(ii) 30 days where 10 or more employees are to be made redundant over a period of 30 days or less;

(iii) 28 days in any other case, e.g. for fewer than 10 employees.

(c) The employer must inform the Secretary of State, not later than the times shown in (a), in order that the Department of Employment may assist in redeployment or retraining or possibly avoid or minimise the effects of the redundancy. If the Secretary of State is not informed the employer may be prosecuted and fined.

(d) An employee who accepts an offer of a different job in the same company may have a trial period of four weeks (or longer by agreement) in the new job, without loss of the right to redundancy pay (*see* 11).

Finally, under the Employment Protection (Consolidation) Act 1978, an employee may complain of unfair dismissal if it is believed that he or she has been unfairly selected for redundancy, for example if the employer has not followed the agreed procedure or has not considered the possibility of offering alternative employment. In selecting workers for redundancy, employers are expected to take into account each worker's:

> age
> length of service
> capabilities
> qualifications
> experience
> past conduct
> suitability for alternative employment within the firm

Progress test 16

1. What period of notice should be given to a dismissed employee? **(2, 6)**

2. What are the main reasons why a dismissal may be unfair? **(7–9)**

3. Define redundancy. **(11)**

4. How can a company try to avoid making its employees redundant? **(12)**

17
Labour turnover

1. Definition

Labour turnover is the movement of people into and out of the firm. It is usually convenient to measure it by recording movements out of the firm on the assumption that a leaver is eventually replaced by a new employee. The term separation is used to denote an employee who leaves for any reason.

2. Measurement

Two formulae are in common use for measuring labour turnover.

(a) The separation or wastage rate, which expresses the number of separations during the period (usually one year) as a percentage of the average number employed during that period. It is therefore:

$$\frac{\text{Number of separations during period}}{\text{Average number employed during period}} \times 100$$

(b) The labour stability index, which shows the percentage of the employees who have had at least one year's service. It is usually expressed as follows:

$$\frac{\text{Employees with at least one year's service}}{\text{Number of employees employed one year ago}} \times 100$$

A variation on the labour stability index is the 'fringe turnover index':

$$\frac{\text{Number of employees who joined and left within one year}}{\text{Average number employed during the year}} \times 100$$

This shows the percentage turnover of short-term workers.

Another method of measuring labour turnover is to study a group of employees recruited during a certain period (usually three months) and record the rate at which they leave the company. An example is shown in Table 17.1 based on the assumption that the company engaged 500 new employees during the period.

Table 17.1

Quarterly periods of service			Number of leavers	% leaving	% remaining
First	(1–13	weeks)	200	40	60
Second	(14–26	weeks)	100	20	40
Third	(27–39	weeks)	50	10	30
Fourth	(40–52	weeks)	25	5	25
Fifth	(53–65	weeks)	15	3	22
Sixth	(66–78	weeks)	10	2	20
Seventh	(79–91	weeks)	5	1	19
Eighth	(92–104	weeks)	5	1	18

These figures are sometimes presented graphically by plotting the percentage leaving against quarterly periods of service. The result is called a *survival curve*.

A useful application of survival curve computations is the determination of the 'half-life' survival rates of workers in various employment categories. A half-life survival rate is the time that elapses before 50 per cent of a particular cohort of workers who all began work at the same time have left the organisation. Half-life survival rates may then be compared for different departments, age groups, etc. in order to ascertain the 'staying power' of each cohort.

3. Use of turnover measurements
The separation rate is easy to calculate and is widely used. It

also has the great advantage of indicating costs because separations and replacements can involve the company in considerable expense (*see* **4**). It can be somewhat misleading, however, for two reasons.

(a) Recently engaged employees are more likely to leave than long service employees (*see* Table 17.1), and therefore an increase in the separation rate may simply be due to some increased recruitment a few weeks previously rather than to a sudden deterioration in worker satisfaction.

(b) Some jobs in the company may be vacated and filled several times during the year. Suppose, for example, that in a company employing 1000 workers 250 leave during the year, giving a separation rate of 25 per cent. The true position might be as follows:

150 jobs vacated and filled once	=	150 leavers
25 jobs vacated and filled twice	=	50 leavers
10 jobs vacated and filled three times	=	30 leavers
5 jobs vacated and filled four times	=	20 leavers
Total: 190 jobs vacated during year		Total: 250 leavers

In such a case the separation index can give a false impression because 100 of the 250 leavers are short-service employees (though the cost of replacing them can still be considerable).

The stability index is best used in conjunction with the separation rate, showing the extent to which the company is retaining its experienced employees. On the figures shown above, the stability index would be

$$\frac{1,000 - 190}{1,000} \times 100 = 81\%$$

Survival rates always show that the tendency for employees to leave is greatest during their early weeks with the company; they are useful in showing if the company is losing a particularly large number of employees early in their service compared with a previous period. It is often instructive to compare survival rates in different departments or different employee categories, e.g. by age groups or occupations.

4. Cost of labour turnover

Separations and their consequent replacements can be surprisingly expensive. The cost of labour turnover increases when employees are more specialised, more difficult to find and require more training. It is made up of some or all of the following components:

(a) lower production during learning period;
(b) lost production while the employee is being replaced;
(c) payment to other employees at overtime rates while waiting for a replacement;
(d) possible diversion of efforts of more highly skilled employees while waiting for a replacement;
(e) possible sub-contracting of work;
(f) cost of scrap and spoiled work while job is being learned;
(g) cost of recruitment, selection and medical examination;
(h) training cost;
(i) administrative cost of removing from and adding to payroll.

Therefore, when the separation rate is high the employer can incur considerable costs which are not always immediately obvious.

5. Reducing labour turnover

All employers expect to have a certain degree of labour turnover; without it the company would stagnate. The average age of employees would increase (meaning also that a large number of employees might retire simultaneously); and there could be insufficient new blood coming into the organisation. No doubt many companies would be content if their separation rates lay between 10 and 15 per cent, though few rates in the private sector of industry and commerce are as low as this. If an employing firm wishes to reduce its labour turnover because it considers it is excessive for the district and the industry, it may take the following action.

(a) *Recalculate* the separation rate for various categories of the firm's employees, e.g. departments, age groups, occupations, to see if turnover in any of these categories is particularly high; if so it can be specially investigated.

(b) *Ensure* that selection procedures are adequate; suitable employees are more likely to stay than unsuitable.

(c) *Ensure* that the immediate supervisor, by being involved in selection, feels some responsibility towards a new employee.

(d) *Check* that employees are being fully utilised — some may be leaving because of boredom or job dissatisfaction.

(e) *Overhaul* pay structure, perhaps using job evaluation (*see* Chapter 21).

(f) *Introduce or improve* an induction course (*see* 14:21).

(g) Give new employees appropriate *training*.

(h) *Show that prospects* in the company are good by promoting from within wherever possible.

(i) *Ensure that physical working conditions are adequate.*

In general, an increase in job satisfaction (*see* 2:27) and in the cohesiveness of working groups (*see* 7:9) will decrease the rate of labour turnover.

Progress test 17

1. State two formulae by which labour turnover may be measured. (2)

2. Which labour turnover formula indicates costs? (3)

3. What items make up the cost of labour turnover? (4)

4. State some ways in which labour turnover may be reduced. (5)

18
Appraisal

Traditional appraisal methods

1. Definition

Appraisal is the judgment of an employee's performance in a job, based on considerations other than productivity alone. It is sometimes called merit rating, more frequently when its sole object is to discriminate between employees in granting increases in wages or salaries.

All managers are constantly forming judgments of their subordinates and are in that sense continuously making appraisals; the term is, however, applied in personnel management to a formal and systematic assessment made in a prescribed and uniform manner at a certain time.

2. Purpose of appraisal

The principal uses of appraisal are:

(a) to help a manager decide what increases of pay shall be given on grounds of merit;

(b) to determine the future use of an employee, e.g. whether the employee shall remain in his or her present job or be transferred, promoted, demoted or dismissed;

(c) to indicate training needs, i.e. areas of performance where improvements would occur if appropriate training could be given;

(d) to motivate the employee to do better in his or her present job by giving the worker knowledge of results, recognition of merits and the opportunity to discuss work with his or her manager.

3. Types of appraisal

Appraisal reviews are usually categorised into three types.

(a) *Performance reviews*, which analyse employees' past successes and failures with a view to improving future performance.

(b) *Potential reviews*, which assess subordinates' suitability for promotion and/or further training.

(c) *Reward reviews*, for determining pay rises. It is a well-established principle that salary assessments should occur well after performance and potential reviews have been completed, for two reasons:

  (i) performance reviews examine personal strengths and weaknesses in order to improve efficiency. If salary matters are discussed during these meetings, they might dominate the conversation;

  (ii) ultimately, salary levels are determined by market forces of supply and demand for labour. Staff shortages could cause the firm to pay high wages quite independent of the objective worth of particular workers.

4. Appraisal methods

There are many kinds of appraisal schemes, though usually they are elaborations or variations on one of the following.

(a) *Ranking*, which requires the manager to rank subordinates in order of merit, usually on their total ability in the job but sometimes according to a few separate characteristics.

It is quite easy for a manager to use this method for a small number of subordinates, and usually quite close agreement about the rank order is found among various judges who know the subordinates well. It can be used to decide pay, and to some extent to determine future use, but not to identify training needs or provide motivation. However, although it puts subordinates in order of merit it does not show how much better the first is than the last.

(b) *Grading*, which allots employees into a predetermined series of merit categories — usually five — on the basis of their total performance.

It works reasonably well for a homogeneous group of subordinates, and a fair agreement among raters is usually obtained. There is, however, a strong tendency for extremes to be avoided (the central tendency), i.e. very few subordinates are rated poor or exceptional. To overcome this, a forced distribution is sometimes used; managers are instructed to ensure that subordinates are put into the five categories in the following proportions, ensuring that the assessment of merit is distributed normally:

Poor	Below Average	Average	Above Average	Exceptional
10%	20%	40%	20%	10%

The forced distribution is, however, an unsound method to use if the number of subordinates is below about 40. Grading has the same uses and limitations as ranking.

(c) *The rating scale* is by far the most common method of appraisal. It consists of a list of personal characteristics or factors against each of which is a scale, usually of five points, for the manager to mark his or her assessment of the subordinate. An example is shown in Appendix 2. Instead of entitling the points of the scale 'poor', 'below average', etc., they are frequently defined (as shown in Appendix 2) to encourage consistency of judgment among the raters. The factors are also defined, and there are sections at the end of the form for general remarks and suggestions for future action.

This method can be used for deciding pay, determining future use and indicating training needs. It is rather difficult to use for motivating an employee, who may well be inclined to argue about the details of the ratings rather than discuss the job constructively.

The rating scale method is in some ways rather dangerous because it gives a false impression of analysis and exactitude. If it is to be successful the managers who use it must be trained, and the factors included in it carefully considered. Some of the faults often found, and ways by which they can be reduced, are described in 5.

(d) *The open-ended* method is a comparatively recent innovation, introduced because of dissatisfaction with rating scales. Instead of requiring a manager to assess a number of personal characteristics, not all equally relevant, the method emphasises the way the job is performed and expects the manager to write a few sentences about the subordinate rather than put ticks in columns. The method has many varieties, a common one being to ask the manager four questions about the subordinate.

(*i*) What are the employee's strong points in relation to the job?

(*ii*) What are the employee's weak points in relation to the job?

(*iii*) What is the employee's promotion potential?

(*iv*) What are the employee's training needs?

Another approach is simply to ask the manager to write a general account of the subordinate's work over the past year and suggest any action that might be taken to improve his or her performance. In some companies subordinates simultaneously write their own versions of the year's work and suggest transfers or training that might help their career. The two documents are exchanged before the appraisal interview (*see* **6**) takes place.

The open-ended method cannot be used directly to decide pay but it fulfils the other purposes of appraisal very well. It is more intellectually demanding than the other methods and is perhaps at its best when the subordinates' jobs are relatively unstructured, allowing differences in performance to be clearly shown. In contrast, the rating scale can be completed with much less thought and seems to be suitable for subordinates who have similar and rather routine jobs.

(e) *Behaviour expectation scales* are an interesting development in appraisal methods. This approach — sometimes referred to as the 'Behaviourally Anchored Rating Scale' technique (BARS for short) — requires the assessor to select some aspect of a subordinate's behaviour considered by the appraiser to be typical of the appraisee's performance in a certain aspect of a job. For example, the superior of an employee being assessed under the heading 'ability to cope with stress' would be asked to complete a form which begins with the words, 'I would expect this employee to behave in the following way', followed by a list of statements from which the appraiser must choose. Among the statements might be:

remain calm and collected	5
become frustrated	4
show irritability	3
act erratically	2
fly off the handle	1

Alongside each statement is a certain number of points indicating the relative desirability of the behaviour. In the example given, 'becoming frustrated' under stress scores 4 points compared with only 1 point for 'flying off the handle', which is much worse. These scale values are said to be 'anchored' against the typical employee behaviour that each statement represents.

BARS systems are complex, time-consuming and difficult to administer. Specific problems include the following:

(*i*) how to select the categories of behaviour (called 'performance dimensions') that warrant assessment;

(*ii*) specification of examples of good and bad behaviour within a category;

(*iii*) deciding how many points to allocate to each example of behaviour (i.e. "anchoring" scale points against appropriate descriptions of expected behaviour).

All methods of appraisal require employees to be matched against the demands of their jobs; therefore it is necessary to have job specifications which include performance standards expressed as precisely as possible.

5. Rating scale problems

Unreliable judgments may be made when using the rating scale method.

(a) Managers are often unwilling to use the extreme ratings (known as the central tendency).

(b) They have different standards of judgment, sometimes influenced by strong prejudices.

(c) They do not all attach the same meaning to the names of the factors, e.g. co-operation and initiative, unless these are carefully defined.

(d) They are strongly influenced by a subordinate's recent behaviour rather than by his or her work throughout the appraisal period.

(e) Their judgment is influenced by any particularly strong or weak characteristic of the subordinate, causing them to take a generally favourable or unfavourable view of the subordinate's other qualities (the halo effect).

(f) It is difficult to design a rating scale which is suitable for all types of employee. The scale shown in Appendix 2 would not, for example, be appropriate for managers.

These problems may be reduced by defining the factors and ratings and by training managers in the use of the rating scale.

6.   Need for appraisals

There has been in recent years a reaction against formal appraisals, largely because of their tendency to decay into routine form-filling, managers sometimes copying what they wrote the previous year.

It has been said that a manager should, as a normal part of the managerial process, continually assess the merits of his subordinates and consider what training they need to improve their performance or meet new demands. The manager should take action, e.g. initiate a transfer, if his or her assessment indicates it is necessary and be ready to give a written appraisal whenever it is specifically required, e.g. if a subordinate has applied for promotion. There is general agreement, however, that an annual meeting between the manager and subordinate to review the latter's work during the year is useful because it gives formal recognition of the subordinate's efforts.

7.   The appraisal interview

In many companies appraisal is one-way and secret; it can therefore only fulfil the first three purposes of appraisal in 2 and cannot be used to motivate the employee by reviewing his or her job performance.

A two-way and open appraisal requires that an interview takes place between manager and subordinate based on the techniques described in Chapter 5. A problem-solving approach is usually recommended, encouraging the subordinate to talk freely about his or her successes and failures over the period. The self-criticism that may occur in this process is much more likely to lead to action by the subordinate to remedy faults than criticism by the manager.

On the other hand, it is said that in many companies relations between manager and subordinate are not good enough to permit a problem-solving interview to take place. The subordinate will try to hide shortcomings rather than discuss them. Managers who have the time, patience and social skills to conduct problem-solving interviews are also rather rare. Moreover one of the functions of a manager is to assess subordinates and tell them if their work is unsatisfactory; subordinates expect the manager to do this and will not respect that person if he or she appears to avoid the task.

When conducting an appraisal interview a manager should adhere to the following guidelines.

(a) Begin the interview with an outline of its purpose, the assessment criteria the company has chosen to apply, and state that the object of the exercise is to improve performance, not to bully or harass the employee.

(b) Put the subordinate at ease, emphasising the positive aspects of his or her work during the review period.

(c) Offer an opinion of the subordinate's performance and ask whether the subordinate has any thoughts on how it could be improved. This request may bring to the surface any major difficulties experienced; if it does not, the topic of poor performance should be raised circumspectly, concentrating on *issues* rather than personal failings.

(d) Diagnose the causes of problems and root out the histories of specific failures.

(e) Ensure that all relevant information is available during the interview (appraisers should be well-prepared and fully briefed on the details of incidents of poor performance).

(f) Apply identical criteria when assessing subordinates of the same grade, avoiding favouritism, bias and subjectivity when interpreting information.

Management by objectives

8. Introduction

Management by Objectives (MBO) is a system which attempts to improve the performance of the company and motivate, assess and train its employees by integrating their personal goals with the objectives of the company.

9. Method

The employee agrees with the manager what his or her performance objectives should be over a set period. The objectives are ideally expressed quantitatively and are taken from key areas of the job, i.e. tasks which if done well will cause the whole job to be done well. At the end of the period the employee and manager review jointly the achievement or non-achievement of the objectives.

10. Advantages

MBO is intended to encourage employee participation and increase job satisfaction by giving the employee a sense of achievement and involvement with his or her work (*see* 2:**3, 17** and **8:13**). The manager can appraise the employee by referring to specific performances rather than by making subjective judgments. Training needs may also emerge during the discussion at the beginning and end of the review period. Other advantages are that:

(a) employees are forced to think hard about their roles and objectives, about why tasks are necessary and how best to get things done;

(b) targets are clarified and the crucial elements in each job identified;

(c) superiors and subordinates are obliged to communicate with each other, and there is forced co-ordination of activities between various levels of management, departments and between short- and long-term goals.

11. Disadvantages

Many managers and employees find the joint objective setting and performance review interviews difficult and sometimes inconsistent with the general management style of the company. The system may then degenerate into a routine in which the manager simply instructs the employee which objectives to pursue. Quite often it is difficult to find new objectives which offer a challenge, and the system may encourage individual, selfish effort to the detriment of the working group. Further possible problems include the following.

(a) Attempts to quantify performance in activities that are not really quantifiable (advisory duties or the work of a receptionist, for example).

(b) Concentration on short-term measurable goals while neglecting important but less precise long-term objectives.

(c) Difficulties arising from subordinates being given objectives;

but not the resources, information and authority needed to achieve them.

12. Effects of MBO
Few companies now practise MBO in its entirety but it has left a beneficial legacy to the appraisal schemes which succeeded it, achievement of objectives being emphasised much more than the rather indefinable qualities of energy, co-operation, initiative, etc. It has encouraged the use of open-ended appraisal methods (*see* **3(d)**)) and the appraisal interview (*see* **7**). Salaries or bonuses of senior managers are sometimes influenced by their performance against objectives set for them each year.

Assessment centres

13. Assessment centres
A special form of appraisal intended to identify potential for promotion is the assessment centre. It consists of a series of exercises such as leaderless group discussions (*see* **4:13**), in-tray exercises (*see* **20:10**), role-playing (*see* **20:2**), business games (*see* **20:16**) and ten-minute speeches. A group of candidates is brought together at a fairly isolated spot (for example, a country hotel) where they go through the exercises over a period of one to three days. They are judged by assessors who are usually managers of the company who have received appropriate training. Assessment centres are sometimes used for initial selection of supervisors, managers and sales staff.

The advantages of assessment centres are that:

(a) they offer assessors far more information about candidates than is available from conventional interviews;
(b) they present suitable environments for the evaluation of candidates' interpersonal skills, e.g. persuasiveness, assertiveness, ability to cope with stress, communication skills, etc.;
(c) candidates have time to settle into the assessment process and thus (hopefully) will not be as nervous as otherwise might be the case;
(d) attendance at an assessment centre can itself be a useful and interesting learning experience for candidates;

(e) there should in principle be a higher *probability* of selecting the correct candidates than with any other selection method.

Problems with assessment centres include the following.

(a) They are expensive because they must be carefully designed to suit the company's special requirements and because staffing them takes up a considerable amount of management time.
(b) Arguably, the personal characteristics examined *via* assessment centre exercises (many of which have a psychological base) cannot be measured accurately, even over a period of three or four days.
(c) Assessors might not be fully familiar with the details of the work that successful candidates will have to undertake. Hence the wrong qualities may be assessed.
(d) Assessment of a candidate's personality and other characteristics must inevitably depend to some degree on the assessors' subjective value judgments.

Progress test 18

1. What are the purposes of appraisal? **(2)**

2. Describe the rating scale method of appraisal. **(4)**

3. Describe the BARS system of performance appraisal. **(4)**

4. What are the difficulties in conducting appraisal interviews? **(7)**

5. What are the main advantages and disadvantages of Management by Objectives? **(10, 11)**

6. What are assessment centres? **(13)**

Training principles and administration

The systematic approach

1. Purpose of training

Under favourable circumstances, training has the important dual function of utilisation and motivation. By improving employees' ability to perform the tasks required by the company, training allows better use to be made of human resources; by giving employees a feeling of mastery over their work and of recognition by management their job satisfaction is increased. When circumstances are unfavourable, these results may not be obtained, for example when the trainee sees no purpose in the training (*see* 3:6), when it is regarded as a punishment or a sign of displeasure or when the training seems irrelevant to the trainee's needs.

In detail, the gains which it is hoped training will bring are:

(a) greater productivity and quality;
(b) less scrap or spoiled work;
(c) greater versatility and adaptability to new methods;
(d) less need for close supervision;
(e) fewer accidents;
(f) greater job satisfaction showing itself in lower labour turnover and less absence.

It is always desirable to attempt to validate a training course to see if any of these results have been achieved (*see* 10).

Arguments against training are that it is expensive (often, trainees are not producing while they are being trained, and they might leave the company as soon as their training ends) and that individual firms can sometimes recruit competent employees at low cost from outside. Also, workers' job expectations typically increase in consequence of training, so that if trained employees are not immediately put on to work that requires them to exercise their recently acquired competencies they might become disaffected and look for other jobs where they can use their new skills.

2. Reasons for training

Sometimes training is a routine, e.g. all new employees in certain jobs automatically go through a training course. More often training is given as a response to some event, for example:

(a) the installation of new equipment or techniques which require new or improved skills;

(b) a change in working methods;

(c) a change in product, which may necessitate training not only in production methods but also in the marketing functions of the company;

(d) a realisation that performance is inadequate;

(e) labour shortage, necessitating the upgrading of some employees;

(f) a desire to reduce the amount of scrap and to improve quality;

(g) an increase in the number of accidents;

(h) promotion or transfer of individual employees.

Training which is routine and traditional sometimes becomes out of date, irrelevant or inadequate. A review may show that the purposes, methods and standards of the training should be changed.

3. The systematic approach to training

Like any other business process, training can be very wasteful if it is not carefully planned and supervised. Without a logical systematic approach some training may be given which is not necessary, and vice versa, or the extent of the training may be too small or too great. When the training is complete, *validation* will show whether it has been successful in achieving its aims and *evaluation* will attempt to measure its cost-benefit.

The systematic approach to training follows this programme.

(a) The job is analysed and defined (*see* 13:1–6).

(b) Reasonable standards of performance are established, perhaps by reference to experienced employees.

(c) The employees being considered for training are studied to see if the required performance standards are being attained.

(d) The difference (if any) between (b) and (c) is considered. It is often called the 'training gap', though it may be partly due to faults in the organisation, poor materials or defective equipment.

(e) Training programmes are devised to meet the training needs revealed in (d) (*see* Chapter 20).

(f) Training is given and appropriate records kept.

(g) The performance achieved after training is measured; if the training programme has been successful the performance standards set in (b) should now be achieved (validation).

(h) An attempt is made to calculate the cost of the training and compare it with the financial benefit gained by the improved performance of the employees. The training programme may be revised if a method can be seen of achieving the same result at lower cost (evaluation).

The following mnemonic may be useful:

> Analyse job
> Performance standards
> Performance attained
> Requirements of training
> Originate training programme
> Administer training
> Check results
> How can training be improved next time?

4. The assessment of individual training needs
The systematic approach to training will show the training needs of an individual employee or a group of employees engaged on the same work.

Careful analysis of the job including the setting of performance standards is the first step; management by objectives is a special example of this (*see* 18:8–12). The performance now being attained by employees can sometimes be measured, but more often it is assessed through an appraisal scheme (*see* 18:1–5). Management by objectives again shows a different technique by reviewing measurable performance in previously agreed key areas of the job. Any disparities between standards and performance levels show possible training needs.

Often, of course, the assessment is done almost by intuition, particularly when an individual employee's performance could obviously be improved by clearcut training action, e.g. giving the worker more knowledge of the product or showing that person how to use an office machine. Validation of the training may be equally straightforward in such cases.

5. The assessment of long-term training needs

Many training programmes, e.g. apprenticeships, are lengthy, and can therefore be wasteful unless plans are made well in advance. A sudden need for skilled engineering crafts workers will not be met by increasing the number of apprentices entering a four-year scheme; on the other hand it is possible for a company to have jobs only for a small proportion of its apprentices when they complete their training because it is reducing or giving up some of its manufacturing activities.

The assessment of long-term training needs, usually carried out for a whole company, is therefore part of human resources planning (*see* Chapter 12). By estimating the expansion or contraction of the labour force, what categories will be affected, the probable number leaving the company and the present utilisation of employees, it is possible to plan what kind of training will be required in the future, when it should begin and how many present or new employees need to be trained. If financial or material resources are limited the analysis may also help to decide which training activities should be given priority.

Training design

6. Training principles

The psychological principles of training have been dealt with in 3:6–10; motivation of the trainee is particularly important and is influenced a great deal by the design of the training programme and the methods which are used.

The first step in designing a training course is to consider the training requirements under three headings:

Attitudes
Skills
Knowledge

For example a shop assistant in a men's outfitters would require a certain *attitude* towards customers, *skill* in selling, measuring, wrapping and displaying, and *knowledge* of stock, sales procedures, current fashions and the company's general policy. Methods of training in these three aspects of a job will be described in the next chapter.

7. On- or off-job training

The methods of training will to a large extent dictate whether the training shall take place on or off the job.

(a) *On-job* training is given in the normal work situation, the trainee using the actual tools, equipment, documents or materials that he or she will use when fully trained. The trainee is regarded as a partly productive worker from the time training begins.

(b) *Off-job* training takes place away from the normal work situation, usually employing specially simplified tools and equipment. The trainee is not regarded as a productive worker from the beginning, the initial work often consisting of exercises. Off-job training may take place on the employer's premises, at a training centre attended by trainees from several employers, or at a college.

8. Advantages and disadvantages of on-job training

(a) Advantages:

(*i*) it is less costly than off-job training because it uses normal equipment in normal surroundings;

(*ii*) learning will take place on the equipment which will be actually used when the trainee is proficient; there are no transfer of learning problems (*see* 3:**9–10**);

(*iii*) the trainee is in the production environment from the beginning; he or she does not have to adjust to it after the rather sheltered conditions of off-job training.

(b) Disadvantages:
  - (*i*) the instructor (usually a supervisor or a nearby worker) may be a poor teacher and may not have enough time to give proper training;
  - (*ii*) if there is a payment-by-results scheme it may discourage the instructor from training and the trainee from learning properly;
  - (*iii*) the trainee may be exposed to bad methods and learn these instead of more efficient methods;
  - (*iv*) a large amount of spoiled work and scrap material may be produced;
  - (*v*) valuable equipment may be damaged;
  - (*vi*) training takes place under production conditions which are stressful, i.e. noisy, busy, confusing and exposing the trainee to comments by other workers. Stress usually inhibits learning;
  - (*vii*) some forms of training can only take place on-job, e.g. job rotation, coaching, and those skills which are so uncommon that it is not worthwhile to set up off-job training facilities for these. Conversely, theoretical training can hardly ever take place on-job; the trainee must attend a college, which is off-job training.

9.   Advantages and disadvantages of off-job training

(a) Advantages:
  - (*i*) as the training is given by a special instructor, it should be of higher quality;
  - (*ii*) special equipment, simplified if necessary, can be used;
  - (*iii*) the trainee can learn the job in planned stages, using special exercises to enable the trainee to master particularly difficult aspects;
  - (*iv*) in the long-term off-job training may be less costly because it enables workers to reach higher standards of speed and quality;
  - (*v*) it is free from the pressures of payment-by-results schemes, noise, danger or publicity;
  - (*vi*) the trainee will learn correct methods from the outset;
  - (*vii*) the trainee does not damage valuable equipment or produce spoiled work or scrap;

    (*viii*) it is easier to calculate the cost of off-job training because it is more self-contained than on-job.

(b) Disadvantages:

    (*i*) the higher costs of separate premises, equipment and instructors can only be justified if there is a regular, fairly large intake of trainees (though this may be overcome by participation in group training schemes in which several employers co-operate);

    (*ii*) sometimes there are transfer of learning difficulties when a trainee changes from training equipment to production equipment and from a training school environment to a production environment;

    (*iii*) no training can be entirely off-job; some aspects of the task can only be learned by doing them in the normal production setting, with its own customs and network of personal relationships. To illustrate this point, training in driving might be given to a very high standard on a private track, but the driver will not be truly expert until he or she has experienced driving on public roads; only then can a learner driver learn to react to the behaviour of other drivers;

    (*iv*) some methods of training which have become important in recent years can only be off-job, for example programmed learning, skills analysis and discovery learning (*see* Chapter 20); even here the final stages of training must be on-job.

Validation and evaluation

10. Validation of training

The systematic approach to training (*see* 3) provides a means of validating a training programme. The trainee may be given a test to see if he or she is now able to reach the performance standards that have been set, or the quantity and quality of the trainee's production may be measured for the same purpose.

Unfortunately, training programmes are often extremely difficult to validate. Many jobs are not measurable in any significant way and therefore validation of training for them can only be subjective. For example, the performance of a manager who has attended a management training course may be assessed by his or her superiors before and after the course. They may well agree that an improvement has occurred, but could this not be due to the fact that the manager is now older? Perhaps his assessors, having sent the manager on a course, will simply assume that he or she must have benefited from it. Another possibility is that since the course began events have occurred which help the manager in the job.

The more specific the training, the easier validation becomes. If the management course referred to above had contained a course in accountancy, a test would show clearly whether this had been effective, in contrast with the more general parts of the course dealing with management principles, etc., which would be impossible to validate objectively.

11. Evaluation of training

By calculating the cost of training and comparing it with the financial benefits to the company from the improved performance of the trainees, validation may be extended to become evaluation. The ease and accuracy of evaluation vary a great deal.

(a) The cost of off-job training is much easier to ascertain than that of on-job training.

(b) The financial benefits of training are easier to estimate for manual than for non-manual workers.

(c) The costs of inadequate training can often be fairly easily measured, e.g. scrap material, spoiled work, customer complaints, overtime working to remedy mistakes.

(d) The benefits of training often go beyond an improvement in job performance (*see* 1). It is, however, difficult to estimate to what extent relaxation of supervision and reductions in accidents and labour turnover are due to improved training. Expressing these benefits in financial terms is even more difficult.

Training administration

12. Paying for training

Prior to 1989 there existed in many industries 'Training Boards' that were legally empowered to maintain lists of all employers in those industries and to impose training levies on firms. Monies received from levies were then used for employee training in the relevant industry. Appeals by employers against being included in a levied 'industry' were heard by Industrial Tribunals. The philosophy behind Training Boards was that since firms can poach trained labour from each other, there is little incentive for the individual business to devote resources to training. Yet trained labour is essential for an industry to survive. Thus, *every* firm in the industry should contribute to the aggregate cost of training its labour; contributions being proportional to the number of workers each company employs.

In 1989, all Training Boards and levies were abolished except for the construction industry. Boards were replaced by 'non-statutory training organisations' (NSTOs), which were voluntary bodies responsible for predicting future skill requirements and for co-ordinating training activities within a specific industrial sector. Currently there are over 100 NSTOs in the UK. They have no legal authority and are funded entirely through voluntary contributions. Some NSTOs provide direct training, others simply monitor and comment upon the quality of training provided by external suppliers.

13. Training schemes

In recent years the government has introduced various schemes intended to provide training for unemployed persons. They are usually engaged by employers to work on an organised training programme which includes a period of off-job training.

Trainees receive an allowance to which the government and the employers each contribute. It is hoped that on completion of the programme they will be better qualified to obtain permanent employment. Examples of such schemes were:

(a) *The Youth Training Scheme*, which endeavoured to find work with training for unemployed 16- or 17-year-old school leavers who were engaged by employers on an organised work/training programme that paid trainees a small weekly wage (provided by the government and financed in part by the European Social Fund).

(b) *The Employment Training Scheme*, that attempted to create individually planned training experiences for the adult long-term unemployed. Trainees spent some time with an employer, but might also have attended college and/or worked on a community project for part of the period. Participants received a small supplement to their normal unemployment benefits.

Responsibility for administering such schemes lies with 'training agents' i.e. government-approved organisations which place individuals with local firms, which do not have to pay wages to trainees or even any national insurance contributions on their behalf. However, firms are expected to contribute a small amount to overall costs. This amount is subject to negotiation with the trainee's training manager, as is the period the trainee will spend with the firm and how long in other training locations. The maximum total training period is twelve months.

In 1990, responsibility for co-ordinating industrial training in various geographical areas passed to *Training and Enterprise Councils* (TECs), which consist of local company managing directors and other senior business executives (who participate on a voluntary basis) plus a salaried civil servant. There are about 80 TECs in the UK. Their task is to provide the country with a skilled workforce. To achieve this they contract training providers (e.g. local colleges or training agents — *see* below) to deliver courses and other training that correspond to specifications laid down by the area TEC. The aim is to match the training provided to the needs of local businesses. TECs do not themselves run training courses.

14. The National Council for Vocational Qualifications (NCVQ)

This is a governmental body established in 1986 to implement a national system for vocational qualifications and to determine standards of occupational competence on a national level. Examining bodies desiring NCVQ accreditation must develop courses that satisfy NCVQ criteria, which are laid down by '*lead bodies*' for various industries or occupations. A lead body is a committee comprising representatives of professional bodies, government departments and major businesses connected with the industry or occupation concerned. Its role is to devise criteria for measuring the competence of employees in a particular field. Currently there are about 140 lead bodies in the UK.

The NCVQ does not itself award certificates or diplomas.

Rather, it 'hallmarks' approved qualifications, indicating thereby that the holder has attained a certain prespecified level of knowledge, skill and understanding of a certain subject. NCVQ-approved qualifications have to be competence-based, i.e. the training undertaken must contribute directly to a person's ability to complete a job. Thus, courses need to cover all the 'elements of competence' associated with a specific type of work. Elements of competence are descriptions of actions, behaviours, outcomes, or knowledge of what should be done in a workplace situation. These elements are then collected into 'units of competence' that form the basis for an NCVQ-recognised award. Each unit of competence is accompanied by 'performance criteria', i.e. definitions of what trainees should be able to do on completion of the training.

15. Responsibility for company training

Because training is so important in the utilisation and motivation of human resources it deserves the special attention of the senior management of the company. One of the advantages claimed for the high level policy adopted by some ITBs was that it 'brought training into the board room', the large amounts being paid to the training board forcing consideration at director level of possible ways of recovering the money. At a lower level, the line manager must regard the training of subordinates as a primary responsibility, since he or she is expected to use the resources at his or her disposal to the best advantage.

Some companies have training officers or departments which advise on policies and methods and may administer some of the training. Consultants are sometimes called in, particularly to give advice about unusual training problems, or to overhaul methods which are obviously inefficient. These various roles in training may be summed up as follows.

(a) Senior management determines a general training policy which is consistent with the objectives of the company. It may be derived from the company human resources plan (*see* Chapter 12) or based on an assessment of training needs to which junior levels of management have contributed.

(b) Line managers have a responsibility for training their subordinates and are often personally involved in giving it because training is always wholly or partly on-job (*see* 8). In some cases they may design and supervise training programmes, while in others the training of their subordinates may be largely off-job, line managers being expected to provide the finishing touches when the employees begin productive work. In all cases it is the responsibility of line managers to ensure that the training which is given, by whatever means, is relevant to the needs of the department and is effective in its results.

(c) Training officers advise senior management on policy by applying their expert knowledge of training to the needs of the company. They frequently conduct surveys or are consulted when changes are proposed which will necessitate training or retraining. They design courses, administering them if they are off-job. They are expected to advise on external education and training facilities, maintaining contact with the ITB (where it exists), colleges, and various training organisations.

(d) Instructors are in direct contact with trainees, and in most cases are concerned with off-job training. They are not responsible for designing the course but they are expected to report any deficiencies it seems to contain. They are usually proficient workers who have taken a short course in training methods.

(e) Consultants tend to be called in when a company is facing unusual training problems, for example poor productivity or the consequences of reorganisation or technical change. They study needs, advise on appropriate methods and set up training procedures which the management of the company can then continue.

Progress test 19

1. What benefits does a company hope to obtain when it trains its employees? (1)

2. Outline the systematic approach to training. (3)

3. Under what three headings should training requirements be considered? (6)

4. Compare on-job and off-job training. (7, 8, 9)

5. Define and distinguish between validation and evaluation of training. **(10, 11)**

6. Describe the place of line managers and training officers in company training. **(15)**

20
Training methods

Training in attitudes

1. The importance of attitudes

The definition of an attitude (*see* **7:12**) is as follows: 'An individual's characteristic way of responding to an object or situation. It is based on experience and leads to certain behaviour or the expression of certain opinions.'

Attitudes determine the general approach of an employee to work; for example, the care that is taken to avoid mistakes, the way customers, clients or patients are dealt with or the degree of persistence shown in achieving work objectives. In some cases the appropriate attitude is already present when the employee enters the occupation in question — a nurse has probably chosen that particular career in consequence of possessing attitudes favouring the care of the sick. In other cases the employee has not felt a vocation towards the job but has perhaps taken it up because it is convenient or respectable. A shop assistant, for example, may have an attitude towards customers which does not produce sales and may injure the reputation of the shop. Unless this attitude can be changed the person will never be a successful employee. The importance of attitudes obviously varies according to the type of job; they are not particularly important when the work is highly structured because so long as the employee is at a work station he or she has little choice about the way the work is undertaken. On the other hand, unstructured work, with its freedom of choice and its opportunity for self-regulation, cannot be carried out successfully unless the employee's attitudes are consistent with the purposes of the job.

2. Attitude training

Attitude training is difficult because many attitudes are deep-rooted and cannot easily be changed in a short time. The usual methods employed are as follows.

(a) *On-job experience within a group of employees* whose attitudes are thought to be appropriate. There is often no practical alternative to this method, but it is slow to produce an effect and will fail if the attitudes of the other employees are unsuitable. It is therefore unwise to put a new employee in a group of disgruntled workers.

(b) *On-job training by attaching the trainee to a senior employee* who has appropriate attitudes and the personal qualities likely to influence their acceptance. Coaching or a period as a personal assistant are examples of this method.

(c) *Off-job training* in which a group of employees discuss case studies designed to emphasise the relevant attitudes. Usually the group is divided into sub-groups or syndicates, each reporting back to the whole group through a spokesperson. A discussion in a small group is thus reinforced by a discussion in a larger group. This method is useful because the case studies can be written with the particular background and needs of the trainees in mind. However, sometimes discussion of imaginary incidents involving imaginary people fails to produce an emotional response. It is also possible for lazy trainees to make no contribution to the discussion and be completely detached from it.

(d) *Off-job role-playing exercises* in which a situation is described up to a certain point of crisis. Participants in the exercise are then asked to act out the parts of the people involved in the situation, extemporising the dialogue and behaving in the way they think is characteristic not of themselves but of the individuals whose roles they are playing. The group might act out situations concerning dismissal, a difficult customer or negotiations with trade unions. This method is usually enjoyed by the trainees, who show emotional involvement, sometimes intense. The training officer can make sure that lazy trainees are included by giving them roles to play, and can use audio or video tapes to record the role-playing so that the participants may discuss their performance afterwards. Non-participant critics may be asked to attempt roles themselves in a repetition of the exercise. It seems that attitudes are often modified by this method; though a great deal depends on the support which is given when the trainee returns to his or her normal job.

(e) *T-groups* are an off-job training method (the T stands for training) which has been in vogue in recent decades. The group of trainees (not more than twelve in number) is told that its sole task is to examine and discuss its own behaviour. After a slow and awkward beginning, the group's discussion generally becomes somewhat emotional, even heated, with members criticising each other's attitudes or indulging in frank self-criticism. Group sessions often continue for several days, and are regarded by some as enjoyable and by others as unpleasant. The purpose of T-group training is partly to bring about a change in attitudes by showing individuals what others think of them, partly to demonstrate the importance of personal behaviour in group processes and partly to improve the social skills of the trainees. This form of training has never been clearly validated; its effects on some individuals have been quite harmful psychologically and many others have found it useless because they have been unable to practise their newly found social skills in an unsympathetic working environment.

Training in skill

3. Definition

The Department of Employment's *Glossary of Training Terms* gives the following definition of skill:

> An organised and co-ordinated pattern of mental and/or physical activity in relation to an object or other display of information, usually involving both receptor and effector processes. It is built up gradually in the course of repeated training or other experience. It is serial, each part from second to second is dependent on the last and influences the next. Skills may be described as perceptual, motor, manual, intellectual, social, etc. according to the context or the most important aspect of the skill pattern.

(Receptor processes provide the sensory input and effector processes the output or response.)

More briefly, skill may be defined as a practised, expert way of perceiving a relevant stimulus and then responding to it (*see* 1:**10(c)**). Skill training therefore comprises the following:

(a) recognition of stimuli, e.g. the sensation of the material feeling smooth;

(b) appropriate responses, e.g. the correct angle at which the carpenter should hold the chisel;

(c) establishing serial performance, each response providing a new stimulus which in turn evokes a new response and so on.

4. Methods of skill training

The traditional method of training in skill is usually known as 'sitting next to Nellie', i.e. the trainee is told to watch and copy an experienced worker. If 'Nellie' uses poor working methods, or if the job includes much that cannot be understood simply by observation, then the method is a bad one. If Nellie uses good methods and if the job is visible, i.e. it can be readily understood simply by observation, then the method can be effective and economical.

Since a very large number of jobs contain non-visible elements and many 'Nellies' use poor methods of work, it is preferable on most occasions to use more organised means of training. One approach is to analyse the key elements of jobs by breaking them down into their essential components. The method proceeds as follows.

(a) A supervisor performs the job him or herself and divides it into reasonably self-contained stages, each of which can be taught as a unit.

(b) He or she examines each stage to identify and describe 'key points', e.g. special difficulties or dangers. An example of a breakdown, (taken from *Recommendations for Training Operatives* published by the Ceramics Industry Training Organisation) is given in Table 20.1. Permission to reproduce the example is gratefully acknowledged.

(c) He or she makes sure that the materials and equipment required for training are properly arranged.

(d) The supervisor talks to the trainee to find out what is already known about the job and arouses the trainee's interest in learning it.

Table 20.1   Job breakdown

Replacing tap washer

Element no.	Stage	Key points
1	Unscrew spindle cover (ferrule) to expose spindle assembly retaining nut	Turn in anti-clockwise direction
2	Support spindle cover (ferrule) in left hand, unscrew spindle assembly from tap body and lift out	Ensure correct size spanner, unscrew in anti-clockwise direction
3	Remove washer assembly and inspect valve seat	Ensure no ingress of foreign bodies
4	Unscrew washer retaining nut and remove — remove damaged washer	
5	Fit new washer, replace retaining nut and tighten	Do not overtighten — might damage new washer
6	Replace washer assembly in tap	Ensure correct seating
7	Replace spindle assembly in tap body and tighten	Ensure washer assembly spindle is located in body of spindle assembly, tighten in clockwise direction
8	Replace spindle cover and tighten	Tighten in clockwise direction

(e) The job is then demonstrated to the trainee in stages, explained slowly and carefully, with particular emphasis on the key points.

(f) The trainee performs the job, the supervisor observing to see that no mistakes are made and asking questions to ensure that the trainee has understood it. It may be necessary for the supervisor to repeat some of the instructions given in (e). The trainee repeats the job until the supervisor is satisfied that performance is adequate.

(g) The supervisor puts the trainee to work, watching fairly closely at first but gradually relaxing supervision as the trainee gains confidence and skill.

The method is cheap, and is suitable for small numbers of trainees. It begins by being off-job, though usually very near the scene of production, but soon becomes on-job. A separate training department with specialist staff is not required. The analysis of the job in (a) and (b) cannot go very deep, and the method is therefore not appropriate for difficult skills, i.e. where the stimulus–perception–response sequence is not obvious. Also, supervisors transmit current working practices from one generation of workers to the next even if the practices are outdated.

It is successful with 'visible' jobs where everything of importance in the job can be observed, the mental processes being relatively unimportant; good examples would be packing or most forms of assembly work. Jobs of this kind contain a low proportion of skill and a high proportion of procedural knowledge.

Further approaches to skills training are the technique of skills analysis (*see* below) and the discovery method (*see* **6**).

5. Skills analysis

This method of training has been developed for those jobs which require a high degree of dexterity and co-ordination of senses and bodily movements. The actions of a highly skilled worker are analysed in great detail to identify and describe:

(a) what actions are performed with each finger, each hand and each foot;

(b) how these actions are combined;

(c) the stimuli he or she recognises which give the signals to begin and end these actions;

(d) the senses by which these stimuli reach the worker;

(e) the possible faults that may occur in the article being produced; these are classified, the reasons for them determined and methods of rectifying and avoiding them analysed.

From this information is compiled a skills analysis breakdown (*see* Table 20.2) and a faults analysis. Exercises are developed to train employees in the recognition of stimuli, the perfection of difficult movements and the co-ordination of those movements.

Skills analysis training has been successful in reducing training times and increasing proficiency. It claims to abolish the learning plateau (*see* 3:7(c)) because its carefully graded exercises allow the trainee to make steady uninterrupted progress.

It is an off-job training method, for obvious reasons, and is expensive and lengthy to prepare because a detailed job analysis must be carried out by expert consultants. A company is only justified in using it, therefore, when there is a large intake of trainees and when training by simpler methods is fairly long, i.e. over one month. In such cases the heavy initial outlay in consultants' fees, special equipment and training premises may be amply justified.

6. The discovery method

This is a technique of skill training which has been developed in recent years and applied with particular success to the retraining of older workers. It is similar in many ways to the newer methods used in primary education.

Discovery learning occurs when the trainee finds out for him or herself the principles of the job and the correct method of performing it; it is claimed to be more motivating than other forms of training because it offers the trainee a challenge followed by the gratification of a discovered solution. The trainer is comparatively passive, giving little formal instruction or demonstration. Another advantage claimed for this method is that it is trainee-centred; it tries to approach training problems from the point of view of a worker who does not yet possess the skill rather than by taking an expert worker as a model, as in skills analysis. During a discovery training programme it becomes very obvious if a trainee does not understand, but when in contrast an instructor explains or

Table 20.2   Extract from skills analysis breakdown

Operation analysis sheet

Job   Linishing of television lenses
Element: Removing surface

Equipment — linishing belt

Left hand	Right hand	Vision	Other senses	Comments
AP to start grind	AP to start grind	Watch build up of ground glass appearing as a white curved line above point of contact with wheel. Density of line indicates amount being ground off. Red area shows point of contact.	K to exert pressure and correct. Vibration of wheel indicates degree of pressure. Touch checks correct pressure being applied	Pressure exerted in a rocking motion to bring radius of face into even contact with belt
Hold	Hold	Check grind off of shear mark Check extent of grind up face 3/4 approx	K to reduce pressure in centre of screen	Extend grind to centre of screen holding elbows as grind reaches top half of screen Increase rate of locking across centre of screen
RG. Slide hand to bottom L/H side 3" from corner	Hold	Follow white line	K to reduce pressure in L/H increase in R/H	
Push elbow away from body to assist rotation of screen	Pull screen towards body rotating screen through 180°	Follow white line to ensure smooth rotation		Weight of screen being taken by belt. Pivot for rotation of screen on belt at crown of screen face
RL and move	RG to top R/H corner, Th. inside touching angle of inside face and edge — 1234 wrap over top edge	Follow white line to ensure smooth rotation	K & T to increase pressure in L/H group	
RG top L/H corner, Th. inside touching angle of inside face and edge — 1234 wrap over edge	Hold	Follow white line to ensure smooth rotation		White line to be horizontal to belt — if at any other angle a cross cut grinding ridge may occur

AP — Apply pressure   RL — Release   K — Kinaesthesis   RG — Re-grasp   T — Touch   Th — Thumb demonstrates a task he or she can never be sure if the trainee has understood or not.

An illustration of discovery learning is the training scheme for menders of worsted cloth described in *Training the Adult Worker* by Eunice Belbin (HMSO). The trainees first learned the detailed patterns of the weaves by copying them using thick elastic instead of thread and then discovered how to mend faults which were introduced into the weaves. The size of the weaves was gradually reduced until it reached actual size; by then the trainees had reached in 12 weeks a standard of proficiency formerly attained in a year to 18 months. According to Belbin, training needs to address five basic requirements: comprehension by the worker of what has to be done, reflex development, attitude formation, memorising, and learning the procedures attached to a job. This is sometimes referred to as the CRAMP approach to training (the acronym for the five elements).

The discovery method, like skills analysis, is an off-job training technique and requires a large intake of trainees if it is to be economically justifiable. It can be used successfully not only for skill but for knowledge training, by presenting the trainee with the opportunity to deduce for him or herself the answer to a problem, or indicating where to find out necessary information. Further advantages are that:

(a) trainees learn how to ask the right questions as well as find answers;

(b) the training is perceived as immediately relevant to trainees' jobs;

(c) results of exercises may be useful for improving the firm's overall efficiency.

On the other hand, discovery training can be difficult and expensive to administer, and positive results cannot be guaranteed.

Training in knowledge

7. Knowledge requirements

No employee can work well without adequate job knowledge; in some cases it can be acquired in informal ways by experience in the job but usually it is imparted more quickly and accurately by formal training. Job analysis will show what knowledge is required, for example under the following headings:

(a) purpose — the function of the job within the total process;
(b) background information — the history, traditions and policies of the company, which may help the employee to understand the significance of the job;
(c) legal requirements;
(d) quality standards — how accurate or how approximate the work should be;
(e) materials of work, e.g. for a salesperson what goods are available, their prices and qualities, for a manual worker the physical properties of the materials being used;
(f) tools and equipment;
(g) technical, e.g. accountancy, scientific or engineering knowledge;
(h) personal contacts — job relationships with other employees;
(i) procedures — the order in which things are done.

In contrast to attitudes and skills, knowledge may be imparted in many different ways, most of which are inexpensive and convenient. The most important methods of knowledge training are described below.

8. Coaching

This may vary from a rather casual "sitting next to Nellie" approach to formal regular sessions in which an experienced employee, usually a manager, explains the job, asks the trainee questions to test his or her knowledge and often exercises general supervision over the trainee to check that he or she is making correct use of the knowledge. The instruction is immediate, direct, inexpensive, convenient and allows two-way communication. Account may be taken of the trainee's special needs, and the pace of the instruction may be varied.

Often, coaching consists of a demonstration followed by the trainee imitating the instructor's actions. The trainee can repeat difficult operations, ask questions, and progressively attain higher levels of skill. Simple tasks should be demonstrated first; then more complex tasks once the simple ones have been mastered.

There is intimate involvement in the training process and the instructor is available to remedy mistakes as they occur.

Two problems arise.

(a) Success depends on the instructor's ability to coach (an incompetent instructor will transmit incorrect working methods).
(b) Coaching is wasted if the trainee fails to pay attention at crucial moments.

A related approach is for the trainee to learn things independently and then be questioned by the instructor in order to expose gaps in the trainee's knowledge. However, such an approach could severely damage a trainee's self-confidence and should not be used unless a congenial rapport exists between coach and trainee before the interrogation.

9. Formal lectures

When a company has a number of trainees in the same kind of work simultaneously, it may arrange for the group to have lectures on the subjects (a) to (f) in 7 by one of its senior employees. When this cannot be done, trainees may attend lectures outside the company, for example at a technical college, though the knowledge they learn here will be more general, and less specific to the company's needs.

Lectures are transmissions of predetermined sets of facts and opinions within a controlled environment. A good lecture will emphasise major points, since only a minority of the points mentioned (about 25 per cent at most) will be remembered by trainees. Most people find it difficult to concentrate for more than an hour at a time. Another possible problem is lack of motivation to learn among trainees.

Technical knowledge (*see* 7(g)) is usually acquired outside the company. As in coaching, the effectiveness of formal lectures depends on their perceived relevance, the ability of the lecturer, the care with which the lectures are prepared, and the extent to which the trainees are encouraged to participate in discussions. Films and other visual aids can make the lecture more effective, and it is customary to give the trainee a hand-out covering the main points of the lecture.

10. Other methods

A number of other devices may be used to help trainees acquire knowledge under **7(a)**, **(b)** and **(h)**. Examples are as follows.

(a) *Visits and tours* whereby arrangements are made for trainees to visit other departments or establishments of the company and talk to employees with whom he or she would normally only deal by letter or telephone. The trainee often benefits by seeing the stages of work preliminary and subsequent to his or her own.

(b) *Manuals and charts.* The trainee is sometimes given a detailed written description of the job, perhaps incorporating charts which show the route the work takes or explain the decisions the employee has to make. Many employees prefer to learn by this method instead of by personal contact, though it is still necessary for someone to be responsible for the trainee, introduce him or her to the work and check progress.

(c) *Simulation.* Instead of putting the trainee immediately to work, he or she may be asked to simulate the job using dummy materials or documents. A programme is devised which grades tasks from the easy and obvious to the more complex. This method often makes formal instruction unnecessary, because skilfully applied it can become very similar to discovery learning (*see* **6**).

(d) *In-tray.* A special version of simulation is in-tray training, in which the trainee is asked to deal with a batch of miscellaneous documents which he or she is supposed to find in each day's in-tray. Decisions of various kinds have to be made, though not of course actually put into effect.

The value of this technique for training depends on the review which should follow, when the trainer discusses with the trainee the decisions made. It is used in management training and occasionally as a means of selecting managers, though the exercise is difficult to score objectively.

(e) *Auto-instruction.* To benefit from this method, trainees need above-average intelligence, persistence and motivation. They are given a programme of assignments or tasks which take them to various parts of the company and require them to obtain information from departmental managers or from company files. The trainees are required to report back to their trainer periodically for a discussion and review.

Like the discovery method, auto-instruction is based on the principle that knowledge gained by exploration and discovery is more likely to be permanent than knowledge imparted by instructors.

11. Programmed learning

This consists of a carefully ordered sequence of units or frames arranged so that the trainee masters each unit before proceeding to the next. It is individual instruction, each trainee working at his or her own pace, and can be presented as a teaching book, teaching machine or a visual display unit controlled by a computer which holds the programme.

Each frame contains some information; the trainee is then asked a question to test whether he or she has learned or understood it. If the answer is correct the trainee moves on to the next frame. Programmed learning thus follows the principles of operant conditioning (*see* 3:5) developed by B. F. Skinner, who has been mainly responsible for this method of instruction. The stimulus is the unit of information with its question, the response is the answer to the question, and the reinforcement is the immediate knowledge of results and in most cases the gratification of having made the correct answer.

(a) *Advantages.* Besides the advantages usually found in off-job training, programmed learning also offers the following:
- (*i*) trainees go at their own pace;
- (*ii*) the training can be decentralised, i.e. the teaching book or the teaching machine can be sent to the trainee instead of bringing him or her to a training school;
- (*iii*) most trainees find the method interesting; research has also shown that its effects are long-lasting;
- (*iv*) it can be designed to meet specified performance standards and is continually being validated by the questions it contains;
- (*v*) it is quicker than most other methods of knowledge training.

(b) *Disadvantages.* These are few but important:
- (*i*) learning programmes are expensive to produce and therefore are economically justifiable only when many trainees will use them;

(*ii*) if the subject is changing rapidly the investment in a learning programme will not be justified;

(*iii*) it is suitable above all for teaching facts and procedures; it is not appropriate for subjects where some discussion and flexibility of approach is desirable, e.g. literary criticism.

12. Computer-based training (CBT)

This is training based on computer software packages. Most CBT programs are 'menu driven', meaning that the user selects from various options that appear on a visual display unit about how the training is to proceed. Typically, packages contain numerous self-check exercises and provide for continuous interaction between user and program. If the user makes a mistake, the program automatically scrolls back to the relevant part of the preceding text. 'Adaptive testing' packages enable trainees to predetermine the depth of the material they wish to cover. For instance, one user might require only a brief overview of a certain subject, while someone else may need extensive and detailed coverage and so would select the option providing this level of depth. Training is thus directly linked to individual training needs.

The advantages of CBT are that trainees usually find it interesting as well as instructional, and that users can work through a package at their own pace. However, much time may be lost as users become familiar with the proclivities of a particular package, and self-discipline is necessary to complete all the exercises from beginning to end.

13. Interactive video

These are videos of simulated interpersonal communication situations in which actors portray various characters in workplace scenes. The background to a situation is mapped out, developing to a climax at which the video stops, leaving the viewer to pretend that he or she is one of the characters in the film, and having to provide the next step. For instance, the video might show a production operative just about to lose his or her temper and then, just at the crucial moment, invite viewers to say how *they* would resolve the problem. The action may, of course, be slowed down or frozen to highlight critical events.

Management development

14. Definition
The *Glossary of Training Terms* gives the following definition of management development:

> A systematic process of development of effective managers at all levels to meet the requirements of an organisation, involving an analysis of the present and future management requirements, assessing the existing and potential skills of managers and devising the best means for their development to meet these requirements.

The definition shows that management development includes:

(a) human resources planning to assess the demand for managers (*see* Chapter 12);

(b) appraisal of managers' present abilities, sometimes using a management by objectives programme (*see* Chapter 18);

(c) appropriate development methods.

It is sometimes regarded as part of *organisation development* — a planned attempt to improve the effectiveness of a company by examining and reforming the way it is organised, its communications and its management style. The systematic approach (*see* 19:3) cannot be applied to development, which aims to prepare for future jobs whereas training is concerned with improving performance in present jobs. Validation of a management development programme is therefore very difficult.

15. Development needs
These can be divided into three categories.

(a) Knowledge required to perform a manager's job in the company concerned, including:
  (*i*) background of company, its organisation and practices;
  (*ii*) company resources available;
  (*iii*) company technology;
  (*iv*) specialist management techniques, e.g. operational research;

    (*v*) relevant law;
    (*vi*) general, social and economic environment.
(b) Planning, analytical and creative skills, which include the following:
    (*i*) recognising objectives and putting them in order of importance;
    (*ii*) assessing the value of available resources, e.g. human, material, technological and financial;
    (*iii*) formulating and administering plans, delegating as necessary;
    (*iv*) discerning and solving day-to-day management problems.
(c) Social skills (sometimes called interpersonal or interactive skills), important because managers may easily spend two-thirds of their time working with and trying to influence others. They include:
    (*i*) communication upwards, downwards and laterally (*see* **9:3**);
    (*ii*) co-ordination within a department or between departments;
    (*iii*) motivation of subordinates;
    (*iv*) awareness of others' needs, attitudes and perceptions.

16. Development methods
Needs may be met either by activities arranged within the company or by external courses. The latter appear to be losing favour because they are unable to take into account a company's particular systems, traditions or general management style. In-company programmes are growing in popularity, especially those which include a team of people who normally work together, or even a whole department. It is, however, often difficult in practice to release a whole team or department at the same time unless the programme is held outside normal working hours.
    Development methods often used in management development fall into three areas.

(a) *Knowledge.* As in training, this is the easiest area to deal with. Company matters are dealt with by secondment, coaching or auto-instruction (*see* **10**), while outside courses are appropriate for specialist techniques and the general environment.

(b) *Planning, analytical and creative skills.* This is the most difficult of the three categories. To a certain extent the acquisition of knowledge will help the manager by showing the factors to be considered and the techniques available, but it seems that planning, analytical and creative skills can only be developed by practice, either in a real job or in a situation which attempts to simulate reality.

In the first case, the manager will feel fully responsible, will take genuine decisions and will deal with their consequences, though the mistakes of an inexpert manager can be disastrous.

In the second case, the manager may be more enterprising but will have little sense of responsibility; his or her behaviour in real life may be entirely different. A simulated situation, however carefully it is described, can never depict, for example, the personalities and organisational climate which are so important in management decision making. Some simulated methods which are used to try to develop these skills are:

(i) *case studies and role-playing* (*see* **2**);

(ii) *in-tray exercises* (*see* **10**);

(iii) *business games* in which two or more teams attempt, for example, to market an imaginary product using the information supplied to them. The effects of their decisions are evaluated (usually by a computer) and fed back to them. The team which has made the largest profit will be the winner.

The following are real-life methods:

(i) *projects*, i.e. special assignments given to managers, who must enquire into a company problem, make recommendations and sometimes put them into practice;

(ii) *junior boards*, in which a group of young managers is given decisions of fairly low importance to make which have been delegated to the group by the main board;

(iii) *action learning*, in which a manager takes over a different job and through doing it learns a new set of management skills. The manager must analyse the problems associated with a job, formulate a solution, implement the solution (under the guidance of an experienced superior) and monitor its consequences;

(iv) *training companies*, usually small subsidiaries of a large group, which are intended to trade profitably, yet give opportunities for young managers to develop their skills in a somewhat protected environment;

(v) *coaching* (*see* **8**) is often used and is frequently successful, but sometimes the experienced manager who is coaching may make decisions so automatically that either he or she does not realise they have been made or cannot explain the reasons for them.

(c) *Social skills.* These have received much attention in recent years and are always dealt with in special courses.

The main methods are as follows.

(i) *Attitude change,* e.g. by T-groups or role-playing (*see* **2**).

(ii) *Team-work and management-style courses,* usually given by consultants, in which groups are formed to carry out simple tasks together and then discuss what lessons about their behaviour can be learned. Examples are:

- Coverdale training, which is a group-training application of the principles of action learning in which a specialist instructor directs a group in completing a straightforward task and then leads discussion after the task's completion;
- group discussions about normal working behaviour in the context of a theoretical framework, e.g. the managerial grid (*see* **8:7**).

(iii) *Analysing individual behaviour* following a formal system, sometimes with a theoretical basis, e.g. transactional analysis.

(iv) *Training in social techniques.* This is the reverse of method (i) in which it is assumed that a change in attitudes will modify behaviour. Instead, training is given in the techniques of hand-shaking, smiling, eye contact, etc. in situations which are as near to reality as possible, e.g. a simulated appraisal interview. The trainee becomes aware of the benefits of the improved techniques in his or her social contacts, and thus modifies basic attitudes.

(v) *Lectures* in the psychology of perception, motivation, groups, etc. usually in conjunction with one of the above methods.

(vi) *Outdoor management training.* This assumes that the qualities needed for successful management may be cultivated through short management development courses involving outdoor pursuits such as rockclimbing, canoeing or orienteering. Such activities are said to enhance participants' abilities to plan, organise, create and manage teams, control others and handle uncertainty.

17. Arguments against management training

Academic management training has been criticised for having few practical applications, for encouraging technical specialisation rather than the overall ability to lead, and for creating unrealistic job and career expectations among junior managerial employees. Opponents of management training allege that the environments in which training occurs are necessarily artificial, and too remote from real life managerial situations to be of practical value. Arguably, most aspects of management can only be learned by doing. In particular, the entrepreneurial attitudes that are essential for commercial success cannot be inculcated through academic management training; many of the most innovative of all entrepreneurs and managers have received no management training whatsoever. Normal competition between managerial employees should ensure the emergence of the most able at the top. Further arguments against management training are that:

(a) the dimensions of managerial competence encompass a vast range of tasks, so that it is not possible to devise courses that comprehensively cover the entire management field;
(b) individuals enter management in so many different ways and from such varied backgrounds that no single programme of studies can meet the highly specified needs of each participant;
(c) management is by its very nature a fast changing subject, so that the contents of any management training course could quickly become out of date, especially if the course does not devote sufficient attention to underlying management principles.

Progress test 20

1. What methods may be used for attitude training? (2)

2. What are the disadvantages of the 'sitting next to Nellie' method of skill training? (4)

3. Why does skills analysis training sometimes eliminate the learning plateau? **(5)**

4. What are the principles of the discovery method of training? **(6)**

5. State three methods of knowledge training. **(7–10)**

6. What are the advantages and disadvantages of programmed learning? **(11)**

7. What are the advantages of computer-based training? **(12)**

8. What are a manager's main development needs? **(15)**

21
Job evaluation

The basis of job evaluation

1. Definition

Job evaluation is the process of placing jobs in order of their relative worth so that employees may be paid fairly. It is concerned with the demands and conditions of the job and not with the personal qualities of the individual who is occupying the job. Since jobs differ in so many respects, numerous problems arise in assessing their relative importance. A 'job' consists of a whole series of tasks, responsibilities and obligations, including the skills, knowledge and mental agility required, qualities of initiative, reliability, ability to withstand stress; capacities for planning, controlling others, co-ordinating the nature of the environment in which the work is completed, and so on. Ideally, jobs should be ranked according to objective criteria — known and understood by all who work in the organisation. The first stage in job evaluation is usually to establish a rank-order for jobs and the second is to apply money values to it.

2. Importance of job evaluation

Payment for work can fulfil many functions (*see* 2:16), from the provision of food and shelter to the recognition that an employee's job has a certain status and value, i.e. it can satisfy both lower and higher needs. Because pay is significant not only for what it will purchase but also for what it symbolises, a company's pay structure is very important to its employees, who will strongly resent what they perceive to be unfairness or injustice. In some companies, for example, pay anomalies have appeared perhaps because of inconsistency of treatment in the past, a merger with another company, or high rates being offered to meet a temporary shortage of a certain type of employee. Sometimes no one can explain the anomalies. The purposes of job evaluation are therefore:

(a) to make pay administration easier by reducing the number of separate rates of pay;

(b) to harmonise internal rates of pay with those found in other companies;

(c) to provide a means by which a reasonable rate of pay can be fixed for new or changed jobs within the company;

(d) to protect the employee from arbitrary decisions by management;

(e) to justify wage differentials and hence avoid frequent invocations of grievance procedures;

(f) to facilitate fair promotion systems based on rationally determined job grading structures (each grade should specify all the qualifications and personal attributes needed to occupy a job within that grade).

In a small company these purposes can obviously be fulfilled without a formal system; no doubt some kind of intuitive evaluation takes place. Large companies, however, with their much more complex organisation and greater variety of occupations will find job evaluation almost essential unless their job structure is completely static, with pay relativities firmly established by tradition. Such firms are rare.

3. Factors determining pay

A wage or salary is influenced by many different factors. Some of these affect the basic pay for the job and others the pay that individual employees receive.

(a) *Supply and demand* — eventually, when the supply of a particular type of labour is scarce, its price, i.e. its wage or salary, will rise, and vice versa. The operation of this economic law is, however, affected by the following:

(*i*) people are often unwilling to move to another district;

(*ii*) pay is not the only reward gained from employment;

(*iii*) knowledge of the various rates of pay offered is not widespread;

(*iv*) training for a new occupation may take some years.

(b) *Difficulty of the job* — it is generally agreed that jobs which require a high level of intelligence, experience, knowledge or skill deserve a high rate of pay.

(c) *Unpleasant working conditions.*

(d) *Cost of living.*

(e) *Government intervention.*

(f) *Productivity, merit or length of service* — often determining the pay received by an individual over and above the basic rate.

4. Job rates and individual rates

Job evaluation establishes a basic rate by considering factors **(a)** to **(d)** in **3**. If it is thought desirable to reward differently the individuals who are doing the same job then additions may be made to their basic rate, perhaps on productivity (using payment by results — *see* 22:**3–5**), merit (by appraisal — Chapter 18) or length of service.

5. Introducing job evaluation

A new or altered job evaluation system is a change which must be very carefully introduced by management (*see* 9:**12–14**) because it affects the vital subject of pay. The method of evaluation must be clearly explained to employees and their representatives, some modifications perhaps being made at the employees' request. It is usual to guarantee that no employee at present employed by the company will receive a reduction in pay, though if the job is found to be overpaid his or her successors in it may be given a lower wage.

Some companies have found that the fairness of the scheme in the employees' eyes is increased if an appeals committee is set up to listen to complaints that jobs have not been given the value they deserve. Employee representatives, e.g. shop stewards, often sit on these committees.

6. Essential requirements

Any method of job evaluation requires two things.

(a) Job specifications for all jobs which are to be valued (*see* 13:**5–6**).

(b) A committee to consider the job specifications and apply to them the particular technique of evaluation which it has been decided shall be used. The committee usually contains a few permanent members, e.g. the personnel officer, the work study officer, the organisation and methods officer together with other members drawn from a panel of managers who have all had training in the technique. Job evaluations carried out by an individual are not likely to be well received; using a committee will reduce the effects of bias and prejudice.

Methods

7. Job evaluation methods
Three methods of job evaluation are in common use.

(a) *Ranking*, a non-analytical method because the job is valued as a whole, an impressionistic view being taken.
(b) *Grading*, a semi-analytical method in which the job specification is examined fairly closely but not exhaustively.
(c) *Points rating*, an analytical method which requires a very detailed examination of the job specification.

8. Ranking
In this method the committee judges each job as a whole and places the set of jobs in order of their worth. Sometimes this process is aided by using as points of reference one or two jobs whose place in the hierarchy is generally accepted.

(a) Advantages:
   (*i*) it is quick and requires no complicated administration;
   (*ii*) it is easily understood;
   (*iii*) it is particularly suitable for fairly homogeneous jobs, e.g. all clerical, or where it is known that the pay structure is already reasonably satisfactory.
(b) Disadvantages:
   (*i*) although the method is easy to understand, its results are difficult to defend as they are based on impressionistic, almost intuitive judgments;
   (*ii*) it is impracticable in large companies or in smaller companies in which jobs are very varied;

    (*iii*) it does not indicate the spaces between positions in the rank order, i.e. job A may be judged to be worth more than job B, but the method will not show how much more.

    (*iv*) this type of system (often referred to as 'felt-fair' evaluation) may provoke industrial tribunal actions initiated under the 1984 revisions to the Equal Pay Act by aggrieved workers who claim they are unfairly paid less than members of the opposite sex who do work of equivalent value to their own. Recent test cases have established unambiguously that the results of felt-fair job evaluation systems will be ignored by courts and tribunals when determining equal pay cases (*see* **14**).

A refinement of ranking is the *paired comparison* method, in which each job is ranked against every other job, taking a pair of jobs at a time. If N jobs are dealt with in this way then $N(N-1)/2$ comparisons have to be made, i.e. to rank 20 jobs will require 190 comparisons. It is usual to distribute the pairs of jobs among several judges and collate the results on a computer. By showing how many times a job has been given first preference, not only may a rank order be prepared but spacing along the rank order will also be shown. The paired comparison method also enables jobs of different types to be evaluated.

The subjectivity of ranking is obvious, though experienced judges using this method very often achieve remarkable agreement.

9. Grading

This method provides a framework into which jobs can be fitted. It is decided in advance how many grades or classes of pay shall be created, and the jobs which should fall into each grade are defined. The lowest grade, for example, will be defined as containing those jobs which require little skill and are closely supervised. With each successive grade skills, knowledge and responsibilities increase. The committee then reads the specification for each job, matching it against the various grade definitions until an appropriate grade is found. Eventually every job in the company has been allotted to a grade.

(a) Advantages:

    (*i*) it is relatively simple, quick and inexpensive;

(*ii*) the decisions of the committee can be supported by the definitions of the job grades.

(b) Disadvantages:

(*i*) complex jobs are often difficult to fit into the system; a job may seem to have the characteristics of two or more grades; like ranking, the method is at its best when a fairly homogeneous family of jobs is being evaluated;

(*ii*) because of the difficulty in (*i*) the original grades tend to be sub-divided into smaller grades, making the scheme more difficult to operate;

(*iii*) the method is less objective than appears at first sight. To a large extent jobs are valued before the specifications are examined because arbitrary decisions have been made that certain features of a job belong to certain grades. For example, an unscrupulous employer could attempt to depress the remuneration of employees by defining the grades in such a way that the majority of jobs fell into the lower grades. On the other hand, this will not occur if the grade definitions have been prepared and published by an independent body, such as the Institute of Administrative Management, part of whose system of clerical workers' job grading is shown in Appendix 3;

(*iv*) semi-analytical schemes have been adjudged inadequate by courts hearing equal pay cases. Courts now insist that firms adopt fully analytical techniques when comparing the value of work done by men and women.

10. Points rating

This is the most widely used method. A number of factors are first agreed against which jobs can be analysed. A very simple set of factors for manual jobs might be:

Skill
Effort
Responsibility
Working conditions.

However, it is usual to sub-divide each of the main factors into about three sub-factors, making about twelve altogether. For example, 'skill' might be divided into education, experience and dexterity. Sometimes non-manual jobs are provided for by extending the factors to include, for example, complexity of duties, contacts with others or requirement to handle confidential information, or sometimes a special set of factors is used for a particular family of jobs.

Each factor carries a range of points; the committee analyses each job specification to decide how many points shall be awarded to the job for each factor. The total of points when set against other totals indicates the position of the job in the hierarchy. An example of a job evaluation scheme for manual workers is shown in Appendix 3.

11. Weighting

The factors chosen for job evaluation may not all have equal importance; skill, for example, may contain the three sub-factors training, experience and dexterity of which experience is thought to make the greatest contribution to the value of a job.

Weighting is the name given to the process by which some factors can be given greater emphasis than others. It can be carried out in two ways.

(a) A multiplier is introduced so that the points value given to a factor can be doubled, trebled, etc. Each factor carries the same range of points, e.g. 1 to 10, but the value given to, say, experience might be multiplied by 4 and that for training by 2.

(b) Factors judged to be more important have a wider range of points attached to them. This is the practice followed in the scheme shown in Appendix 3.

12. The choice of factors and weights

The choice of factors and weights is intuitive rather than objective. A company with no experience of job evaluation will probably begin by using a scheme borrowed from another company, or one which has appeared in a book. If the results of evaluating a few well-known jobs do not agree with commonsense or tradition the company will change the factors or weights until an acceptable set of relationships is obtained.

Different jobs require different factors; it is very unusual for a company to be able to evaluate all its jobs by the use of one scheme only. For example, factors for evaluating management jobs would be quite different from those shown in Appendix 3, consisting perhaps of:

Judgment
Qualifications and experience
Extent of decision-making
Control of staff
Contacts with others.

These factors would probably be sub-divided.

13. The subjectivity of points rating

The justification for the points rating system of job evaluation is that it works, not that it is objective or scientific. There are several subjective elements in the method, some of course being found in any job evaluation system.

(a) The job specification may reflect the bias of the job analyst.
(b) The members of the job evaluation committee, although guided by detailed job specifications and carefully-described factors, still make subjective judgments about the worth of a job.
(c) The selection of factors is based originally on imitation or conjecture and confirmed by intuition.
(d) Weights are selected according to the same principles.

In spite of its subjective elements points rating usually provides acceptable and consistent results if job specifications are well prepared and the committee is thoroughly familiar with the system.

14. Legal considerations

Under the 1984 amendments to the Equal Pay Act any person is entitled to the same remuneration and conditions of service as a member of the opposite sex who is doing similar work, or *work which is of a similar value*, as judged under a *job evaluation* exercise. If a job evaluation has not already been undertaken within the organisation, the employee has the legal right (regardless of length of service, current grade or whether part-time or full-time) to apply to an industrial tribunal for an order (which is legally enforceable) that a job evaluation be carried out by an independent expert appointed by and reporting to the tribunal.

This evaluation will consider the effort, skills and responsibility needed to take decisions and so on attached to the post, and the demands made on the individual worker in this job compared to jobs done by the firm's other workers.

Apart from the report submitted by the independent expert appointed by the tribunal, other reports may be submitted to the tribunal by each side based on the job evaluation studies undertaken by their own (paid) experts. These are presented as evidence in support of each party's case. The tribunal's decision is legally binding: wages *must* be increased and jobs regraded if the tribunal orders that this should occur. Moreover, Article 119 of the Treaty of Rome (which overrides UK domestic law) explicitly demands 'the application of the principle that men and women should receive equal pay for equal work'.

The revised Equal Pay Act clearly states that job evaluations must use *analytical methods*, i.e. they must examine 'in terms of the demands made on the worker under various headings (for instance, effort, skill, decision) the jobs to be done by all or any of the employees in an undertaking'. In other words, overall ranking or felt-fair classification will not be regarded as satisfactory. This is a point of great significance for employers, since it means that any non-analytical study is open to challenge in the courts.

The law as it stands requires the complainant whose job has been rated as *unequal* by an analytical study to demonstrate that there was a fundamental flaw in the analytical techniques adopted. But if the job evaluation was non-analytical, there is no need to demonstrate a flaw in the method. It is automatically assumed that the study was inadequate and that it did not meet the requirements of the Act. In consequence, it cannot be used as a barrier against a claim in an industrial tribunal — the aggrieved party may simply ignore the fact that the evaluation occurred and can proceed directly to the tribunal without having to prove the study was faulty. Moreover, recent test cases have upheld complaints that certain analytical evaluation exercises which resulted in pay differentials between jobs were not in fact analytical enough. The details and methodology of job evaluations are today increasingly questioned by the courts.

15. Measuring equal value
Even if an analytical job evaluation fairly demonstrates that

two jobs done by members of the opposite sex differ in content, a claim can still be made if the jobs have equal value in terms of the effort, skill, decision making, etc. required to undertake them but they are not equally paid. The amended Equal Pay Act emphasises that the relevant yardstick in determining equal value is whether the jobs are equivalent with respect to the *demands made on the employee* when doing the job rather than the perceived value of the work to the employer. In other words, it is the *nature* of the work actually done that matters.

The Equal Opportunities Commission's own guide to the amended Equal Pay Act offers examples of possible similar and dissimilar demands made on the workers undertaking two hypothetical jobs. These are reproduced below.

Examples of similar demands

Job A	Job B
Responsible for contact with public	Responsible for staff
Lifts heavy weights occasionally	Lifts small weights continuously
Diagnoses machine faults	Analyses written reports
Checks stocks and orders replacements	Checks work done by subordinates and allocates tasks
Uses drilling machine	Uses typewriter
On feet most of day	Has to concentrate on numbers

Examples of dissimilar demands

Job A	Job B
Drives a van	Examines customer complaints
Sweeps up	Chooses fabric for new designs
Decides shift rosters	Responsible for packing and despatch

Cases that go before tribunals are judged on their individual merits, though all rely heavily on the results of independent analytical job evaluation studies. Already, such studies have determined that the work of a factory nurse was of equal value to that of a skilled fitter, that a secretary's work had equal value to a scientific assistant's, that an administrator's job was equal to a data analyst's, and that the demands made on a seamstress were of equal value to those made on a fork-lift truck driver. Other pairings have involved quality controllers and technical trainers, and the comparison of catering assistants with drivers. There are no limits on the jobs that can be compared, and every organisation must be fully cognisant of this when devising job evaluation procedures.

Job evaluation and pay

16. Grading jobs

After evaluation has been completed by the ranking or points rating method the jobs appear in an order of value. They are then divided into groups or grades, the object being to allot to each grade a particular basic pay rate or pay-range. If the grading system of job evaluation is used this division will have been done already.

17. Grades and pay

In very many cases it is found that most jobs contained in any grade are already paid at about the same rate; the few jobs for which pay is inconsistent are then brought into line.

Occasionally a job appears to be in one grade by job evaluation but in a considerably higher grade according to its present pay. If after checking the job specification and evaluation this difference remains it is usual to regard the discrepancy as being due to temporary abnormal market conditions; employees in that job are shown in the company's pay records as receiving pay for their grade plus a special allowance to bring their total remuneration to the market rate.

18. Pay surveys

Some companies regularly make comparisons between their own rates of pay and those paid by other companies for similar jobs, e.g. rates are compared for the copy-typists, forepersons or accountants employed in those companies. These rates are then applied to pay grades. This procedure can be misleading because:

(a) pay is not the only reward from a job — some companies may have low rates of pay but a high reputation for security (*see* 2:30);
(b) the jobs compared may in fact be similar only in title; the duties and responsibilities may be different;
(c) it is not logical for a company to evaluate its jobs systematically

and then base its pay structure on the wages or salaries paid by a company which may have made no attempt to bring order into its remuneration system.

Progress test 21

1.   What are the purposes of job evaluation?   **(2)**

2.   Name the most important factors determining levels of pay.   **(3)**

3.   What do all methods of job evaluation require?   **(6)**

4.   Describe briefly the ranking and grading methods of job evaluation.   **(8, 9)**

5.   How are factors and weights chosen in the points rating method?   **(12)**

6.   In what circumstances might an industrial tribunal regard a job evaluation as sexually discriminatory?   **(14, 15)**

7.   How are the results of job evaluation expressed in monetary terms?   **(17, 18)**

22
Wages and salaries

Wage structures

1. Definition
A wage is the payment made to manual workers. It is nearly always expressed as a rate per hour.

2. Wage structures
The foundation of a manual worker's earnings is his or her basic time wage, which is sometimes fixed by job evaluation but is subject in most industries to minimum rates agreed in national collective bargaining (*see* 26:9) or laid down by wages councils (*see* 26:**14**). The worker is paid the hourly rate for every hour of attendance at work, though he or she may be fined for lateness by quartering, i.e. for being five minutes late the employee loses quarter of an hour's pay.

In addition to the basic rate the worker will often receive other payments, the most common examples of which are as follows.

(a) *Overtime pay* for any work done beyond normal hours. It is usually paid at premium rates, at time and a quarter, time and a half, double time, etc., the rate varying according to the time of the day on which the overtime is worked. (*See* also 23:**10**)

(b) *Shift pay* for employees who work unusual or changing hours, to compensate them for inconvenience and hardship. The amount of shift pay varies in different industries, but seems to range from about 10 to 20 per cent of the basic rate. (*See* also 23:**11**.)

(c) *Special additions,* e.g. danger money, dirt money or wet money which are paid to the employee during abnormal working conditions. Since the circumstances which justify these additions are hard to define, many employers find it preferable to allow for these contingencies in the job evaluated basic rate rather than give special extra payments which are often difficult to take away again.

(d) *Merit or length of service additions* to employees either on the results of appraisal (*see* Chapter 18) or on completion of a certain period of service. Merit payments are not very popular with wage-earners, who feel they are influenced by prejudice and subjective judgments. Length of service payments have an approximate relationship with merit, encourage employees to stay with the company, and can be precisely defined.

(e) *Cost of living allowances* are given quite commonly in response to a rise in the general price level or to employees who work in high-cost areas, e.g. London. In many cases they are eventually consolidated into the basic wage.

(f) *Policy allowances* cover miscellaneous extra payments, like the addition to the job evaluated rate for temporarily scarce employees (*see* 21:17).

(g) *Payments by results bonus*, i.e. an extra payment based on the output of the worker or of the group to which he or she belongs (*see* 3).

In private industry, about 70 per cent of a manual worker's total earnings are on average accounted for by the basic wage and about 30 per cent by a selection from the additional payments shown above.

Total earnings have increased at a faster rate than basic wages (a phenomenon known as wages drift) because the additional payments have become proportionately larger. It should be noted that they are decided entirely within the company, often at a fairly low level of management, and are not easily influenced by government action.

Payment by results

3. Principles of PBR

In nearly all methods of payment by results the employee receives a basic rate to which is added a variable payment based on output. For each job a standard is set expressed either as a quantity produced per unit of time or as the time taken to do the job; bonus becomes payable when the employee exceeds this standard.

If a company installs a PBR system for the first time it therefore needs to take the following steps.

(a) The scheme is communicated to the employees with perhaps some modifications after consultation with representatives. Supervisors and managers are trained in its use.

(b) A standard rate of output is set for each job by measuring the reasonable time taken to do it and making allowances for rest periods and personal needs. There are various methods of setting standards, from intuitive judgment to detailed analysis of bodily movements.

(c) Administrative arrangements are made to record each employee's output, calculate his or her bonus, and add it to the worker's basic wage.

The cost of running a PBR scheme, including work study, clerical work and dealing with disputes arising out of it, can be considerable. Some schemes are also rather complicated to compute and difficult to understand because the bonus does not increase proportionately with output but at a faster or slower rate.

4. Advantages of PBR

A well-designed and well-maintained scheme will increase productivity from the same number of employees and the same equipment and thus reduce unit costs. The work study which it requires may well show more efficient methods of production, and the supervisor need not control subordinates so closely because the monetary incentive makes human control unnecessary.

The popularity of PBR is shown by the fact that about 40 per cent of manual workers are paid by this method. To operate at its best, however, it requires a steady flow of measurable work, the pace of which is within the control of the worker.

5. Disadvantages of PBR

There has been a reaction against PBR in recent years because the advantages described above are sometimes outweighed by the following disadvantages.

(a) A PBR system is exceptionally liable to decay; new methods

and materials, introduced gradually, may slowly cause a standard to become loose so that workers can earn high bonuses very easily.
(b) It is a constant source of shopfloor conflict, both when a new rate is being fixed and when a worker is asked to move from a job where the rate is loose to another where the rate is tight.
(c) Supervisors are tempted to show favouritism in allocating jobs when it is easy to earn bonus in some but difficult in others.
(d) It is difficult to reward fairly the labourers and skilled setters or maintenance workers whose output cannot be measured although their work influences the output of others. Such workers are usually paid a lieu bonus, based on the average bonus earned by the PBR workers.
(e) Salaried supervisors sometimes earn less than their subordinates who are paid by PBR.
(f) Output norms are frequently found. A group of employees decides that no one shall exceed a certain level of output, on penalty of unofficial sanctions, e.g. ostracism, hiding or spoiling tools, damage to clothing. Output is restricted because:
  (*i*) loose rates are not so obvious;
  (*ii*) employment is safeguarded;
  (*iii*) by reducing discrepancies in performance, the unity of the group is maintained (*see* 7:8).
(g) Earnings can fluctuate because an employee is not given a steady supply of work; at certain times therefore he or she is not able to earn bonus.
(h) Quality and safety may be adversely affected.

6. Group bonus schemes
In some forms of PBR the standard is based on the performance of a group rather than an individual. The bonus earned by the group is shared among its members sometimes equally, sometimes in proportion to basic pay. The advantages of group bonus schemes are:

(a) they can include indirect workers, e.g. labourers or maintenance workers;
(b) they improve team spirit;
(c) they encourage flexibility, because individuals are more willing to move to other jobs within the group;

(d) they simplify clerical work;

(e) they are particularly suitable for jobs which are carried out by a team of workers of various levels of skill, e.g. electric cable jointing.

Group bonuses tend to be unsatisfactory when the group becomes large, when its members constantly change or when it contains a mixture of very fast and very slow workers.

7. Plant-wide PBR

Some companies have PBR schemes which are virtually group bonus schemes extended to cover a whole plant, bonus being payable according to the extent by which factory output exceeds a given standard.

Two other schemes are used in this country, though not widely, which do not require output standards to be fixed by work study methods; these are the Scanlon and the Rucker plans, both of American origin.

(a) *The Scanlon Plan* first requires the following ratio to be calculated:

Sales value of production: Total payroll

A bonus becomes payable when in any month that ratio is exceeded, i.e. when payroll costs as a proportion of production value have decreased. It therefore becomes the aim of everyone to increase production and decrease labour costs, e.g. by reducing overtime or allowing numbers to run down. A network of suggestion committees puts up ideas to improve efficiency.

(b) *The Rucker Plan* is similar except that the ratio is:

$$\frac{\text{Sales value of production} - \text{Value of bought-in materials}}{\text{Total payroll}}$$

This meets the objection that under the Scanlon Plan employees can receive a bonus because prices have been increased to cover the increased cost of raw materials and components.

Both schemes work best when market conditions are favourable; if the company cannot sell its products bonus will be reduced or will disappear.

8. Measured daywork

This system is sometimes introduced as a substitute for a conventional PBR scheme. It has several variations, but essentially it offers the employee a fixed weekly wage in return for an undertaking to produce to an agreed level of performance. Since the company is committed to paying high wages it will do its utmost to provide the employees with a steady supply of work, the scheme thus encouraging managerial efficiency. Employees are more ready to move to other work temporarily or accept changes of method because they do not have to consider such questions as tight and loose rates. Industrial relations, it is claimed, also improve because there are fewer causes for dispute.

The scheme gives a more responsible role to the supervisor, who is expected to interview employees who do not reach their agreed performance to find out the reasons and rectify them as soon as possible. Difficulties have sometimes been reported when a large number of employees all fail to reach the output standards they have previously agreed to.

Levels of pay often have to be fixed at quite a high level when measured daywork is introduced because they must take account of pay anomalies and previous high individual bonus earnings. Some companies which have adopted the scheme say that the heavy financial commitment is justified by the improved attitudes that are found in management and employees; others found that their measured daywork schemes have not been successful and have reverted to conventional PBR, though often on a group rather than an individual basis.

9. Stepped pay systems

Productivity levels achieved under measured day work have often been disappointing, as there is no incentive for the employee to work to a level above the contracted rate. To overcome this problem some companies have introduced a more complicated system, often called the 'stepped pay band', which defines several levels of performance with a rate of pay for each. Employees may choose the level they work on and are checked from time to time to ensure that this performance is being maintained. They may ask to move up to a higher level if they feel they are capable of working at that rate. This method combines regular levels of pay with individual incentives.

Wages law

10. Payment of wages

Rules determining how wages may be paid are specified in the Wages Act 1986. This removed all previous restrictions on employers paying their workers by means other than cash (or cheque or credit transfer in appropriate circumstances), although the actual method of payment is a matter for negotiation. Under the Act it is generally illegal to deduct money from an employee's pay or for the firm to require the employee to pay back money received in wages except in the following circumstances.

(a) Deductions for income tax and national insurance; or if a court has ordered that part of a person's wages be paid to a third party (e.g. to settle a fine or money owing under a court judgment).

(b) Payments requested in writing by the employee, such as trade union or sports clubs subscriptions.

(c) Agreed deductions for lateness or poor work, provided the agreement is incorporated into the employee's contract of employment.

(d) Accidental overpayment of previous wages or expenses.

(e) For *retail employees only*, deductions to make good cash shortages (e.g. money missing from the cash till) or stock deficiencies. 'Retail employment' means anyone involved in the sale and supply of goods or services. Hence, the Act covers not just shop assistants, but any employee handling cash transactions with customers — bus conductors, milk deliverers, booking office clerks, bank counter staff, etc. Deductions must not exceed more than 10 per cent of the wages due on any one pay day (except the last pay day before the employee leaves the firm) and the deduction must be made within twelve months of the detection of the shortage or deficiency.

The Wages Act covers self-employed contractors as well as employees. If an employer makes an unauthorised deduction, the worker or sub-contractor may apply to an industrial tribunal for recompense.

Salary structures

11. Definition
A salary is a fixed periodical payment to a non-manual employee. It is usually expressed in annual terms, implying a relatively permanent employment relationship, though normally paid at monthly intervals. In many ways, it resembles a retaining fee. Salaried workers are usually termed staff.

12. Characteristics of salaries
A salary differs from a wage in many respects, reflecting the different attitudes traditionally held by an employer towards the firm's non-manual compared with manual employees.

(a) A salary is usually all-inclusive; there are no additional payments of danger money or productivity bonus, for example.

(b) A salary is progressive, in most cases increasing annually, whereas a wage-earner reaches the standard rate for the job early in adult life and does not receive annual increases.

(c) A salary is often regarded as personal to the individual, but a wage is the sum paid to all workers at a particular job.

(d) A salary is often confidential, but there is no secret about a wage.

(e) In the private sector of employment, salaries are less likely than wages to be the subject of trade union negotiations.

13. Salary administration
This comprises a set of processes for determining, controlling and monitoring the salaries paid to employees. It is particularly concerned with the design and operation of salary structures (including the choice of criteria for salary grade), with determining relations between fringe benefits and basic salary, the timing of salary reviews, and the administration of salary progression systems. The objectives of salary administration are as follows.

(a) To enable the organisation to forecast accurately its future salary bills and to control these effectively.

(b) To establish fair differentials between various grades of staff.

(c) To provide incentives to employees through offering them a career ladder through which they may progress.

(d) To relate salaries to employees' contributions to the organisation.

(e) To attract, retain and motivate employees of the appropriate calibre.

An effective salary system will keep the organisation's salary levels in line with market levels; will adjust salaries as the cost of living changes; will be consistent yet sufficiently flexible to allow for additional salary increases for employees of exceptional merit; and will be easy to operate and clearly understood by all salaried staff.

14. Salary administration methods
Implementation of a salary system requires the following:

(a) A survey of the salary levels offered by comparable firms.

(b) Determination of salary budgets for various employee categories.

(c) Job analysis and evaluation (*see* Chapter 13).

(d) Decisions concerning salary ranges and overlaps.

(e) Policies regarding merit and performance related pay increases.

There are a number of ways in which a company can administer its salaries.

(a) *Ad hoc*, in which there is no attempt at any kind of job evaluation to assess a fair level of salary for a job. Increases in salary are given erratically, often at the demand of the employee rather than at the initiative of the company. In a small company this method is workable, but in a large company it can produce an illogical and unfair salary structure which will cause discontent and jealousy. For obvious reasons salaries paid by this system are intended to be confidential.

(b) *Merit review*, usually found in medium and large companies in the private sector. After job evaluation, a salary range is attached to every staff job. Employees are appraised and given personal merit increases each year which will move their salaries at varying speeds through the range, In this way individual effort and merit are rewarded. However a large amount of administrative work might be needed to assess the merit increases of all employees in the organisation, and if this task is delegated to heads of department substantial discrepancies in the amounts awarded to equally worthy individuals might emerge. Also, if very many employees simultaneously receive high merit increases the organisation is presented with a large unexpected wages bill. It is customary for salaries under this system to be kept confidential; in most cases the employees do not know the maximum salary it is possible to earn in their jobs.

(c) *Incremental scale*, found above all in the public sector, e.g. the civil service, local government and nationalised boards, though its use appears to be increasing in the private sector. All staff jobs are evaluated and graded, the salary range appearing as, for example, £17,000 x £500 – £21,500 indicating that there is a standard increment of salary each year of £500. Most schemes permit a manager to award double increments for exceptional merit or withhold an increment for unsatisfactory work or conduct, but as a rule the standard increment is given automatically. In this system long service and loyalty are encouraged by regular salary increases and merit by the speed of promotion to a higher grade. Sometimes grades overlap, creating the opportunity to reward long-serving workers whose ability levels make them unsuitable for promotion. It is customary for salaries in the incremental system to be non-confidential.

(d) *Rate for age*. This is an incremental scheme frequently applied to young workers, who receive pay rises of a predetermined amount on each of their birthdays up to a certain age (usually 21 years). Thus it assumes that the employee's contributions to the firm increase according to his or her experience and maturity. Provision for merit increases may be incorporated into the system.

Control over the firm's aggregate salary expenditures might be exercised through the following devices.

(a) Setting overall salary budgets for various sections, departments, functions or activities.

(b) Restricting the total amount available for salary increases to the amount generated by improvements in employee productivity.

(c) Careful forecasting and the statistical analysis of relationships (referred to as 'maturity' or 'salary progression' curves) between employees' ages and salaries (hence enabling the firm to predict future salary costs as the average age of its workforce alters).

(d) Deliberate salary attrition. Here the firm imposes a rule that resigning employees shall not be replaced until the expiry of a minimum period (six months, for example) during which colleagues are expected to cover the ex-worker's duties. This creates additional resources for the payment of merit increases to remaining staff. Note, moreover, that new starters are normally appointed in the bottom part of a grade whereas leavers will often be at a higher end of the scale.

A common procedure for monitoring trends in aggregate salary movements is the use of the 'compa-ratio' (short for comparative ratio). The mid-point of each salary grade is taken as the target salary for that grade. Then, the extent to which average salaries in a grade deviate from the mid-point is measured using the following formula:

$$\frac{\text{Average of all salaries in the grade}}{\text{Mid-point of the salary range}} \times 100$$

Thus, a compa-ratio of 100 would mean that the average salary within a grade is exactly equal to the mid-point. A high value indicates the presence of a large number of long-serving employees in a particular grade, and/or too many new appointments in the top end of the grade category. Low compa-ratio values could mean that the firm is paying salaries that are no longer competitive, or that there are too many recently recruited (and thus inexperienced) workers.

Other pay legislation

15. Equal Pay Act 1970

This Act requires employers to give equal treatment regarding terms and conditions of employment to men and women if:

(a) they are employed on like work; or
(b) they are employed on work of equal value (*see* 21:15).

16. Maternity pay

Under the Employment Protection (Consolidation) Act 1978,

a woman who has had at least two years' service with an employer must not be dismissed because of her pregnancy unless she is unfit to do her normal job and suitable alternative work cannot be found. In most circumstances she will receive maternity pay at the standard rate for a period not exceeding eighteen weeks, but if she has had at least two years' service with the company, has continued to work up to the eleventh week before the baby is due and has given her employer at least three weeks' written notice of absence, she will receive for the first six weeks of absence maternity pay at a higher rate, i.e. nine-tenths of her normal pay. After six weeks she will receive (for not more than twelve weeks) maternity pay at the standard rate.

If the woman is qualified to receive maternity pay at the higher rate she also has the right to her former job (or a similar one) if she informs the employer in writing of her wish to return within 29 weeks after the baby's birth. She must also, if requested by her employer not later than 49 days after confinement, confirm in writing that she intends to return, and whether requested or not provide a further confirmation 21 days before she proposes to return. Complaints about these provisions may be made to an industrial tribunal.

17. Guarantee payments

The Employment Protection (Consolidation) Act 1978 also gives employees, who have been laid off or put on short time because of a shortage of work, the right to continue to receive pay for a limited period, i.e. for up to five days in any period of three months. Many employers have made agreements with their employees which provide for guarantee payments more favourable than this.

18. Suspension on medical grounds

Employees who are suspended under certain health and safety regulations because their health is endangered are entitled under the Employment Protection (Consolidation) Act 1978 to receive a normal week's pay for every week they are suspended up to a maximum of 26 weeks. An employee will lose the right to this pay if he or she unreasonably refuses to do any suitable alternative work that the employer offers.

Progress test 22

1. Name possible extra payments a manual worker may receive in addition to a basic wage. **(2)**

2. What must a company do when it introduces a payment by results scheme for the first time? **(3)**

3. What are the main advantages and disadvantages of PBR? **(4, 5)**

4. For what kinds of job is a group bonus scheme particularly suitable? **(6)**

5. Define measured daywork and state why it is sometimes introduced to replace PBR. **(8)**

6. State the main provisions of the Wages Act 1986. **(10)**

7. How does a salary differ from a wage? **(1, 2, 11, 12)**

8. What is an incremental salary scale? **(13)**

9. Summarise the Equal Pay Act 1970. **(15)**

23
Safety and conditions of employment

Safety

1. Accidents at work

Figures issued by the Department of Employment indicate that the number of fatal accidents occurring at work currently averages between 500 and 600 per annum, and that each year there are approximately 300 to 400 thousand serious industrial accidents. The cost of accidents at work is enormous, both in human suffering and in lost production, and the management of every company should give special attention to improving safety.

2. Safety programmes

As the concept of accident proneness is now largely discredited (*see* 6:7–8), safety programmes concentrate as far as possible on ensuring that the employee is suitable for the job and that work is conducted in a safe environment. The following are often included in a safety programme.

(a) *Thorough investigation of all accidents*, to try to prevent the same accident occurring again. Therefore a system of reporting all accidents is required; in some companies near misses as well as actual accidents have to be reported.

(b) *Continuous review of accident prevention measures*, bringing them up to date particularly when there is a change in process or materials, and ensuring that machines are guarded, gangways kept clear, electrical equipment insulated, etc.

(c) *Careful selection of new employees* to eliminate those who are physically or mentally unsuitable.

(d) *Training which includes safety as an integral part* rather than as an afterthought.

(e) *Safety devices and clothing* which are acceptable to employees; if they hinder the performance of the job or make the wearer feel clumsy and conspicuous, they will not be worn.

(f) *Consideration of the possible effect of PBR schemes on safety.* If workers frequently remove safety guards or adopt dangerous practices in order to earn high bonuses it may be necessary to abandon PBR and pay time rates only if the company can find no way of making the process completely safe.

(g) *Propaganda campaigns*, e.g. posters, safety suggestion weeks, etc., are sometimes used, but there is general agreement that their effects are short-lived.

(h) *Provision of adequate first-aid and medical services* to mitigate the effects of any accidents which occur.

3. Safety officers

Some employers have appointed a safety officer, but safety officers are compulsory on construction sites above a certain size.

The effectiveness of a safety officer depends on the following:

(a) The speed and completeness of the accident reporting system;
(b) relations with shopfloor workers and supervisors;
(c) his or her technical knowledge and training;
(d) above all, the extent to which he or she is supported by, and can influence, the senior management of the company.

4. Law regarding safety

The Health and Safety at Work, etc. Act 1974 covers not only all people at work (except domestic workers in private employment) but also the general public who might be affected by the work of others. It is mainly an enabling measure, laying down general principles of safety and providing the power to make detailed safety regulations. For the time being the previously existing safety legislation continues in force, in particular the Factories Act 1961 and the Offices, Shops and Railway Premises Act 1963.

The most important general duties laid down by the 1974 Act are as follows.

(a) Employers must maintain safe plant, safe systems of work and safe premises. They must also ensure adequate training and supervision in safety matters.

(b) A written company safety policy must be prepared and made known to all employees. Employers must let employees know the arrangements for putting that policy into effect.

(c) A company must be conducted in such a way that the health and safety of persons not in employment there are not affected.

(d) Manufacturers and suppliers of articles for use at work must ensure that they are safe when properly used.

(e) Employees have a duty to take responsible care to avoid injury to themselves or to others, and they must co-operate with employers in meeting statutory requirements.

(f) Safety representatives from among the employees may be appointed by recognised trade unions. They must be consulted by the employer on health and safety matters, they may inspect the employer's premises, and they have the right to be informed by the safety inspectors of any matters found to affect health and safety. If at least two safety representatives require it, the employer must set up a safety committee.

> NOTE: The Health and Safety Commission recommend that in companies where trade unions are not recognised, a safety committee should nevertheless be set up consisting of members drawn from management and employees. The employee representatives on such a committee would not have the rights of inspection and information described above.

5. Accident reports

There are government regulations which compel employers to report all serious accidents (and other accidents involving more than three days' absence from work) within seven days. Approved report forms may be purchased from commercial stationers or from HMSO (form F 2508). Records of accidents, dangerous occurrences and outbreaks of certain specified industrial diseases have to be kept for at least three years.

Accident reports are useful for identifying and preventing the recurrence of dangerous activities. Also, formal records are needed to investigate subsequent claims for compensation from injured employees. Every firm employing more than nine persons, or less than nine if the firm is covered by the Factories Act, is legally obliged to keep an accident book. Reports should be completed as quickly as possible after the incident (before memories fade) and give full details of the victim (age, sex, occupation, etc.) and of the accident (time, date, circumstances). It should list witnesses, describe the injuries sustained, first aid administered and note whether (and if so when) an ambulance was called and when it arrived and departed. The cause of the accident should be stated, with details of whether safety rules were followed, whether protective clothing was actually worn, machinery properly guarded, etc.

Copies of the report should be circulated to the worker and his or her union, to safety representatives and to the personnel department. Collectively, accident reports should be analysed to identify recurring causes and the effects of changes in machinery, working methods, paces of production, shift work pattern, etc. on the frequency of accidents.

6. The Health and Safety Commission

This was set up under the Act to develop health and safety policies. It consists of representatives of employers, employees, local government and appropriate professional bodies. The Commission's policies are operated by the Health and Safety Executive, which enforces the relevant legislation and inspects premises. The separate inspectorate, which previously existed under various safety Acts, are now combined in one body under the Executive.

7. Enforcement

If an inspector discovers a contravention of the Act, one of the previous Acts or a safety regulation he or she may do one of the following.

(a) *Issue a prohibition notice*, requiring the employer to stop a process which carries the risk of serious personal injury until remedial action has been taken.

(b) *Issue an improvement notice*, requiring the employer who contravenes a statutory provision to remedy matters within a certain time. Appeals against an improvement notice or a prohibition notice may be made to an industrial tribunal.

(c) *Seize, render harmless or destroy* any substance or article that is considered a cause of imminent danger or serious personal injury.

(d) *Prosecute* any person contravening a relevant statutory provision, in addition to or instead of serving a notice as in (a) and

(b) above. For most offences a fine is levied, but serious cases may be prosecuted on indictment in the Crown Court, with the possibility of an unlimited fine or imprisonment for up to two years. The powers given under the Act to prosecute a person rather than a company apply not only to a director or manager but also to any employee who does not co-operate in safety matters for his or her own or for colleagues' protection.

8. Compensation for accidents at work

An injured employee who considers his or her injury to be due to the negligence of the employer may bring an action for damages against that person under common law. The employer is also held liable for accidents caused to employees by the action of other employees, provided that this behaviour was in the course of their employment. If the employee's action is successful he or she will be awarded a lump sum depending mainly on the severity of the injury. The Employers' Liability (Compulsory Insurance) Act 1969 requires employers to take out insurance against such claims.

Legal claims of this kind are independent of any action a health and safety inspector may bring against the employer, though of course if the inspector has taken action as in **7**, the claimant's case will be greatly strengthened.

Working conditions

9. Hours of work

Manual workers in most companies work longer hours than non-manual workers, partly because they are expected by custom to start earlier in the morning and partly because they do more overtime. Statistics published by the Department of Employment show that on average, male manual employees work about seven hours a week longer than male non-manual, and female manual employees about three hours a week more than female non-manual.

10. Overtime

A company asks its employees to work overtime for the following reasons:

(a) to maintain production when there is a shortage of labour;
(b) to increase production temporarily or seasonally without increasing the number of employees;
(c) to enable maintenance to be carried out on plant and equipment while its users are not working.

Therefore, when properly managed, overtime can add considerably to the efficiency of the company. Research shows, however, that much overtime is worked not in response to one of the above needs but as a means of supplementing employees' incomes. It then becomes an inefficient practice because factory services have to be maintained beyond normal working hours for no gain in production.

Some companies have reduced or abolished overtime by negotiating with their employees a higher basic rate of pay so that earnings without overtime become approximately the same as total earnings were previously. A salaried worker is often not paid for overtime; when this is the case, the rate is usually plain time or a very low premium rate.

11. Shift work

During the last 30 years, no doubt because expensive capital equipment now being used must be continuously operated to cover its costs, there has been a steady increase in shift work, i.e. an arrangement in which one set of workers takes over from another to enable the production process to continue operating without a break.

It takes the form either of 'double day shifts' in which there are two successive shifts but no night shift, or three shift working, in which the process continues for the 24 hours without a break.

Three shift working can bring the following problems.

(a) Supervisors require special training because management is not there to support them outside normal working hours.
(b) An incoming shift frequently blames an outgoing shift for bad work, an untidy workplace, etc.
(c) Canteens, first aid and security services must be provided.
(d) Machinery may break down more frequently because it is in constant use.

(e) Travelling to and from work by public transport is often difficult at shift change-over times.

Shift work, moreover, can cause significant problems to the individual employee, including:

(a) disruption of biological rhythms (adrenalin secretions, sleep/waking patterns, body temperature, etc.);
(b) reductions in the quantity and quality of sleep, accompanied by constant tiredness;
(c) digestion problems and possible loss of appetite;
(d) disruptions of family life, anxieties about child care, social isolation and worsening social relationships.

Shift workers, on average, have more severe accidents than others, and the quality of their output is sometimes poor.

12. Flexible working hours

A comparatively new development, sometimes called flextime or flexitime, allows employees to choose within limits what hours they work. Schemes differ in detail, but they frequently contain the following features.

(a) Employees must all be present during a certain part of the day, usually called *coretime*, e.g. from 10 a.m. to 12 noon and from 2 p.m. to 4 p.m.
(b) They may choose when they arrive or leave within limits set by the company, e.g. not before 8 a.m. or after 7 p.m.
(c) They may vary the length of the lunch break.
(d) Hours worked in excess of the standard total for the accounting period (usually a month) may be taken on whole or half-day holidays.

The advantages claimed for the system are that it improves employee satisfaction by giving considerable freedom for individuals to arrange their hours to suit their own circumstances, that it reduces absenteeism and that it enables the place of work to be staffed outside the usual hours. On the other hand, lighting and heating will cost more, and those employees who attend early or late may not be able to work normally because other people on whom they depend are not there.

Fringe benefits

13. Definition

A fringe benefit is a reward to an employee apart from a wage or salary. It usually provides, at the expense of the employer, goods or services which the employee would otherwise have to pay for him or herself. The most important fringe benefits are described below.

14. Company pension schemes

The development of company (or occupational) pension schemes in this country has two main characteristics.

(a) Far more non-manual workers are covered than manual.
(b) Individual schemes vary widely in their contributions, conditions and benefits, manual workers' schemes in general being inferior to those for non-manual workers.

Since April 1988 all employees have had the right to choose whether they wish to stay in a company pension scheme, and it is no longer possible for an employer to insist that a worker belong to a particular scheme as a condition of employment. Thus, workers (especially young workers who are likely to change companies frequently) can elect for a personal private pension rather than a company specific plan. Note, however, that company pensions will remain the best choice for very many employees because they usually offer attractive benefits and the employer adds a significant amount on top of the worker's contribution.

15. Sick pay

Most non-manual workers receive payment from their employers when they are absent from work through illness; a lower proportion of manual workers do so. In most cases the benefits provided by sick pay schemes for non-manual workers are superior to those for manual workers. There seems to be no difference in the amount of sickness absence between employees who are covered by a sick pay scheme and those who are not.

Employers' sick pay schemes are, of course, additional to the sickness benefits provided by the state. These are governed by the Social Security and Housing Benefits Act 1982 and require employers to remit statutory sick pay (SSP) to workers for up to twenty-eight weeks. The firm pays the SSP to the employee and then reclaims 80 per cent of this from the DHSS (except for small firms, which may reclaim 100 per cent).

16. Subsidised meals
A very large number of companies either provide meals on their premises at less than cost price or give their employees vouchers for full or part payment of meals in restaurants.

17. Company goods at a discount
Employees of companies which are either manufacturers or traders often have the opportunity to buy goods at reduced prices. A similar practice is the reduction in fares offered to their employees by railways and airlines.

18. Company cars
The use of a car is necessary in some jobs, e.g. sales representative, and when the company, as it often does, allows the employee to use the car for private purposes it adds considerably to the employee's real income, even though it is subject to income tax. The value and prestige of having a company car makes this fringe benefit probably the most highly prized of all.

19. Characteristics of fringe benefits
The following are the most important characteristics of fringe benefits.

(a) They are not related to merit but they often improve with status and length of service.
(b) They do not necessarily benefit all employees, e.g. the person who has good health or who does not need company products.
(c) They are not established or amended after rational analysis but follow fashion or moral principles.
(d) They are not universal; large companies usually have a wide range of benefits while small companies tend to have very few.
(e) Once established they are difficult to abolish and become accepted by the employees as a normal condition of service rather than a benefit.
(f) There is no evidence that candidates are attracted to a

company by its fringe benefits, but it is possible that fringe benefits discourage employees from leaving.

(g) They probably increase job satisfaction, but will certainly bring about dissatisfaction if they are inconsistently and carelessly administered, giving rise to accusations of favouritism, unfairness or meanness.

20. Employee welfare

Workers' morale and feelings of attachment to an employing organisation may be greatly enhanced through the provision of welfare services. Examples of such services are:

(a) payment by the employer of subscriptions for employees' membership of private medical schemes;

(b) provision of a welfare officer able to counsel employees in relation to their private problems (including bereavement and retirement counselling);

(c) occupational health screening;

(d) social and recreational facilities;

(e) having a company lawyer provide free legal advice to employees in approved circumstances;

(f) rehabilitation schemes for injured workers;

(g) availability of company loans to workers, benevolent funds and the provision of financial help with housing or transport costs.

Staff status for manual workers

21. Equalising status

In recent years some companies have begun to employ manual workers on the same conditions of service as non-manual, showing that they regard them as having the same status. The most important effects on manual workers' conditions are as follows.

(a) Fringe benefits, particularly pensions and sick pay, are improved.

(b) Hours of work are shortened.

(c) Control becomes less strict; for example, manual workers are no longer required to clock on.

(d) A salary is paid instead of a wage, though often the employees prefer it to be paid weekly rather than monthly.

(e) Overtime is paid at a lower rate; the natural resistance to this change is often dealt with by a simultaneous productivity agreement which abolishes or greatly reduces the amount of overtime worked (*see* **10**).

22. Benefits

The following reasons are often given for equalising status.

(a) In many companies improvements in work methods have made the boundary between manual and non-manual employees much less distinct.
(b) Staff status will reduce labour turnover among manual workers.
(c) Jealousies between manual and non-manual workers will be reduced.
(d) Industrial relations within the company will be improved.

The last three reasons are hopes rather than certainties because deep-rooted attitudes cannot change rapidly. A much more important reason is the belief that it is morally wrong and logically indefensible to treat manual workers in an inferior way.

Suggestions

23. Procedure

Many companies have formal arrangements to encourage their employees to submit suggestions regarding efficiency, safety or welfare. It is usual to have a committee consisting of representatives of managers and employees to assess the suggestions and recommend whether they should be adopted, perhaps after taking expert advice. The originator of a successful suggestion receives an award.

24. Benefits of suggestion schemes

(a) The company may be able to use more efficient methods.
(b) There may be fewer accidents.
(c) New uses may be found for scrap.
(d) Two-way communication is encouraged.
(e) Use is made of the employees' ingenuity and creativity.

(f) The recognition of these qualities will give the employees greater job satisfaction.

25. Problems of suggestion schemes

Interest in a suggestion scheme will flag unless the management actively encourages it. Steps which may be taken are:

(a) publicity for every successful suggestion, perhaps with a circulated description and photograph of the formal presentation of the award;

(b) occasional suggestion campaigns asking for ideas to solve specific problems;

(c) generous awards, e.g. 25 per cent of annual savings;

(d) careful treatment of unsuccessful suggestors, i.e. full explanations of the reasons for rejection;

(e) a scrupulously fair procedure for assessing suggestions;

(f) a convenient channel through which suggestions can be submitted, e.g. a suggestions box.

Maintaining a lively suggestions scheme is expensive in time and money but many companies have found that the ideas which have come forward bring financial benefits which outweigh the expense many times.

Justice

26. The importance of justice

Personnel policies and procedures designed to utilise, motivate and protect the human resources of a company will fail unless they are perceived by the employees to be just and fair in themselves and applied in a just and fair way. Justice in this context will provide:

(a) similar treatment to employees in similar circumstances;

(b) greater rewards to those who merit them or are particularly deserving;

(c) the opportunities to express an opinion which management will consider and possibly act on.

Job satisfaction is reduced and industrial relations deteriorate when employees perceive injustice and unfairness in company personnel policies and the way in which they are applied.

27. Fair procedures
Injustice will be minimised if the following conditions are observed.

(a) Job and personnel specifications are accurate and unbiased; performance standards, if set, are reasonable.
(b) New employees are not engaged at rates of pay higher than those received by present employees doing the same work, or offered exceptional privileges.
(c) Promotion, transfer, demotion and retirement policies are open and uniformly applied.
(d) Dismissal procedures (including those for redundancy) are clearly defined and if possible negotiated with employee representatives.
(e) Appraisal schemes give employees the opportunity to discuss their progress with their manager.
(f) Selection for training is regarded as a reward rather than a punishment.
(g) Rates of pay are appropriate to the job and to the individual employee, i.e. they are based on job evaluation, with recognition to the individual by means of a well-maintained payment by results scheme, merit rating or length of service increments.
(h) Fringe benefits and working conditions are applied uniformly.
(i) Communications are two-way in all appropriate circumstances and participation is used where practicable.
(j) Disciplinary procedures are carefully applied, beginning with the disciplinary interview (*see* 5:**20–21**). There are warnings and provisions for appeal, and penalties are not disproportionate to the offence or capriciously applied. The Code of Practice published by the Advisory, Conciliation and Arbitration Service gives useful guidance here.

Disparities between departments in the treatment of e.g. time-keeping, pay increases or leave of absence cause great resentment. Departmental managers have the difficult task of dealing with their subordinates in ways consistent with those elsewhere in the company yet responsive to the circumstances of individuals.

Progress test 23

1.   Outline a safety programme suitable for a manufacturing company.   **(2)**

2.   What duties regarding safety does an employer have under the Health and Safety at Work, etc. Act?   **(4)**

3.   Name the benefits of overtime working to an employer.   **(10)**

4.   What problems are found in three shift working?   **(11)**

5.   Name the most important fringe benefits.   **(13–18)**

6.   In what ways do fringe benefits differ from wages and salaries?   **(19)**

7.   What benefits does a company hope to obtain from giving staff status to its manual workers?   **(21–22)**

8.   What are the benefits of suggestion schemes?   **(24)**

9.   Give some examples of the importance of justice in personnel procedures.   **(26, 27)**

24
EC dimensions of personnel management

1. Introduction

British membership of the EC affects personnel management in several important areas, particularly *vis-à-vis* possibilities for the cross-border recruitment of employees (*see* **2**); new training requirements (*see* **3–4**); redundancy (*see* **9**); and Community proposals for compulsory employee participation in management decision making, including worker directors (*see* **12**) on the boards of large firms.

Community law on matters pertaining to personnel management overrides UK legislation, and comes in three forms: Regulations, Directives and Decisions.

(a) *Regulations* are precise laws that apply immediately and equally in all member states.

(b) *Directives* are edicts which specify a necessary outcome (e.g. to have equal pay for work of equal value completed by men and women) but then allow each Community member to introduce its own specific legislation to achieve the desired objective.

(c) *Decisions* are rulings of the European Court of Justice on test cases, and have the same effect as Regulations.

Additionally, *Draft Directives* are issued. These are proposals of the European Commission, accepted in principle by most EC nations, but not yet implemented in consequence of opposition by one or more Community members. A number of Draft Directives will profoundly affect UK personnel management if they become binding, particularly those concerning part-time workers (*see* **14**), night and shift work (*see* **16**), and employee representation on the boards of large companies.

It follows that the personnel manager of the future will require:

(a) European perspectives;

(b) a working knowledge of all EC Regulations and Directives affecting personnel management;

(c) awareness of the implications of Draft Directives which, if adopted, will significantly alter personnel management practice;

(d) knowledge of EC training and recruitment opportunities, particularly in areas affected by domestic skills shortages;

(e) the capacity to understand and manage a multinational EC workforce;

(f) the ability to devise and implement training programmes to develop employees' skills and competencies in certain fields; notably in language training, export marketing and administration, European logistics, knowledge of EC markets and business methods, etc.;

(g) the ability to assess the skill levels and capacities of job applicants from other EC countries.

2. Cross-border recruitment

A major consequence of the Single Market is that EC citizens may freely reside in any Community country of their choice and seek employment in that state. They are entitled to unemployment and retirement benefit in the nation of their employment, and to equal access to public housing and education for their children on a par with local workers. Free mobility of labour makes possible the recruitment of workers from other EC countries, particularly of workers possessing skills and competencies not available locally. This will lead to the following consequences.

(a) Personnel managers will require knowledge of recruitment practices in various EC countries and need to be familiar with:

    (*i*) pan-European job advertising media capable of reaching good quality foreign EC workers;

    (*ii*) levels of pay and conditions of service necessary to attract high calibre Continental applicants;

    (*iii*) foreign EC educational and other qualifications.

(b) Possibilities for training staff *via* courses held in other EC countries, especially for training in European business practices, European transport and distribution systems, negotiation and tendering procedures in various EC states, etc.

(c) Community-wide headhunting (*see* 14:12).

Cross-border recruitment can occur through placing job advertisements in foreign newspapers or trade magazines, personal recommendations from foreign business contacts (such as suppliers, customers or banks), extension of a firm's 'milk-round' to include Continental educational institutions, and by taking foreign EC students for sandwich-course or other work-experience placements.

3. Euro-executives

These are multi-lingual managers who feel at home in any European Community country, are familiar with EC business laws and practices, and regularly move between companies and countries. Qualities of Euro-executives include:

(a) cultural adaptability, i.e. the ability to blend quickly into the local culture of any EC member nation;

(b) wide-ranging experience of European business management resulting from several changes of jobs and location;

(c) possession of generalist rather than function-specific management competencies;

(d) ability to communicate effectively and to exercise interpersonal management skills;

(e) knowledge of individual EC markets;

(f) selling and negotiating skills, and the ability to conduct hostile negotiations in more than one language;

(g) familiarity with EC product standards;

(h) knowledge of the documentation and procedures attached to cross-border EC marketing, including those needed for transport and distribution across the Community;

(i) willingness and ability to cope with rapid technical, organisational and environmental change;

(j) capacity to get on with fellow workers of different nationalities and to contribute to multinational project teams;

(k) acceptance of a lifestyle involving much foreign travel, frequent relocation and disruptions to normal family routines.

Problems attached to the employment and use of Euro-executives are as follows.

(a) Their high salaries (resulting from their short supply) which create large differentials between Euro-executives and other managers. Euro-executives are hired in consequence of their superior competencies and will demand remuneration packages comparable to those available in other countries. Additionally, they could demand compensation for the high cost of accommodation in prosperous areas (London, for instance), for the cost of sending children to private schools that cater for a particular nationality, and for the loss of a spouse's earnings.

(b) Fitting them into conventional line and staff organisation systems, which might stifle their initiative and creativity.

(c) A high probability of their being headhunted (*see* **14:12**) by other firms.

(d) Their lack of intimate knowledge of their employing companies and associated products or of the local economy and local business cultures. Euro-executives might not stay in a country long enough to develop networks of contacts with local business people, banks, ancillary services, etc.

(e) Possible conflicts arising from different approaches to business adopted by Euro-executives compared to locally-recruited managers.

Euro-executives, moreover, could experience significant domestic problems that might reduce their usefulness to employing firms, for example:

(a) reluctance to accept a fresh assignment in another EC country because the manager's children have only just settled into a local school;

(b) opposition to an intended move from the manager's spouse, who may regard it as interference with his or her own career;

(c) traumas and tribulations attached to regularly moving house and resettling in other cultures;

(d) practical problems connected with finding suitable housing, arranging for pension transfers, tax arrangements, etc.

4. Higher Education Diplomas (HEDs)

These are professional qualifications obtained after at least three years' study and recognised in all EC countries. Their purpose is to facilitate the mobility of professionally-qualified workers within the Community. In the past, member states restricted the right of entry to certain professions (e.g. accountancy, law, medicine) to persons who studied and qualified within their own national territories. HEDs, however, should enable these restrictions to be lifted. The training, examination and other requirements for specific professions are being harmonised across member states, and anyone possessing the appropriate HED will be free to practise his or her profession in any Community country (although some 'topping-up' of qualifications may be required in certain specified circumstances). Accordingly, professionally-qualified people will be able to offer their services on a European scale, possibly resulting in:

(a) greater competitiveness among professionals, and an increased supply of professionals in job markets offering the highest reward;
(b) recruiting companies advertising for professionally qualified staff throughout the Community;
(c) rapid transmission among professionals in different countries of new ideas and working methods.

Moreover, a number of Directives are in force which compel member states to recognise 'Certificates of Experience' relating to experience obtained in a particular industry in another member state and issued by the authorities of that country.

Legal obligations*

5. Equal rights for men and women

Perhaps the most significant of EC interventions in the personnel field lies in its continued promotion of (gender) equal opportunities. Article 119 of the Treaty of Rome demanded equal pay for equal work, and this (in principle, at least) is mandatory in all member countries. The Council of Ministers has also directed that there shall be equal pension rights and social security benefits for men and women – this has been interpreted by the Court of Justice to mean equal retirement ages for men and women.

6. Health and safety at work

UK health and safety legislation (*see* Chapter 23) is extensive, detailed, and not normally affected by minimum EC standards because UK requirements are generally above these basic levels. Nevertheless, the number of EC Directives concerning health and

---

* *See European Community Law* by P.A. Kent in this series.

safety is increasing rapidly, partly since EC health and safety Directives may be approved by a majority (rather than unanimous) vote of Community members. Already there exist important Directives on visual display units (*see* below), eye protection, the manual lifting of heavy loads, protective equipment, and workplace safety. More are expected soon, possibly increasing the complexity of bureaucratic rules and the costs to employers of complying with health and safety laws.

7. Directive on visual display units

This specifies minimum health and safety requirements for work with display screen equipment. The UK is incorporating the requirements of the Directive *via* amendments to the Health and Safety at Work, etc. Act 1974. Under the Directive, employers must:

(a) analyse display screen workstations to identify potential hazards and take measures to remedy any health and safety problem discovered;

(b) train employees in the proper use of display screen equipment, inform workers of relevant facts, and consult employee representatives about VDU matters;

(c) plan VDU operators' daily schedules in order to interrupt long periods of screen work and to create changes of activity;

(d) ensure that workstations satisfy the technical requirements of the Directive in relation to screen sizes and luminosity, keyboard design, working environment, etc.

(e) provide employees with eye and eyesight tests prior to their commencing VDU work and at regular intervals thereafter. Firms must supply special spectacles if employees' normal spectacles are not suitable for display screen jobs.

8. The Framework Directive

In addition to *specific* Directives on health and safety, the Community enacted in 1989 a 'Framework Directive' which contained a statement of *general principles* concerning the protection of employees' health and safety at work. It obliged employers to take 'appropriate measures' to satisfy these principles, according to detailed rules imposed by national authorities. Under the Framework Directive, employers must ensure the prevention of occupational risks, eliminate dangers, inform and consult with workers, and invite the 'balanced participation' of employee representatives when dealing with health and safety matters. The British government considers the UK Health and Safety at Work, etc. Act 1974 to meet the essential requirements of the Framework Directive.

9. Directive on mass redundancies

This 1975 Directive requires that companies give prior notification of group redundancies scheduled for implementation over a period of 30 days or less. Additionally, consultation with employee representatives concerning the mechanics of imposing large-scale redundancies and on measures for avoiding them (e.g. through natural wastage or redeployment) is required. All the provisions of the Directive were embodied in the UK Employment Protection Act 1975, and in the Employment Protection (Consolidation) Act 1978 (which actually go considerably further than the Directive demands (*see* 16:**11**)).

10. Directive on safeguarding employees' rights following the transfer of ownership of undertakings

The purpose of this Directive is to protect employees' rights and to compel management to inform and consult with employee representatives on the transfer of the ownership of a business. General information about the transfer must be disclosed, plus specific facts regarding its effects (redundancies, for example) on particular groups of workers. Information must be transmitted early enough to permit proper discussions with employee representatives to occur. Employees' terms and conditions of service cannot be altered at the time of transfer, and workers may only be declared redundant if this can be objectively justified at the moment the business changes hands. If redundancies are necessary, the new owner *automatically* assumes full responsibility for making statutory redundancy payments (*see* 16:**11**) to the people involved.

11. Directive on the protection of employees following an employer's insolvency

All the requirements of this 1990 Directive had already been incorporated into domestic UK legislation by the time of its implementation. The Directive obliges the state to pay to workers dismissed in consequence of an employing firm's insolvency all outstanding maternity pay, holiday pay for up to six weeks accumulated over the previous twelve months, up to eight weeks' arrears of wages, amounts due as compensation for redundancy or unfair dismissal, and pay for employees' statutory minimum periods of notice.

Directives not yet unanimously agreed

12. Draft Directive V on company law

The laws of certain EC countries (Germany, for instance) require large companies to have two boards of directors: an 'executive board' consisting of managerial employees responsible for tactics and operational management and, above that, a 'supervisory board' which takes strategic decisions. Importantly, elected worker directors must by law be invited to sit on supervisory boards in these countries.

Originally, this proposed Directive would have required all EC companies employing more than 1,000 people to set up a two-tier board of directors with compulsory employee representation on the supervisory board, or worker participation in management through a separate 'works council' with representation on the board, or an equivalent body established by collective agreement (provided the body affords at least the same rights as alternative devices). However, the Draft was subsequently amended to offer companies the option of a single board with a majority of non-executive directors (empowered to appoint and dismiss executive directors) instead of having a two-tier board. Between one-third and one-half of a single or supervisory board would consist of employee representatives.

Objections to the Draft Directive have included the following.

(a) It could jeopardise the 'voluntarist' tradition of UK industrial relations.

(b) Conflicts might be created between agreements reached by worker and other directors at the board level, and settlements concluded *via* plant level collective bargaining in divisions and subsidiaries of the firm.

(c) Companies operating in several EC countries would experience severe practical problems resulting from their boards having to include employee representatives from several countries, speaking different languages (thus requiring the presence of interpreters at board meetings), from widely disparate trade union backgrounds, and with contrasting cultural perspectives.

(d) Businesses affected by the Directive would need to train employee representatives in the principles of management, company structure, finance, market environments, etc. in order to enable them to understand board-room discussions.

(e) Agendas of board meetings could become dominated by personnel management and industrial relations issues, at the expense of considering strategic and operational matters.

13. Draft Directive on employee information (the 'Vredeling' proposal)

This would require that each year the managements of firms with more than 1,000 workers give to employee representatives information on their overall employing organisations, plus specific information on their own subsidiaries or establishments. Information provided would need to include details of company structure, the firm's financial situation and its demand for labour, intended major new investments, and current trends in sales and production. Also, managements would have to consult employee representatives about decisions likely to have serious consequences for workers' interests. At least 30 days' notice of intended changes in working practices or plant closures would be necessary, and during this period 'adequate consultation' with workers would have to take place.

In February 1991 the Commission drafted a further proposal concerning consultation with employees, suggesting that companies with more than 1,000 workers in total and which employ at least 100 people in any two or more EC states should be obliged to establish works councils at the request of management or employee representatives. Councils would meet at least once a year and would have to be consulted about any management proposal with serious implications for workers' interests.

14. Draft Directive on part-time employees

The Commission is anxious to improve the employment rights and terms and conditions of employment of part-time workers. Accordingly, the Draft Directive on this matter provides for:

(a) wages for part-timers that are strictly proportional to wage levels paid to full-time workers doing the same work;

(b) equal access to vocational training;

(c) making it unlawful to discriminate unfairly against part-timers when selecting employees for promotion;

(d) equal access to occupational pension schemes;

(e) equal rights in relation to health and safety at work;

(f) proportional entitlement to paid holidays, sick pay, redundancy and retirement benefits;

(g) the right of part-timers to claim unfair dismissal (*see* 16:9) on the same basis as full-time workers.

The proposal applies to all part-timers working at least eight hours a week. An employer intending to use part-time (or temporary) workers would have to inform employee representatives about this in good time. Employers would also be required to advise part-time (and temporary) workers of any permanent full-time vacancies that arose.

Similar provisions apply to a Draft Directive on temporary and fixed-contract workers, who would become entitled to social security benefits identical to those of permanent employees. Individuals engaged under temporary contracts would have to be informed of the reasons for their being on temporary rather than permanent contracts. Additionally, the client companies of employment agencies would be made liable for the pay and national insurance contributions of temporary agency workers following an employment agency's collapse. All EC health and safety legislation would apply equally to full-time, part-time and temporary workers.

Objections to these Draft Directives have included the following.

(a) Many part-timers work this way through preference rather than inability to find full-time jobs. Extension of employment protections to part-time workers will reduce the number of firms willing to engage such employees, thus lessening the availability of part-time work.

(b) The cost of employing part-timers will increase dramatically if the proposal becomes law; leading to lower international competitiveness of UK firms. In particular, the Directive would oblige employers to pay national insurance for *all* workers employed more than eight hours a week, including those earning less than the current NI threshold. Up to two million UK workers could be affected by this change.

15. Draft Directive on the protection of pregnant women
This 1990 proposal provides for the following.

(a) Employers would have to adapt a pregnant employee's hours, duties and/or working conditions, without loss of pay, in order to ensure her health and safety.

(b) Pregnant employees normally engaged on night work would need to be given alternative day jobs for a 16-week period, of which eight weeks must be prior to the expected date of birth of the child.

(c) fourteen weeks' maternity leave on 100 per cent pay would be available to pregnant workers, with no loss of employment rights (including the right to reinstatement). Two weeks of the leave must be immediately before the expected date of birth.

(d) Pregnant employees would be protected from dismissal on the grounds of pregnancy, regardless of their lengths of service.

(e) Exposure of pregnant women to certain harmful substances and physical risks would be outlawed.

16. Draft Directive on night and night shift-working
This would impose statutory daily and weekly rest periods on night workers plus controls on the amounts of overtime they are allowed to complete. Under the proposal, night workers would not normally be able to work more than eight hours in any 24-hour period, and overtime would not be permitted without special permission (if permission is granted, the overtime working must not last more than six months).

Nightworkers would be entitled to free medical examinations prior to starting night shifts, and periodically thereafter. Also, they should be given additional time off to compensate for their unsocial hours, must have a daily rest period of at least eleven *consecutive* hours, and at least one day off work each week.

Objections to the proposal have included the following.

(a) Rest breaks within a shift might be unworkable in continuous process operations where plant cannot be left unattended.

(b) Opportunities for overtime could be an important incentive necessary to induce employees to accept night-shift working.

(c) Overtime night-shift working is a convenient means whereby firms facing labour shortages can satisfy short-term increases in the demands for their products.

17. Contracts of employment

A Draft Directive of February 1991 suggests that employers be required to issue to workers written contracts of employment (*see* 16:1) within one month of their recruitment, provided they work more than eight hours a week.

The social framework

18. The social dimension of the European Single Market

A major requisite of the Treaty of Rome is that EC countries actively seek to raise the living standards of their citizens. Measures adopted to achieve this aim are collectively known as the 'social dimension' policies of the EC. Such policies include:

(a) job creation and training schemes;

(b) equal opportunities programmes;

(c) provision of information on opportunities for employment and training;

(d) legislation on industrial health and safety.

19. The European Social Charter

In December 1989 the European Council voted by eleven to one (the UK being the dissenting member) for the adoption of a Community Charter of fundamental social rights. The effect of this 'Social Charter' would be to establish uniform employment conditions throughout the Community, including matters relating to remuneration, training, living and working conditions, access to company information, consultation, and participation in management decision making. The philosophy underlying the Charter is the belief that the Single Market will only succeed if both sides of industry (employers and labour) are fully involved in creating a new united Europe.

It is important to note that under the Single European Act 1987 (which amended the Treaty of Rome so as to facilitate the rapid completion of the Single Market), any proposal regarding employee rights and interests, and/or the free movement of people, requires unanimous agreement among member nations before it becomes legally binding. Accordingly, acceptance of the Social Charter is *voluntary*, and may not be imposed on a Community state against its wishes. The Charter itself would guarantee individual rights to the following.

(a) Fair remuneration. This would involve the specification of rules for establishing a fair wage.

(b) Health, protection and safety at the workplace.

(c) Access to vocational training throughout a person's working life, including the right to retraining.

(d) Freedom of association and collective bargaining, i.e. to belong or not belong to a trade union and for unions to have the right to bargain with employing firms.

(e) Integration into working life of disabled people. The provision of training for the disabled, accessibility to work premises, availability of special transport, and explicit consideration of disabled people during the ergonomic design of equipment.

(f) Information, consultation and worker participation in company decision making, especially in enterprises that operate in more than one Community country.

(g) Freedom of occupation, residence and movement of workers, including equal treatment *vis-à-vis* local taxes and social security entitlements.

(h) Improvement in living and working conditions. This embraces equality of treatment for part-time and temporary workers (*see* **14**), controls on night working (*see* **16**), and requirements for weekly rest periods and paid holidays.

(i) Social protection, including adequate unemployment and other social security benefits.

(j) Equal treatment of men and women.

(k) Protection of young people, with a minimum working age of 15 years (16 for full-time employment) and a ban on night work for those under 18.

(l) Reasonable living standards for senior citizens, with a specified minimum income underwritten by the state.

20. Advantages and problems of the Social Charter

Implementation of the Charter will create a social partnership between the two sides of industry and will improve social cohesion within the Community, hence raising living standards and the skill levels of workers and greatly contributing to increased productivity.

Some of the subjects dealt with in the Charter are already covered by existing EC Directives, but the Charter will pull together into a unified whole a variety of currently fragmented employment and social policies.

If adopted, the Charter will be more than a statement of intentions; it will become *legally binding* in all EC states – which will have to legislate to ensure that the rights it embodies are guaranteed within their frontiers. Also, the draft Charter insists that member countries commit themselves to 'mobilise all the resources necessary' to implement its provisions.

Objections to the Social Charter have included the following.

(a) Some of its requirements violate the 'principle of subsidiarity',i.e. the EC's agreed position that laws be imposed at the Community level *only* if social policy objectives *cannot* be achieved *via* government action within each member state.

(b) Matters pertaining to consultation, employee representation, etc. are perhaps best resolved through *voluntary* collective bargaining between employers and trade unions.

(c) The operating costs of certain businesses could increase dramatically following the Charter's implementation, making EC companies uncompetitive compared to companies in Pacific rim countries and the USA.

(d) Application of some of the charter's provisions would necessitate the creation of large bureaucracies within government departments and much administrative inconvenience within firms.

(e) Intervention and control go against the spirit of free enterprise that supposedly underlies the decision to create a Single European Market.

(f) Currently, social protection is greatest in the more affluent Community states. As laws on social protection are harmonised there could be a tendency to 'harmonise upwards' towards higher (and more expensive) common standards, thus imposing unbearable additional costs on poorer EC countries.

Progress test 24

1. Explain the difference between an EC Regulation and an EC Draft Directive. **(1)**

2. What are the characteristics of Euro-executives? **(3)**

3. List the main requirements of the Framework Directive on health and safety in employment. **(8)**

4. How would the adoption of the EC's $\underline{V}$ Draft Directive on company law affect UK enterprises? **(12)**

5. What is the 'Vredeling' proposal? **(13)**

6. Describe the disadvantages of the European Social Charter. **(20)**

25
Personnel records and statistics

Personnel records

1. Purposes
Personnel records provide the following.

(a) A store of up-to-date and accurate information about the company's employees.

(b) A guide to the action to be taken regarding an employee, particularly by comparing the worker with other employees.

(c) A guide when recruiting a new employee, e.g. by showing the rates of pay received by comparable employees.

(d) A historical record of previous action taken regarding employees.

(e) The raw materials for statistics which check and guide personnel policies.

(f) The means to comply with certain statutory requirements, e.g. the Contracts of Employments Act 1972 and the Redundancy Payments Act 1965.

Specific information about individual employees (i.e. their biographical details, training, educational qualifications, disciplinary records, etc.) is called *item* information. Summaries of item information on groups of employees which enable the company to define the general characteristics of various types of workers (e.g. age and sex distributions in certain departments, differences in educational levels between workers in various grades, etc.) is known as *profile* information.

2. Documents
An employee's personnel record begins with the application

form which he or she completes when applying for a job (*see* 14:**15**). To this is added the copy of the letter formally offering the job and the employee's acceptance. These papers are usually put into an envelope or folder which becomes the *personal file*. From time to time other documents are put into the personal file, e.g. appraisal reports, applications for promotion, sickness certificates, etc.

A summary of the information in the personal file is made on an *employee record*, which is set out in such a way that it is easily read and compared with other employee records. It is usually filed departmentally, unlike personal files, which are filed alphabetically.

3. The employee record

The essential details to be included in the employee record are as follows:

(a) Personal data:
- (*i*) name, address and telephone number;
- (*ii*) clock or company number (if any);
- (*iii*) sex;
- (*iv*) date of birth;
- (*v*) marital status;
- (*vi*) disablement registration number (if any).

(b) Company data:
- (*i*) date of joining company;
- (*ii*) past and present departments and dates;
- (*iii*) past and present job titles;
- (*iv*) past and present wage or salary;
- (*v*) reasons for changes;
- (*vi*) absence record;
- (*vii*) accident record;
- (*viii*) hours of work;
- (*ix*) holiday entitlement;
- (*x*) retirement date and pension scheme membership;
- (*xi*) disciplinary warnings.

(c) Qualifications and skills:
- (*i*) formal education;
- (*ii*) qualifications;
- (*iii*) training record;
- (*iv*) appraisals.

(d) On leaving the company:
    (*i*) date of leaving and reason;
    (*ii*) name of new employer (if known);
    (*iii*) suitability for re-employment.

Once included in the employee record, any information must be kept up to date, which in many cases is a considerable clerical task. Therefore, before adding new items, it is important to consider how often the information would be used, whether it could be obtained quickly from some other source, how easy it is to keep up to date and whether there is room to show it.

4. Manual employee records
In many companies employee records are kept in card indexes or loose-leaf binders. Many proprietary systems are available which provide quick identification of particular types of employees, e.g. the registered disabled, by attaching coloured signals to their records and are successful in showing all the information listed in 3 in quite a small space. Particularly in small companies manual records are quite satisfactory, being flexible, quickly amended, convenient and comparatively cheap.

5. Computer records
A computer can store many times more information than a card index system. It has the following advantages.

(a) In a modern system, information is immediately available either on a visual display unit or a printer.
(b) Lists of employees can be quickly produced according to a desired category, e.g. all over age 60 or disabled persons.
(c) Summaries, e.g. the number of employees in each category, and employee statistics can be easily produced.
(d) Ready-made programs may be purchased and personnel staff can easily be trained to interrogate the computer or insert new and changed information.

Data Protection Act 1984

6. Summary of the Act
It protects the individual against the misuse of personal details

held on a computer or word processor and gives a remedy if the details are inaccurate. It covers almost the whole field of automatic data processing but is especially relevant to personnel records. All data users (i.e. persons or organisations which hold personal details on a computer) must register with the Data Protection Registrar, informing the Registrar of what kind of personal information is held, the use made of it, to whom it may be disclosed and how it is obtained. The Registrar must try to ensure that the user observes the eight Data Principles which are based on a Council of Europe Convention. They may be summarised as follows.

1. The information must be obtained and processed fairly.
2. Data shall be held only for specified and lawful purposes.
3. Data shall be used and disclosed only in the manner described in The Register.
4. Data must be adequate and relevant.
5. Data must be accurate and up to date.
6. Data must not be kept longer than is necessary.
7. An individual may be entitled to be told what information is held about him or her and to have it corrected or erased, if appropriate.
8. Data must be held securely.

The data user has 40 days in which to comply with any request for disclosure. A court may order data users to pay compensation for damage caused by lost, destroyed or inaccurate data or by unauthorised disclosure, i.e. to a person or organisation not named in the registration.

Inaccuracy will be excused if the data user can show either that the information was obtained with reasonable care, or that it was obtained from the person concerned (the 'data subject') or a third party. Other exemptions which are of interest to personnel departments are as follows.

(a) Although data which expresses an *opinion* about an individual is covered by the Act, indications of the user's *intentions* for the individual are not.
(b) The Act does not apply to data held only for the purpose of calculating payroll or pensions.
(c) Individuals have no right of access to data held solely for

research or statistical purposes, providing the results cannot identify any person.

7. Application to personnel records

A company of any size should appoint a co-ordinator to ensure that the Act is observed and to deal with requests for disclosure from employees. It should be noted that data subjects will include unsuccessful job applicants and former employees, if information regarding them is held on the computer.

(a) *Communication*. Employees should be told about their rights under the Act and the limitations on those rights. An explanatory section could be included in the employee handbook, if one exists, or made easily available on the same lines as the detailed conditions of employment (*see* 14:21). When an employer comes under the provisions of the Act for the first time its effects should be explained and discussed with employee representatives. It is important to establish a simple procedure for employees to use, involving either the co-ordinator or a named person of senior status in the company.

(b) *Review of data*. The information held on the computer must be checked to see if it complies with the Data Principles. It should be noted that information not held on the computer, for example on handwritten record cards, is not subject to the Act. The important steps to be taken as regards computer-held data are as follows:

  (*i*) an opinion about an employee should be clearly distinguished from a statement of intention about his or her future. 'Fit for early promotion' could be both, and its disclosure might be embarrassing if because of unforeseen circumstances early promotion proved to be impossible. If the results of appraisal are fed into the computer rather than recorded manually the wording or coding must show clearly whether a statement is an opinion or an intention;

  (*ii*) the source of the data supplied by the data subject or a third party should be indicated; this indication is known as the 'received status marker'. An example is information extracted from an application form (*see* 14:15). This safeguard ensures that data subjects cannot claim compensation for damage caused by inaccurate information they supplied themselves. Employees should be given the opportunity to check the accuracy of information supplied about them by third parties, for example former employees;

(*iii*) it is important to keep data up to date, in order to comply with the fifth Data Principle;

(*iv*) data held on the computer for research and planning should not contain clues to individual employees – for example, job title, age, length of service – so that it may be exempt from disclosure;

(*v*) if the results of appraisal are held on the computer, i.e. data which expresses opinions, employees will be entitled to ask for disclosure. Appraisal schemes which have previously been secret or partly secret will now become open, and managers will be obliged to discuss the computer-held ratings with their staff. Training in the appraisal interview may perhaps be necessary (*see* 18:**6**).

Statistics

8. Essential statistics
The following are the statistics which are essential.

(a) Statistics required by official bodies, e.g. Department of Employment and the Department of Health and Social Security.
(b) Total number of employees, subdivided as far as possible into departments, geographical location, age groups, male or female, etc. and showing the gain or loss over the previous period.
(c) Number of accidents reported to the health and safety inspector, analysed by department and cause.
(d) Labour turnover and stability rates (*see* 17:**2**).
(e) Days lost through absence (expressed as a percentage of the total number of working days during the period) and the number of spells of sickness, both analysed departmentally.

These statistics are usually compiled at monthly intervals.

9. Optional statistics
The following provide useful information for management, but are not so necessary as those listed above.

(a) Numbers of employees in various wage or salary grades. It is not essential to compile these at monthly intervals but it is common practice to do so annually when remuneration is reviewed. Pay statistics are sometimes needed for a special purpose, e.g. if a trade union makes a claim for a wage increase.

(b) The figures described in 14:32 show efficiency in recruitment and selection.

(c) For human resources planning purposes, an analysis of employees by skill, training, place of residence, etc. If redundancy is expected, an analysis by length of service.

All personnel statistics carry much more weight if they are accompanied by a report which describes and explains them, and perhaps suggests future action.

Progress test 25

1. What is contained in the personnel file? **(2)**

2. List the information which should appear in the employee record? **(3)**

3. What are the advantages of keeping employee records on a computer? **(5)**

4. What is the main purpose of the Data Protection Act? **(6)**

5. What defence might a data user have against a claim for damages due to the use of inaccurate data? **(6)**

6. Why is it important to distinguish between opinion and intention in computer-held data? **(7)**

7. Name the most important statistics relevant to personnel work. **(8)**

Industrial relations

1. Nature of industrial relations

Industrial relations (IR) may be regarded as all the rules, practices and conventions governing interactions between managements and their workforces, normally involving collective employee representation and bargaining. The rules of IR define procedures for settling wages and conditions of work, for resolving disputes and dealing with conflicts, and for implementing a wide range of grievance and disciplinary processes. Rules may be written or verbally agreed; internally formulated or externally imposed, e.g. through government legislation. Accordingly, IR involves management and unions, lay workplace employee representatives (*see* 10), government agencies such as ACAS (*see* 19), employers' associations (*see* 6), and (increasingly) detailed government laws and EC Directives.

Unions and employers

2. Trade unions

Over ten million employees belong to trade unions, of which there are currently about 400 within the UK (though the 25 largest unions account for over 80 per cent of total membership). A trade union is an association of workers formed to protect their interests in employment situations. Unions have very specific objectives: they seek better wages and working conditions for their members, greater job security, and improved welfare benefits. Hence unions wish to negotiate with managements on many issues, and may also have wider social aims: higher social security provisions, employment protection legislation, more employee participation in management, and so on.

In a typical union a member is attached to a branch, usually in the nearest large town, which elects representatives to a district or regional committee. A national committee is elected to implement the policy of the union. There are permanent employees at district or regional level (called organisers or officers) and at headquarters (the general secretary and administrative, statistical and legal staff). The policy of the union is intended to be an expression of the views of its members rather than the decisions of its national committee or general secretary; it is a democratic rather than an authoritarian organisation, in contrast to a company.

Because a union caters for a particular type of worker, usually in a certain group of occupations, and a company includes workers of many different kinds, it is quite common for more than one union to be represented in a company. About 80 per cent of trade unionists work in multi-union companies.

3. Reasons for joining trade unions
Employees join a union for the following reasons.

(a) To try to improve their working conditions.
(b) To gain some control over working environments.
(c) In some cases, because of pressure from present union members. An employee is less likely to join a union if he or she is an isolated worker, feels his or her status is high, or has a conscientious or religious objection.

4. Effects of unions on management
When a substantial number of its employers are members of trade unions the effects on the management of a company are that:

(a) decisions and policies are subject to challenge and negotiation;
(b) management powers are limited, and they may be used more cautiously;
(c) decision-making may become centralised so that a unified company industrial relations policy can be formulated and practised;
(d) the management may be required to give certain information about the company to union representatives (*see* **26**).

The main subject-matter of industrial relations has traditionally been working conditions, especially pay, but in recent years it has grown to cover practically all the personnel management practices dealt with in Chapter 12 to Chapter 23.

5. Trades Union Congress

The TUC is a voluntary association of over 100 unions. Its policy is decided by its constituent unions at the annual congress, usually lasting a week, when debates on industrial relations matters take place and the general council of 38 members is elected.

The TUC has very few powers over its constituent unions, its chief functions being:

(a) to agree and express a policy for the trade union movement;
(b) to promote legislation to protect and benefit its members;
(c) to be consulted by the government;
(d) to deal with inter-union disputes.

6. Employers' associations

Employers within a certain industry usually form an association, partly for trade and information purposes and partly to negotiate on industrial relations matters for the industry. Some large companies prefer to remain outside the association for their industry while others, like the gas and electricity boards, cover the whole of their respective industries.

7. Confederation of British Industry

The CBI is in many ways the counterpart of the TUC, being a voluntary confederation of employers' associations. It was formed in 1965 by an amalgamation of some existing employers' federations. Unlike the TUC it deals with other matters besides industrial relations as its general purpose is to promote the prosperity of British industry.

8. Staff associations

Managements that do not wish to deal with trade unions sometimes set up company 'staff associations'. There are, however, difficulties associated with this strategy from management's point of view.

(a) Staff association representatives acquire experience of negotiation, disputes procedures, etc. (ideal training for future trade union officers) at the firm's expense.

(b) Formation of a staff association itself draws attention to the *need* for collective staff representation, and in so doing may strengthen the demand for a *bona-fide* trade union. It could even provoke a union into attempting to enter an organisation it had previously ignored.

(c) If they are to be effective, staff associations will inevitably begin to behave 'as if' they were trade unions. Demands increase, and the representatives making these demands may enjoy wider grass-roots support than would a union, simply because the association was established and sponsored by the firm's management in the first place.

Nevertheless, staff associations have proliferated over the last 20 years, particularly in white-collar service trades. There are perhaps two sets of reasons for this. First, managements often greatly prefer to deal with a staff association than with a union – even if the association behaves aggressively towards management at times. Management perceive staff associations as representing 'their' people rather than interest groups beyond the firm. Recognition of a union raises the possibility of third-party intervention in what management regards as its private internal affairs: unions are seen as obstructive and unhelpful; staff associations as reasonable, moderate, and easy to appease. Second, employees themselves might oppose a union's attempts to enter a firm. Staff feel they ought to be represented, but *not* by a trade union. Staff associations offer an attractive solution to this dilemma.

Collective bargaining

The system whereby an employee's terms of employment are settled, not by individual negotiation, but by agreements reached between representatives which apply equally to many employees, is called *collective bargaining*. In this country it is generally carried out at two levels, national and workplace, and results in 'substantive' agreements covering pay, hours of work, etc. and in 'procedural' agreements to regulate the methods applied to resolving disputes and conflicts (the negotiation of a grievance procedure, for example).

9. National agreements

At national level, an employers' association negotiates with the trade unions which have members in the industry, sometimes forming a permanent body, meeting regularly, called a national joint industrial council. An agreement is made for the industry, confined often to the following basic terms of employment:

(a) minimum rates of pay for various categories of employee, often defined very loosely, e.g. semi-skilled;
(b) maximum length of the standard working week;
(c) overtime premium rate;
(d) minimum length of paid holiday.

A national agreement which included in detail a wide range of employment conditions would not be practicable in most industries because of the many differences in technology, size, profitability, etc. that are found among individual employers. The typical national agreement is therefore expressed in outline terms only and is intended to be supplemented by a further stage of bargaining at the workplace to determine the detailed application of the agreement to the particular company. The main functions of national agreements are to guarantee the employee minimum standards and to protect employers from competitors who might otherwise cut prices because they paid low wages.

National collective bargaining is sometimes restricted by government policies of pay restraint, which are either imposed by law or agreed with the TUC and CBI and then observed voluntarily by unions and employers. They usually contain an instruction or a pledge that pay increases shall be limited either to a fixed amount or to a certain percentage of present pay. There may also be a further restriction on the interval between pay claims, e.g. that not more than one increase shall be negotiated in a twelve-month period. Improvements in fringe benefits as a substitute for pay increases are not allowed, but employers are permitted to exceed the standard increases if they have concluded with their employees a self-financing productivity agreement through which improved methods of work (often including the abolition of restrictive practices) can be shown to produce savings at least as great as the total increased expenditure on pay.

10. Workplace agreements

The way in which national agreements are interpreted at company level depends partly on custom and practice, e.g. what categories of employees are to be regarded as skilled or semi-skilled, and partly on negotiations between managers and trade union representatives. In some cases the unions are represented by their full-time district officers, but often the management negotiates with the shop stewards, i.e. employees of the company who have been elected by groups of union members at the place of work to be their representatives and spokespersons.

The position of the shop steward is somewhat anomalous; though given little formal authority by his or her union constitution, in fact the shop steward frequently negotiates and concludes agreements on a wide range of subjects with the union's connivance. The reasons for the importance of shop stewards in industrial relations are as follows.

(a) They are immediately available, unlike the full-time officer, who is generally overworked.

(b) They know the background of the company thoroughly, especially its payment system.

(c) As the elected representatives of the employees, they are likely to express their point of view. Any agreement concluded with a steward will probably be accepted by union members and not repudiated.

(d) Shop stewards are the channel of communication between the members and the union, since very few union members attend branch meetings.

(e) They are the appropriate persons to express the employees' growing wish to participate in decisions about their work.

(f) Managers prefer to deal with someone they know and employ.

If authorised by his or her union, the shop steward will be the representative to whom the employer must disclose information under the provisions of the Employment Protection Act 1975 (*see* 26).

Disputes procedures

11. National procedures
Besides making agreements about conditions of employment (*see* **9**) employers' associations and trade unions also negotiate a programme or procedure to be followed in an industry for settling a dispute at a place of work without resort to industrial action such as a strike. Procedures differ in detail, but the following is fairly typical.

(a) The aggrieved employee asks his or her shop steward or district officer to take up the case with the middle management of the company.
(b) Meeting between the district officer and senior management.
(c) Meeting between union officials and the regional committee of the employers' association.
(d) Meeting between national officials of the trade union and of the employers' association.
(e) In some industries, an independent arbitrator gives a final decision which both sides have agreed in advance to accept, although it is not legally binding.

Each stage of the procedure is used until agreement is reached; if the dispute is settled at stage **(b)**, for example, the subsequent stages will not be used. The procedural agreement states that no industrial action shall take place until all stages have been used.

12. Comments on national procedures
There are great variations in the effectiveness of national procedures. Some work quickly and appear to be respected by both sides. Others are slow, and are sometimes not used or only partly used.

In the later stages of a typical procedure the negotiators become more and more remote from the actual place where the dispute originated. It has been suggested that in order to reduce the large number of strikes which occur in defiance of national procedures, more attention should be paid to improving disputes procedures at the place of work.

13. Workplace procedures
In recent years the growing complexity of payment systems,

the increasing rate of technical change and the wish of employees to take some share in decisions regarding their working conditions have led to more conflict between management and employees, sometimes expressed in industrial action.

For reasons described in 10, the shop steward is prominent in raising these matters and in negotiations to settle them. Sometimes an informal procedure for dealing locally with disputes is evolved between the management and the shop stewards, with the intention of using the official procedure only as a last resort. If in these negotiations shop stewards wish to put pressure on management they have the following sanctions at their disposal.

(a) *Withdrawal of co-operation*, for example the steward will no longer help in solving disciplinary problems or interpreting national agreements.

(b) *Insistence on formal rights*, for example the steward may insist on raising with management grievances that he or she would normally consider too trivial to mention, or may bring back strict demarcation between crafts.

(c) *Restrictions on output or overtime working*. The steward will organise a go-slow in which employees without breaking any terms of the employment contract reduce output by time-wasting methods, unnecessary journeys to stores, etc. They may also refuse to work overtime, or work it only on their own terms, a particularly useful tactic if the company relies on overtime working to meet its production and delivery commitments.

(d) *Withdrawal of labour*, quite frequently only for a few hours as a demonstration of solidarity or as a sign of impatience with the slow pace of negotiations. A strike called by a shop steward on his or her own authority is an unofficial strike because it has not been considered and authorised by the union. It is very unusual for a union to call an official strike unless a dispute remains unresolved after going through the complete national procedure or an employer is considered to have broken an agreement.

The sanctions at the disposal of a shop steward have their counterparts in possible action by the employer, who can also withdraw co-operation, insist on formal procedures being observed, refuse to allow employees to work overtime when they need it to augment their basic pay, or lock them out. These sanctions are seldom used by an employer, who relies instead on the firm's power to refuse all or part of the demands made by the employees.

Statutory regulation of wages and conditions

14. Wages councils

Statutory arrangements have been made to fix basic employment conditions for industries in which most individual places of work are too small and scattered for trade unions to become established. Examples of such industries are hairdressing, catering and retail distribution. Wages councils – which comprise equal numbers of employer and employee representatives plus three independent members, one of whom takes the chair – are government bodies which set legally enforceable minimum wage levels for employees working in certain industries. Two wage rates are established annually for each industry covered: a minimum hourly rate for work up to 39 or 40 hours a week (depending on the industry), and an overtime rate for hours worked beyond 39 or 40. Employers can pay wages above the minimum, but if they pay less they commit a criminal offence for which they may be prosecuted.

Councils have been set up in eleven industry groupings: agricultural wages (and holidays) are controlled by a separate Agricultural Wage Board, which is not actually a wages council. Prior to 1986, councils were able to make orders setting:

(a) holidays and holiday pay;
(b) different rates of pay for different grades of work.

Both these powers have been abolished. Workers in wages council industries no longer have a legal right to paid holidays though if they worked for their present employer before 25 June 1986 on a grade for which the minimum wage specified was higher than the current rate now that grade differentials have been abolished, they can argue to a tribunal that the earlier terms were part and parcel of their contracts of employment. Thus, if the employer cuts the wages of such an employee to the new minimum, then the worker has the options of either suing for breach of contract or claiming constructive unfair dismissal.

Only workers aged 21 or over are covered by wage council

orders which apply equally to full-time and part-time workers, piece workers and home workers. 'Time workers' who are paid by the hour must be paid the minimum rate whether or not there is work available for them to do.

Wages inspectors, who have extensive powers of entry, search and interrogation, visit the premises of employers in wages council industries to check that they provide terms and conditions at least as good as those specified. An inspector may prosecute any employer who fails to do so, and a court may fine the employer and order the firm to compensate the employees affected.

15. The minimum wage

From time to time trade unions, especially those representing low-paid workers, press for the enactment of a national minimum wage. Some other countries already have such legislation. It is not easy to obtain general support for this in a time of high unemployment, and employers in particular fear the possible 'knock-on' effects of a statutory minimum, i.e., that an increase in wages to the lowest paid would have to be followed by increases to the higher paid who wished to maintain their traditional pay differentials.

Statutory bodies

16. Industrial tribunals

These bodies were originally set up to deal with disputes arising from the Industrial Training Act 1964, but they now deal with an extremely wide variety of employment matters such as unfair dismissal, redundancy, discrimination, equal pay and safety.

They consist of an independent legally qualified chairperson, an employers' representative and a trade union representative. Their proceedings are informal and it is not necessary for the parties in a case to be legally represented. Their purpose is to decide what is reasonable in all circumstances of the case, and appeals from their decisions, which are heard by the Employment Appeals Tribunal (*see* 17), can only be on points of law.

If doubt exists concerning a tribunal's ability to hear a case (e.g. if an employer claims a dismissed worker has not completed two years' continuous service), then a 'preliminary hearing' may be convened to consider this matter. Also, if following a brief examination of a case a tribunal feels that one of the disputants has no chance of winning, it may order a 'pre-hearing assessment' to establish agreed facts and, if appropriate, warn the erring party that its case is bound to fail. The party receiving the warning is entitled to proceed before a different tribunal, but if it loses could be made to pay the costs of the hearing (normally each side pays its own costs). Under the Employment Act 1990, tribunals are empowered to require an applicant to pay a deposit of up to £150 if a pre-hearing review considers a case to have been brought frivolously, vexatiously or to be entirely unreasonable.

17. Employment Appeals Tribunal
This body, which is a court rather than a tribunal, consists of a judge and lay members representing both sides of industry and was set up by the Employment Protection Act 1975 in place of the National Industrial Relations Court.

It hears appeals on points of law from industrial tribunals and on decisions made by the Certification Officer (*see* **21**). Unlike the decisions of industrial tribunals, the decisions of the Employment Appeals Tribunal establish precedents.

18. Central Arbitration Committee
This body, also set up under the Employment Protection Act, comprises people experienced in industrial relations. It will arbitrate in disputes referred to it by the Advisory, Conciliation and Arbitration Service, ACAS (*see* **19**), and also adjudicate on claims that an employer has not disclosed to union representatives information requested for collective bargaining purposes (*see* **25**).

19. Advisory, Conciliation and Arbitration Service
This is an independent body governed by a Council which consists of members appointed after consultation with workers' and employers' organisations. It has the following powers and duties.

(a) The general duty of promoting the improvement of industrial relations and the extension of collective bargaining.
(b) Employers and trade unions can request its help in a possible or actual trade dispute.

(c) It may on its own initiative enquire into any industrial relations matter and publish its findings.

(d) It may enquire into a complaint by a recognised trade union that adequate information for collective bargaining purposes has not been disclosed (*see* 26).

(e) It prepares and publishes Codes of Practice giving guidance for improving industrial relations.

An important duty of ACAS is to seek out-of-court settlements for unfair dismissal cases due to be heard before industrial tribunals. All applications to industrial tribunals are copied to ACAS officers who, if they believe the exercise will be worthwhile, will contact both parties to the dispute – separately and confidentially – to ascertain each side's minimum terms for an out-of-court settlement and/or whether grounds for reconciliation exist.

Industrial relations law

20. Definitions

The following are shortened versions of the definitions appearing in the Trade Union and Labour Relations Act 1974, as amended by the Employment Act 1982.

(a) *A trade dispute* means a dispute between workers and their own employer concerning terms and conditions of employment, engagement, non-engagement or dismissal of workers, allocation of work, a procedural agreement or trade union membership.

(b) *A trade union* is an organisation consisting wholly or mainly of workers, whose principal purposes include the regulation of relations between workers and employers or employers' associations. It is not a corporate body but has the power to make contracts and to sue or be sued in its own name.

(c) *An employers' association* is an organisation consisting wholly or mainly of employers or proprietors whose principal purposes include the regulation of relations between employers and workers or unions. It may be either a corporate body or an unincorporated association, in the latter case having the same powers as a trade union.

In all the definitions 'worker' means any employee, manual or non-manual.

21. Independence and recognition

The Trade Union and Labour Relations Act 1974 defined an independent trade union as one which was not dominated by an employer because of the provision or withdrawal of financial or other support. A union is not independent, therefore, unless it is autonomous and financially self-supporting.

A Certification Officer was appointed under the Employment Protection Act 1975 to consider applications by trade unions for certificates of independence. A union certified as independent receives certain benefits under that Act.

A recognised union is one with which an employer negotiates with the object of reaching agreements. Very many companies have voluntarily recognised a union, or several unions, for a considerable time, but others have refused recognition. There are no statutory provisions for obtaining or enforcing recognition.

22. The closed shop

By the early 1970s nearly half the trade unionists in this country worked in a closed shop, i.e. a place of work where membership of a particular trade union was necessary in order to obtain or retain a job.

Closed shops have been brought about, usually by pressure from the unions, as a means of increasing their bargaining power and establishing their organisations within a company, but sometimes voluntarily by managements because of the efficiency and convenience of dealing with one or just a few recognised unions.

In the last ten years, however, closed shops were criticised for interfering with individual liberty, constraining management's rights to manage in a company's best interests, and causing industrial inefficiency through encouraging overstaffing and the propensity of local union officials to initiate strikes.

The Employment Act of 1988 makes the dismissal of a worker for non-union membership *automatically* unfair. This means the dismissed worker will automatically win a claim for unfair dismissal in an industrial tribunal and, because the case concerns a closed-shop agreement, will be entitled under the Employment Act 1982 to a level of compensation considerably higher than is available in most other unfair dismissal cases. The 1988 Act (*see* **27**) states, moreover, that industrial action to enforce or maintain any kind of closed shop is unlawful. In consequence, a union is now liable to be sued by an employer for damages arising from acts undertaken by the union against the employer for:

(a) employing a non-union member;
(b) considering employing a non-union member;
(c) employing or considering employing someone who is not a member of a *particular* union;
(d) failing to discriminate (under union pressure) against an employee in categories (a) or (c).

Pre-entry closed shops, i.e. situations where job applications have to be members of a union in order even to be considered for a vacancy, were declared unlawful by the Employment Act 1990.

23. Legal immunities

When a lawful strike, as defined in **20(a)**, takes place, the trade union, its officials or any workers concerned in the dispute are immune from legal action for:

(a) inducing or threatening a breach of contract, including a commercial contract or employment contract;
(b) interfering with, or threatening interference with, the performance of a contract;
(c) civil conspiracy, where two or more persons support non-tortious actions.

These immunities are contained in the Employment Act 1982 but the Trade Union Act 1984 removes them in cases where the trade union did not hold a ballot before authorising or endorsing the strike. The ballot must be held not more than four weeks before the strike begins.

The Employment Acts of 1980 and 1982 make unlawful 'secondary action' to bring about a breach of a commercial contract. 'Secondary action', defined as an inducement or threat to break a contract of employment with an employer outside the trade dispute, is only lawful when it is directed against a supplier or customer of the original employer with the aim of disrupting the flow of goods and services between them and is likely to achieve that purpose.

The 1980 Act also reduces the immunities hitherto given for picketing. Picketing a place of work in order to persuade someone to work or not to work carries legal immunity for actions in tort only if the pickets consist of:

(a) employees who normally work there;

(b) former employees, if the trade dispute concerns their dismissal, redundancy or resignation;

(c) employees who have no fixed place of work, or who cannot picket their own place of work – they may in these cases picket their employer's premises or the premises from which their work is administered;

(d) a trade union official accompanying a member of a union involved in the dispute.

The picketing must be in contemplation of furtherance of a trade dispute.

It should be noted that picketing solely to obtain or communicate information does not involve possible breach of contract and is therefore free from the restrictions stated above. However, picketing can sometimes become a criminal offence if, for example, it is violent or causes obstruction of a public highway.

24. Other legal rights of employees

Under the Employment Protection (Consolidation) Act 1978 it is unfair to dismiss an employee for trade union activity or for refusing to join a non-independent trade union.

If the employee is unfairly dismissed for refusing to join a union in a closed shop he or she is eligible for compensation at a higher rate than normal. The worker may make the union party to the dismissal proceedings where it is claimed that the union put pressure on the employer to dismiss that person.

The Employment Protection Act 1975 also gives an employee the right not to have any action short of dismissal taken against him or her:

(a) to prevent or deter the worker from joining or being active in an independent trade union;

(b) to compel the worker to join a trade union.

The activities mentioned in (a) must take place either when the employee is not required to be working, e.g. lunch breaks, or at other times with the employer's permission. This protection is designed to help employees to organise where there is at present no recognised union or no union at all. However, once a union has been recognised its members must be given reasonable time off during working hours to take part in union activities.

Complaints that these rights have been infringed are made to an industrial tribunal, and a copy of the complaint sent to a conciliation officer in case the matter can be settled without a tribunal hearing. If the case is heard by a tribunal the onus will be on the employer to show that the firm has not infringed the employee's rights. If the decision is against the employing firm it may have to pay compensation to the employee, and the tribunal may make a 'declaration' which will form the basis of the employer's future policy towards trade union activity.

The Trade Union and Labour Relations Act 1974 states that a collective agreement is to be presumed not legally enforceable unless it clearly and in writing states otherwise. Voluntary rather than legally enforceable agreements have always been preferred in this country, though the Industrial Relations Act 1971 tried unsuccessfully to change this attitude.

25. No-strike clauses

The 1974 Act also states that a 'no-strike' clause in an agreement can only be part of individual contracts of employment when the agreement:

(a) is in writing;
(b) expressly provides for the inclusion of the clause in individual contracts;
(c) is reasonably accessible to the employee at the place of work;
(d) is made with independent unions only.

The individual workers' contracts should include the no-strike clause either expressly or by implication.

No-strike clauses are increasingly attached to 'single union' agreements whereby an employer offers exclusive bargaining rights within a complete establishment to just one union (plus other concessions, including perhaps 'staff' status and benefits for manual workers) in return for an undertaking not to withdraw labour. Pendulum arbitration is an essential feature of such agreements. This means that:

(a) both sides agree on an independent arbitrator (who may be an individual person or an outside agency) whose task it is to settle disputes, including wage disputes;

(b) each party presents its demands to the arbitrator, e.g. the union may ask for an X per cent wage increase whereas management offers only Y per cent;

(c) the arbitrator then selects one solution or the other – there is *no haggling or compromise*;

(d) this settlement is binding on both sides.

The advantage claimed for pendulum arbitration is that it forces the parties to be realistic in their demands; there is no 'splitting the difference' as commonly occurs with conventional collective bargaining. Thus, a union which claims a ridiculously high pay increase (as an opening gambit prior to accepting something less) is bound to lose under this system provided management does not submit a proposal that is equally absurd. Management also must take care not to offer too little or the arbitrator will 'swing the pendulum' towards the union's more reasonable demand.

26. Disclosure of information

The Employment Protection Act 1975 obliges an employer to disclose to representatives of an independent *recognised* trade union ('recognised' means that the employer has already negotiated with the union on *any* matter, not necessarily concerned with pay and conditions of employment), on request, certain information for the purposes of collective bargaining. It includes information which should be disclosed in accordance with good industrial practice or which, if withheld, would impede the union representatives in bargaining. Union representatives are not, however, entitled to information which:

(a) would be against the interests of national security;

(b) would be illegal to disclose;

(c) had been obtained in confidence;

(d) relates to an individual (unless consent has been given);

(e) had been obtained for the purpose of legal proceedings;

(f) would be likely to cause substantial injury to the employer's undertaking.

The Code of Practice on this subject prepared by the Advisory, Conciliation and Arbitration Service recommends that the employer should disclose information on pay and benefits, conditions of service, human resources, performance, e.g. productivity, sales and orders, and financial matters. It suggests that unions should identify and request the information before negotiations begin, stating why they consider it relevant. Employers are advised to be as open as possible and to present the information promptly and clearly.

A union which believes it has not received adequate information may complain to the Central Arbitration Committee, which may then refer the matter to the Advisory, Conciliation and Arbitration Service. If conciliation fails, the Committee will hear the case and make a declaration on whether or not the complaint is well-founded.

The Committee in making its decision will consider to what extent the Code of Practice has been followed, although the recommendations in the Code impose no legal obligations. If an employer refuses to comply with a declaration that certain information should be disclosed, the Committee may at the request of the trade union make an enforceable award of terms and conditions on behalf of the employees concerned.

It should be noted that the law affects national and workplace agreements equally, provided that recognised unions are involved.

27. The Employment Act 1988

Apart from removing a union's immunity from civil actions in closed-shop disputes (plus the measures outlined in **22**) this Act establishes the following new rights for trade union members.

(a) A member who claims the union has called a strike without holding a ballot may apply for a court order which, if granted, will compel the union to withdraw its strike action.

(b) Members are given the legal right not to be unjustifiably disciplined by their union should they:

(*i*) not participate in or support a strike (e.g. by crossing a picket line);

(*ii*) fail to go-slow on union orders if this would contravene a contract of employment;

(*iii*) initiate legal actions against the union or encourage others to do so. Union 'discipline' is defined as expulsion, fines, withdrawal of benefits or services, telling other unions not to accept an individual as a member, or 'other detriment'. The aggrieved person must complain to an industrial tribunal within three months of the incident, and the tribunal may award compensation of up to 30 weeks' average pay (though a ceiling is imposed on the value of a week's pay) plus an extra award to compensate for future loss of earnings, mental distress, etc. An upper ceiling also applies to the latter figure.

(c) All members can now inspect the union's accounting records.

(d) Employees have the right to insist that their employers stop deducting union subscriptions from their wage packets. If deductions continue, the employer is deemed to be in contravention of the Wages Act 1986 (*see* 22:**10**).

Under the Act it is unlawful for a union to use its funds to compensate a member for the consequences of his or her unlawful conduct during a dispute, e.g. by paying a member's fine, or even to promise to do so. And the statutory procedures for electing members to important union committees (known as 'principal executive committees') are generally tightened. In particular:

(a) every candidate must be able to prepare an address and have this delivered to all members – by post if necessary;

(b) postal ballots, under the supervision of an independent scrutineer, must be used wherever 'reasonably practicable';

(c) a strike scheduled to cover several different places of work *must* be sanctioned by a postal ballot.

The Act creates the position of *Commissioner for the Rights of Trade Union Members*, whose task is to assist individual trade unionists to claim their legal rights. Accordingly, the Commissioner is empowered to pay all the expenses and legal costs (including the fees of a solicitor and barrister) incurred in bringing a case that, in the view of the Commissioner:

(a) involves a major point of principle; *or*
(b) is so complex that it would be unreasonable to expect the individual to handle it personally; *or*
(c) concerns a matter of substantial public interest.

28. Further legislation

The Employment Act 1989 removed a variety of restrictions on the employment of women in certain industries (e.g. coal mining) and on the hours of work (including night work) of young people between 16 and 18 years of age. The Employment Act 1990 outlawed the pre-entry closed shop by making it unlawful to refuse employment to an individual simply because he or she is not a member of a trade union. Additionally, the Act removed immunity from civil actions against workers engaged in secondary actions other than *lawful* and peaceful picketing, and unions became liable for the torts of *all* their officials (including shop stewards) unless they formally repudiate the erring officials' actions in a prescribed manner. Moreover, the Act rescinded the rule that striking workers may be 'fairly' dismissed (*see* 16:9) only if *all* strikers are sacked and not just some of them (e.g. if the employer wishes to make an example of a few individuals), although the new regulation only applies in circumstances of 'unofficial' industrial action. Persons subsequently striking in support of someone dismissed on these grounds are now liable to be sued for damages by employers and other interested parties. Unofficial action means industrial action not approved by the striker's trade union or, if the striker does not belong to a union, not approved by the union of fellow strikers. Note how this aspect of the 1990 Act cannot apply if *none* of the strikers is a member of a union.

Progress test 26

1. Describe the nature of industrial relations. (1)

2. What are the effects on management of the existence of active trade unions in the company? (4)

3. Outline the scope of a typical national agreement. (9)

4. What is the relationship between national and workplace agreements? **(9, 10)**

5. What is a wages council and what are its powers? **(14)**

6. What are the main functions of an industrial tribunal, the Employment Appeals Tribunal and the Central Arbitration Committee? **(16, 17)**

7. Define an independent trade union. **(21)**

8. In what respects is a union immune from legal action? **(23)**

9. Under what conditions must an employer give information to a trade union? **(26)**

10. What are the major provisions of the Employment Act 1990? **(28)**

Appendices

Appendix 1

Example of a job specification

Job description

Cement mixer operator   **XYZ Pre-cast Concrete Ltd**

Operates a cement mixing process which is largely automatic but requires checking to see that it is functioning correctly.

Manually adds colour to the mix when required.

Cleans interior of mixer at end of each day.

Keeps record of coloured mixes (normal mixes are recorded automatically.)

Responsible to the plant supervisor.

Not responsible for any other operators.

Job specification

Major responsibilities

The operator is responsible for the production of satisfactory mixes and for the routine cleaning of the equipment. About 120 mixes should be produced per day, including colour mixes when required. The operator must be prepared to correct or stop the process manually if it is apparent that unsatisfactory mixes are being produced or if mechanical or electrical faults occur.

Routine duties

Starts process each day by operating controls.

By observing mixer control panel and appearance of mix, judges whether process is working correctly or if manual adjustments need to be made.

When instructed by supervisor produces coloured mixes by

adding colour from small pre-weighed bags. Enters details in record book daily.

Cleans equipment in last hour of the day.

Training (off-job, with an experienced operator) lasts two weeks. Should be able to work unsupervised after a further four weeks.

No unusual physical demands are made on the operator except that cleaning the equipment necessitates some bending and stretching.

Non-routine or infrequent duties

During annual overhaul of plant assists for about a week in cleaning and dismantling.

May occasionally be required for general labouring duties, e.g. snow clearing.

Working conditions

A seat is provided by the mixer control panel but the operator frequently needs to stand or walk short distances to inspect the quality of the mix or to prepare coloured mixes.

There is some heating in winter from a hot water pipe running through the control area, which is under cover but draughty because of the entrance and exit points for the materials used in the process.

The work is occasionally dusty while the process is operating but very dusty while the equipment is being cleaned, necessitating the wearing of a mask.

There is a moderate noise and vibration, but it does not impede communication because the operator receives instructions re coloured mixes in writing.

The work area is adequately lit.

Tools and materials used

The materials for the mix (except colour) are delivered and controlled automatically.

No tools are used except a hose, brushes and scrapers when cleaning.

Personal contacts

The operator is isolated except for very occasional visits from the supervisor. The operator can see operators in other parts of the plant through the windows.

Performance standards

120 mixes per day.
Colour mixes as required.
Satisfactory quality of mix.
No breakdowns due to inadequate cleaning.
Records of coloured mixes legible, accurate and up to date.

Appendix 2
Example of an appraisal rating scale

Name _____   Department _____

Job _____   How long in dept. _____

Date of birth _____   How long in company _____

Please tick the ratings you think appropriate, after reading carefully the definitions of the factors and grades. You should add any general remarks in the space provided at the end of the form. Base your judgment on the requirements of the job and the employee's performance in the job.

1. KNOWLEDGE OF JOB
(Present knowledge of job and of work related to it.)

Knows only routine repetitive work. Will not learn   _____
Knows routine work and some parts of other jobs   _____
Knows most jobs but relies on others for special
knowledge   _____
Good knowledge of practically all aspects of the work   _____
Complete grasp of all aspects of the work   _____

2. ACCURACY
(Standard of work compared with standard expected, degree to which work must be checked.)

Work is inaccurate; requires constant checking   _____
Careless at times; requires frequent checking   _____
Usually accurate; requires occasional checking   _____
Accurate except on very difficult jobs   _____
Accurate on all jobs   _____

3. SPEED OF WORK
(Speed at which work is accomplished in relation to the standard expected in the job.)

Very slow; always fails to meet requirements   _____
Slow; often below requirements   _____
Average speed; meets requirements as a rule   _____
Above average speed; usually exceeds requirements _____
Fast; always exceeds requirements   _____

4. CO-OPERATION
(Ability to work with others at all levels; readiness to try out new ideas and methods; response when asked for a special effort.)

Difficult to work with; often touchy and
unco-operative   _____
Occasionally difficult to work with   _____
Normally co-operative; raises few difficulties   _____
Always tries hard to co-operate; easy to work with   _____
Co-operates extremely well with others at all
levels   _____

5. INITIATIVE
(Resourcefulness; ability to work without detailed instructions; readiness to offer ideas and suggestions about work.)

Requires detailed supervision; waits to be told   _____
Requires frequent supervision; asks for instructions   _____
Requires occasional supervision, sometimes offers
ideas   _____
Rarely requires supervision; resourceful, offers ideas _____
Never requires supervision; has many ideas,
solves problems unaided   _____

TRAINING NEEDS
(Suggest any training course or in-company experience which
might improve the employee's performance.)

PROMOTION POTENTIAL
The employee is an excellent promotion candidate
because   _____
The employee is a good promotion candidate because _____
The employee is a border-line promotion candidate
because   _____
The employee is unlikely to be promoted because   _____

GENERAL REMARKS

GENERAL RATING

Assess employee's job performance in his or her *present* job:

[ ]   [ ]   [ ]   [ ]   [ ]

Poor   Average   Excellent

Signed _____ Position ____ Date _____
Countersigned _____ Position ____ Date _____

Appendix 3
Examples of job evaluation schemes

Office job evaluation

The Institute of Administrative Management has developed a grading scheme for office staff which is described fully in its publication *Office Job Evaluation*. Extracts from the scheme are shown below, by kind permission of the Institute.

Nine job grades are defined as follows.

A. Jobs which require no previous work experience and are either

(a) simple enough to require very limited training; *or*
(b) simple but still require a training period and will be closely controlled by supervision or self-checking procedures.

B. Jobs which by virtue of their composition remain simple but develop the ability of the job holder beyond the initial level through extended training both theoretical and on the job. Will consist of standard routines less closely controlled.

C. Jobs which necessitate a length of experience to enable a special aptitude to be used. Routines will continue to be standardised but rulings can start to be relaxed to allow for initiative to be developed.

D. Jobs requiring considerable experience thereby relaxing standardised routines but remaining within predetermined procedures. Limited initiative is to be encouraged resulting in a material reduction in control procedures.

E.   Jobs which require either or both of the following, dependent upon the percentages of total time spent on specialist, technical and work control activities:

(a) technical or specialised knowledge applied where the occasional use of discretion and initiative is necessary;
(b) control of work procedures distributed over up to, say, five lower-grade staff.

F.   Jobs which require the application of both knowledge and experience in one or more of the following:

(a) technical or professional operations at intermediate qualification level of an appropriate professional institute;
(b) performance or control of work of developing complexity whether secretarial, technical or administrative where judgment and initiative is called for;
(c) supervision requiring leadership, guidance on work procedures, training of others and motivation covering a team where control of work alone is delegated to a lower-level grade.

M   1.   Jobs where requirements equate to one or more of the following:

(a) professional or specialised knowledge beyond the Intermediate level examination of an appropriate professional institute but not necessarily to a final qualification of such institutes;
(b) performance or control of work of wide complexity including non-routine decisions and regular use of judgment within determined policy;
(c) management of sufficient numbers of staff to require F-level activities carried out by more than one position.

M   2.   Jobs requiring one or more of the following:

(a) the final qualification of an appropriate professional institute equivalent to a university degree;
(b) performance or control of work of significant complexity and importance requiring regular non-routine decisions based upon initiative leading to the development of policy changes;
(c) management of specialist functions where more than one level

of supervision is necessary to control the range of activities involved.

M   3. Jobs requiring one or more of the following:

(a) in addition to a final qualification and/or equivalent university degree a period of experience consistent with the level of authority;
(b) performance or control of work over a series of functions demanding a high level of generalist expertise and involved in policy-making at the highest level.
(c) management of a series of specialist functions where management level jobs report in for guidance, control and monitoring.

The Institute gives examples of the application of the grading scheme to various types of office jobs. The following show how a variety of office jobs might be graded.

Typing and secretarial

A. –

B. Preparation of straightforward documents by copy-typing from a clear statement, including manuscript, at about 35 words per minute.

C. Word processor operation requiring the organising of adequate space on storage systems in a single word processor unit requiring an understanding of standard records and systems.

D. Preparation of statements which require careful layout of both words and figures from author's draft, including the correction of grammar and punctuation, in order to produce a finished document.

E. Secretarial work requiring the receipt of dictation and its transcription for members of management covering correspondence, reports, etc. Other activities include making appointments, filing and generally working on own initiative.

F. Supervision of a group of typists including training, distribution of work and maintenance of standards.

M 1. -

M 2. -

M 3. -

Accounting

A. –

B. Sorting documents, preparing ledger entries and assisting with the filing thereof after input. Processing details of new accounts for authorisation, changes of address, etc., all under the control of higher-grade staff.

C. Checking input documents, in that quantities and terms are accurate, calculating extensions and discounts agree with orders and contract terms, etc.

D. Maintaining control accounts to ensure that all ledgers input has been correctly processed. Making necessary corrections within knowledge and experience, referring other queries to higher grade staff.

E. Preparing cost and departmental accounts, having responsibility for investigating queries and noting abnormal resulting figures for attention.

F. Supervision of work of a section of clerical staff dealing with the administration of customers' or suppliers' accounts involving dealing with queries which emerge.

M 1. Preparation of statements on the effects of price increases on profit margins which involve knowledge of products and processes as well as management accounting principles and practices.

M 2. Preparing reports to develop complex annual budgets requiring a detailed knowledge of both financial and management accountancy.

M 3. –

Computing

A. –

B. Microcomputer operation entering data and/or text using the keyboard and simple commands under the guidance of an experienced operator and where input is subject to check.

C. Computer operation loading disks onto disk drives, paper into printers, operating VDUs to give simple operating commands in accordance with prescribed procedures.

D. Writing specialist programs for particular systems, e.g., personal computers, optical mark/character readers, etc.

E. Investigating current systems which are straightforward and expected to need a small computer to improve flow of work and productivity. Examining alternatives and preparing statements of requirements.

F. Supervising and operating with a team or shift of computer operators for a medium-sized installation. Ensuring that procedures are adhered to, records are maintained, faults reported and work scheduled in accordance with priorities.

M 1. Defining systems requirements for major projects. Controlling the work of a section of programmers, liaising with systems analysts and designers together with senior management and users.

M 2. Planning large scale or complex data processing systems covering a significant area of the operations of an organisation, including negotiations with departments about projects.

M 3. Control and management of a computer system comprising mini and mainframe computers together with a complex network of more than 250 VDUs.

Miscellaneous

A. Collecting and assembling outgoing mail, collecting and delivering internal mail to a timetable.

B. Sorting and filing in alphabetical and numerical order, preparation of files and extraction of files, etc.

C. Share registration activities involving despatching completed certificates after sealing and maintaining records accordingly. Distribution operations, taking orders over the telephone and responding to delivery queries.

D. Personnel records involving compiling regular statistics for management on sickness and overtime etc.
Maintenance of insurance registers of policies to ensure renewal within the prescribed period.

E. Maintaining statistical records of sales performance and circulating such information to appropriate departments.
Control of work of a small team of purchasing clerks, progressing orders and maintaining records.

F. In property management, calculating maintenance claims and preparing information on property values.
Supervision of staff involved in the calculation and payment of pension benefits.

M 1. Evolving and running suitable training courses for staff up to supervisory level, assessing success and maintaining records of a financial and personnel nature related to the courses.

M 2. Preparing complex reports on major aspects of business activity which involve the interpretation of information and calculation of forecasts for discussion at senior management meetings.

M 3. Management of multi-discipline activities whereby monitoring and control procedures result in policy formulation.

The examples shown above are brief, and only provide a rough guide to the type or level of job in each grade. Fuller information may be found in the Institute's book *Office Job Evaluation*.

Points rating scheme for manual jobs

The following is an example of a scheme used in industry for evaluating manual jobs. Note that the sub-factors under the heading working conditions are intended to cover outdoor as well as indoor jobs. A company in which nearly all manual jobs were under cover or free from contamination and noise would have a different set of sub-factors under this heading. The reader may wish to use this scheme to evaluate the job described in Appendix 1.

	Max.	
Skill and knowledge	*points*	
Education and training required	25	
Experience required	60	
Dexterity	15	
	–	100
Effort		
Energy and stamina required	60	
Working position	40	
	–	100
Responsibility and mental requirements		
For material and equipment	20	
For the work of others	25	
Concentration and alertness	20	
Need to act on own initiative	15	
Need to work steadily	20	
	–	100

Working conditions

Temperature and humidity	20	
Exposure to climatic conditions	20	
Atmospheric contamination (dust, dirt, smell, etc.)	25	
Noise and vibration	15	
Monotony and isolation	10	
Nervous strain, hazards	10	
	—	100

Appendix 4
Examination technique

1. Practice

Candidates who have not attempted an examination for some years, or who have not had recent experience in essay writing, often fail to do themselves justice in the examination room. Practice in answering previous questions, e.g. those in Appendix 5, will add to self-confidence and give a better result.

2. Revision

If a long series of previous examination papers is available candidates may attempt to forecast what topics are likely to be included in the forthcoming examination; for example most examinations in this field contain questions about recruitment and remuneration, with other topics appearing in rotation. Quite often questions are set on subjects which have been discussed in recent articles in the relevant professional journal.

The progress tests at the end of each chapter of this book can be used to check that a student's revision has been thorough. Revision up to the last moment before an examination or late the previous night is not recommended; in the first case the student may remember clearly only those subjects he or she has just read and in the second he or she is too tired to think clearly. Students are often advised to stop revising three days before the examination and then relax completely, though few have been known to take this advice.

3. The question paper

Many candidates fail because they have not read the question paper thoroughly, perhaps producing good answers to questions which have not been set. The questions must be read carefully, then read again, noting particularly the following points.

(a) If a question asks for a comparison or a comment a mere description is not enough.

(b) When an examiner asks for a discussion of a quoted statement, some criticism is expected, not complete approval of it.

(c) All parts of a question must be answered; if it asks for a description, a comparison and suggestions for improvement it is probable that each of these parts will be given approximately equal marks. Candidates should attempt them all.

(d) A question paper is a useful source of information. For example, a candidate faced with the question 'What benefits would a company expect to gain from training its employees?' might well find that elsewhere in the paper there are questions on motivation, supervision, accidents and labour turnover which remind the student of points to make.

4. Timing

After allowing about ten minutes for settling down and reading the questions, the candidate can calculate how much time to allot to each question, e.g. 170 minutes divided by five questions gives 34 minutes per question – half an hour of writing and four minutes for checking.

Although candidates may feel that they could write for longer than half an hour they will lose marks if they do so; a quarter of an hour's extra work on a question may bring two or three marks but the same time spent on a new question, even though it is difficult or uncongenial, can easily earn ten marks or more.

5. Planning the answers

Examiners do not have a high opinion of answers which consist of a number of disconnected and repetitive sentences apparently in random sequence. Candidates will avoid producing answers of this kind if they first spend a few minutes considering which topics they wish to deal with, and putting them in logical order, e.g. advantages, disadvantages, summing up, or description followed by discussion.

6. Irrelevant material

No marks will be given for parts of an answer which are not relevant to the question. Sometimes in response to a question asking for a discussion of one specific aspect of, say, training a candidate pours out all he or she knows about the whole subject of training, often failing to discuss adequately the particular point raised.

7. Illustrative examples

Examples to illustrate procedures or behaviour which have been taken from the candidate's own experience or from what he or she has read will add some individuality to an answer and show that the candidate understands the subject under discussion. While preparing for an examination, therefore, a candidate is well advised to look out for and note any incidents or methods in his or her employing company which can be used as examination material.

8. Style and presentation

Illegible handwriting, poor spelling, complicated sentences and frequent corrections tend to irritate examiners, who are usually working under pressure. Submitting essays for criticism by others will help to remedy these faults, particularly if they have been written under mock examination conditions, i.e. without reference to books or notes and within a strict time limit.

The ideal examination answer is clearly written, expressed in short, direct and grammatical sentences which follow a logical order, illustrated by real-life examples and, of course, relevant to the question which has been asked.

Appendix 5
Specimen examination questions

The following questions are included with the kind permission of the professional bodies listed below:

IAM   Institute of Administrative Management
IMS   Institute of Management Services
LCCI London Chamber of Commerce and Industry
ICSA Institute of Chartered Secretaries and Administrators
CBSI Chartered Building Societies Institute
CII   Chartered Insurance Institute

1. At his performance appraisal interview, one of your staff strongly denounces the appraisal system. He states that he and most of his colleagues are only interested in the salary award.

Discuss the role of money as a motivator and explain how you would respond to the individual concerned.

(CII)

2. (i) Identify five main divisions into which the personnel department of a large manufacturing company can be subdivided.

(ii) Outline the main areas of responsibility normally assigned to each of the divisions identified.

(LCCI)

3. As the demand for a company's products is expanding rapidly the personnel director is to formulate a manpower plan and review the selection and training procedures, so that the company can meet continuing increases in demand.

Discuss the contribution that you would expect to make as a management services officer.

(IMS)

4. One result of technology has been to increase the number of boring jobs. What factors would you consider essential when looking at job design?

(IAM)

5. "Tests can, however, measure some attributes which are difficult to assess by interview. They can thus help to reduce the areas of subjective judgement and of possible human error in the selection process as a whole".
(Plumbley - Recruitment and Selection).

    (i) Explain the uses in employee selection of each of the following tests and attempt definitions of the italicised words:
        (*a*) General *intelligence* tests;
        (*b*) Special *aptitude* tests;
        (*c*) *Attainment* tests;
        (*d*) *Personality* tests.
    (ii) State and briefly discuss two objections to the use of psychological testing in personnel work.

(IAM)

6. (i) What do you understand by "employee commitment"?
    (ii) How can the fundamental human needs for power, achievement and affiliation be harnessed to develop employee commitment to an enterprise and its goals?

(IAM)

7. Explain the importance to the working group within industry and commerce of:

    (*a*) attitudes;
    (*b*) leadership;
    (*c*) motivation.

(LCCI)

8. (*a*) "A sound performance appraisal scheme is an essential requirement for management development to be effective." Discuss.

(*b*) What other functions does an appraisal scheme fulfil in an organisation?

(CBSI)

9. You have applied for a senior vacancy in the Job Evaluation Section of your Personnel Department and anticipate an interview question on job design.

State what you understand by this term and explain the importance of Job Descriptions and Job Specifications in this context.

(CII)

10. The roles of a personnel department may be classified under four headings, (1) provision of specialist advice and counsel; (2) provision of services to other organisational functions; (3) development of personnel policies and procedures and (4) audit and control.

 (i) Briefly distinguish between each of the four personnel department roles identified above
 (ii) Show, using suitable examples, how the exercise of these responsibilities by the personnel department may lead to friction with other inter-organisational functions and briefly indicate how the personnel department may minimise such conflict.

(IAM)

11. (*a*) Identify, with brief examples, *four* organisational causes of individual stress.

(*b*) Make recommendations for the management of stress in the work situation.

(IAM)

12. Your organisation is proposing to make extensive changes involving the introduction of new technology. The Chief Executive has asked you to prepare a report outlining the advantages and disadvantages of using external consultants for the purpose of advising what changes are required and the appropriate strategies for their implementation. Outline the points you would probably make.

(IAM)

13. "The world of work has changed . . . We need to take notice." (Charles Handy) In what ways (*a*) has the world of work changed over the past decade, and (*b*) will the world of work change over the next ten years? What are the implications for personnel specialists? (You may answer this question in relation to the UK or to any other country with which you are sufficiently familiar.)

(ICSA)

14. A manufacturing company has expanded over the last few years and now has 1000 employees. In the past there has been scant attention to personnel aspects with concentration on manufacturing. As further expansion is expected it has been decided that a Personnel Department be established.

As the newly appointed Personnel Manager you have the job of setting up the department. Discuss the main functions that you would see your department undertaking and the nature of any changes that may be needed to make it fully effective.

(IMS)

15. Explain the terms "demand and supply forecasting" as used in connection with manpower planning.

Suggest and comment on not more than five factors that may affect the manpower requirements of an enterprise for basic grade clerical staff over the next five years.

Briefly discuss two methods of measuring and analysing labour wastage.

(IAM)

16. You have been asked to recruit six additional technical clerks within the next two months. Describe the main stages of the recruitment process and indicate the problems most likely to arise and how they might be overcome.

(IAM)

17. Broadly speaking, there are two possible approaches to recruitment: the "selection approach" (fitting the person to the job) and the "classification approach" (fitting the job to the person). In what specific circumstances can either of these approaches be justified?

(ICSA)

18. (*a*) Why is it desirable to have a redundancy procedure?

(*b*) How can manpower planning contribute to the avoidance of redundancy?

(CBSI)

19. A manufacturing company intends to introduce major technological innovations onto the shop floor, with some reduction in manning. The personnel manager is preparing for the first round of discussions with the unions.

Explain how you, as a management services officer, could assist the personnel manager.

(IMS)

20. (i) Distinguish between training policy and training procedures.

(ii) For what purposes may organisations develop and publish training policies?

(iii) State, with reasons, whether you agree or disagree with the statement that "training policies are more often determined by prevailing interest rather than principle".

(IAM)

21. (*a*) What methods exist for identifying the training requirements of an organisation?

(*b*) Why is it important to identify training needs?

(CBSI)

22. A recent article makes the following criticisms of many training and development practices in organisations:

* Training and development are often not fully integrated into the management process.
* Training and development activities perpetuate "introverted" management.

* The priority given to training and development depends too much on the attitudes of individual managers.
* Much training and development is insufficiently related to individual needs.

To what extent do you believe these criticisms to be justified? How can they be prevented or minimised?

(ICSA)

23. (*a*) In relation to administrators review the respective merits and de-merits of training:
    (i) on the job;
    (ii) off the job.
(*b*) Describe in each case, two techniques of "off" and "on the job" training applicable to management development.

(IAM)

24. (*a*) What is job evaluation and what are the benefits that might accrue from its use in a financial services organisation?
(*b*) Describe the points rating method of job evaluation and detail its advantages and disadvantages.

(CBSI)

25. Your firm is considering the introduction of a flexible working hours scheme for all staff below management level. What are the advantages and disadvantages of such a scheme from a management point of view?

(CII)

26. Examine the extent to which computers are currently being used to facilitate the work of personnel departments. What developments do you consider likely over the next few years in this field?

(ICSA)

27. "The pluralistic framework for industrial relations is now completely dead, and the power of unions is insignificant."
Discuss:

(*a*) the accuracy of this remark, both today and in the foreseeable future; and (*b*) its implications for the personnel function.

(ICSA)

28. As part of its training programme a company requires its junior hotel managers to understand the procedures for negotiating with trades union officials and to acquire the necessary skills.

You have been asked to run a one day in-house session for new junior managers. Describe the content of a suitable course.

(IMS)

29. You are the manager of a department which will shortly introduce computerisation of tasks previously carried out manually. What factors should you consider when introducing such a system?

(CII)

30. One of your staff continues to be late for work despite being warned by you. This is now causing friction with other staff. Explain how you would resolve the matter.

(CII)

31. Where racial or ethnic or sex discrimination appear to occur in organisations, how can the existence and extent of such discrimination be measured? What can personnel managers do to remove or reduce the incidence of discrimination?

(ICSA)

32. Health and safety is sometimes regarded as a "luxury" by senior management. What action could be taken, on the initiative of the personnel department, to change this view? How would you go about formulating health and safety policies and procedures which have genuine importance in an organisation?

(ICSA)

33. (*a*) Draft a model disciplinary procedure.

(*b*) Write an accompanying set of guidance notes for line managers which concisely explain the purpose and operation of the procedure.

(CBSI)

34. (*a*) Distinguish between "disciplinary" and "grievance" procedures.

    (*b*) What guidelines would you lay down for the conduct of:
      (i) disciplinary procedures?
      (ii) grievance procedures?

                                                            (IAM)

35. Early in 1990, the Institute of Personnel Management identified four issues and priorities for personnel managers in the United Kingdom: demographics, competitiveness, Europe and the role of personnel in business strategy. From where you are (in the UK or overseas) what do you think are the major issues and priorities for personnel managers in the next decade, and what should personnel managers be doing to meet these challenges?

                                                             (ICSA)

Appendix 6
Glossary of human resources management terms

ACAS (Advisory, Conciliation and Arbitration Service). A government agency established to improve UK industrial relations. It mediates in industrial disputes, seeks out-of-court settlements in cases of alleged unfair dismissal, and publishes *Codes of Practice* on employment matters.

Access to Medical Reports Act 1988. Legislation compelling firms to obtain the consent of employees prior to their being required to take medical examinations.

Achievement test. A selection test intended to establish whether a person possesses a particular *skill* or ability (e.g. typing or driving).

Action learning. An approach to training that requires trainees to collect, evaluate and deal with information relevant to real-life problems.

Actions short of dismissal. Disciplinary sanctions other than the sack, (e.g. demotion, denial of pay increases, loss of fringe benefits, or refusal of requests for time off).

Actuarial selection. Employee selection based on objective statistical data about candidates.

Additional award. Extra compensation awarded by *industrial tribunals* to unfairly dismissed workers whose ex-employers refuse to re-engage them.

Affect structure. A pattern of interpersonal attractions which determines the extent and nature of associations within a group.

Alienation. Extreme job dissatisfaction that causes an employee to feel that work is neither important nor relevant to his or her life.

Alternance. According to the European Commission, the extent to which a training programme mixes off-job training and work experience (e.g. within a sandwich course).

Analogous tests. *Achievement tests* that seek to replicate key aspects of a certain type of employment (e.g. shorthand tests for applicants for secretarial jobs).

Analytical job evaluation. Techniques of *job evaluation* which attempt to quantify the effort, skill and responsibility attached to a job.

Annualised-hours contract. A contract of employment whereby an employee works a certain number of hours during the year; the actual weekly hours varying from week to week within the 12-month period.

Any difference rule. The legal principle that a dismissal is fair even if the procedures leading up to it were unfair (e.g. an employer failing to give proper warnings), provided the outcome would have been exactly the same had no procedural defect occurred.

APL (assessment of prior learning). Pre-testing of trainees to ascertain how much they already know and to evaluate their past activities and achievements.

Apprentice. An employee who receives substantial on-job training for a craft or trade. In return, the apprentice accepts a relatively low wage until he or she is fully competent.

Arbitration. Resolution of a dispute through having an independent outsider examine all its aspects and impose a ruling.

Associated employers. Any pair of companies where one is directly or indirectly controlled by the other or where both are controlled by a third party.

Attitude. An inclination to perceive, interpret and evaluate people, events and issues in a certain manner.

Attribution. The mental processes through which individuals explain their own or other people's behaviour.

Authority. Formal rights to control others that result from appointment to a management position.

Automatically unfair dismissal. Dismissal for joining or refusing to join a trade union; for being pregnant; or because a business has changed hands. *Industrial tribunals* will automatically award compensation to the victims of such sackings.

Banded day work. A wage payment system in which management sets a series of bands for pay and performance, each band carrying a certain flat-rate wage.

Bargaining unit. The sections, departments and/or grades of employee to which a collective agreement is to apply.

Basic award. Compensation awarded by an *industrial tribunal* to an unfairly dismissed worker just equal in value to the amount of a statutory redundancy payment.

Behaviour-modelling training. An application of the social learning approach to training wherein the trainee is encouraged to observe and copy the attitudes and behaviour of carefully-selected role models.

Behaviourism. The proposition that human actions are mainly determined by stimulus–response factors.

Benchmark job. A job against which the duties and responsibilities associated with other jobs are compared.

Biodata. Information on a job applicant's lifetime experiences and current personal circumstances.

Blacking of work. Refusing to complete work normally undertaken by striking employees.

Blackleg. A term of abuse directed against strikebreaking workers.

Blue collar workers. A term commonly used to describe manual workers. The name derives from the blue overalls that many manual employees wear.

Branch committee. A committee comprising key members of a branch of a trade union, responsible for dealing with routine branch administration.

Bridlington agreement. An agreement among member unions of the Trades Union Congress not to poach each other's members.

CAC (Central Arbitration Committee). A government body established to arbitrate in disputes referred to it by *ACAS*, and which hears complaints from trade unions over employers' alleged refusals to disclose information reasonably required for *collective bargaining*.

Cafeteria benefits. Packages of company fringe benefits which allow employees to select whichever elements suit them personally, given their particular circumstances at a certain time (e.g. trading off additional maternity leave against reduced pension benefits).

Card vote. A ballot taken at the annual Trades Union Congress whereby each representative of a member union casts a number of votes proportional to the size of his or her union.

Career. A series of jobs that follow a hierarchy of levels of difficulty, responsibility and status.

Certification officer. A government official responsible for registering independent trade unions and for hearing union members' complaints about their union's conduct of ballots and elections.

Chunking. Grouping together items to be learned into meaningful segments in order to facilitate their memorisation.

CIRO method. A training evaluation technique that analyses the effectiveness of an instructional programme under four main headings: context, input, reaction and output.

Classical conditioning. Association of a neutral stimulus with a reflexive response (i.e. one controlled by the autonomic nervous system).

Clinical selection. Employment interviews that rely on judgmental, impressionistic criteria to select the successful candidate.

Closed question. An interview or written question with fixed alternative answers.

Codes of Practice. Documents published by government agencies (e.g. *ACAS* or the Equal Opportunities Commission), or by professional bodies or trade associations to outline model procedures for good practice in a particular field (e.g. health and safety at work, or the removal of unfair discrimination in employment).

Cognition. The mental processes concerned with thinking, reasoning, language, problem solving and perception.

Cognitive dissonance. Inconsistencies in an individual's perceptions of related objects, events or circumstances (e.g. believing that it is raining but not feeling wet).

Collective bargaining. Negotiations between managements and trade unions intended to establish pay and conditions for a large number of workers.

Commissioner for the Rights of Trade Union Members. A government official appointed to assist trade unionists obtain redress following unlawful acts committed by their unions.

Compa ratio. An index showing the degree to which pay levels are clustered around the mid-point of a particular grade.

Compensatory award. Compensation awarded by an *industrial tribunal* to an unfairly dismissed worker and fixed at a level just sufficient to offset his or her lost wages and benefits.

Conciliation. Use of a third party to help settle an industrial dispute (e.g. by suggesting solutions and advising each disputant of the other side's negotiating position).

Concurrent validity. The property of certain selection tests that they have already been tried on employees actually performing the work for which applicants are being tested and have been proven to identify characteristics genuinely relevant to that type of job.

Conflict cycle. The stages through which industrial disputes typically develop; starting with the issue that triggers the conflict, through negotiations, reassessment of each party's position, the emergence of compromises, and final settlement of the dispute.

Conjunctive negotiations. Negotiating situations where the parties have no alternative but to settle.

Conjunctive task. A group task which depends for its successful completion on each group member finishing one or more subsidiary and highly-interdependent operations.

Consideration leadership style. An approach to leadership which focuses on the need for *two-way communications*, concern for subordinates' feelings, and mutual respect between subordinate and boss.

Consolidation of wages. Incorporation into an employee's basic wage of existing fringe benefits, *ad-hoc* bonuses, etc., that were previously regarded as privileges rather than rights.

Conspiracy. A secret plan to commit an unlawful act by two or more persons.

Construct validity. The characteristic of certain selection tests that there exist significant relationships between the test scores achieved by candidates and other evidence regarding their abilities (e.g. possession of academic qualifications).

Constructive dismissal. The resignation of an employee caused by the employer's unreasonable behaviour (e.g. sexual harassment) that represents a fundamental breach of the employee's contract of employment. The aggrieved worker may then claim to have been unfairly dismissed.

Content theories. *Motivation* theories that seek to define and explain the needs the attempted fulfilment of which is assumed to motivate workers.

Content validity. The desirable property of a selection test that the questions it asks (or the tasks it requires be performed) directly relate to the personal qualities the test is attempting to measure (e.g. a numeracy test for applicants for trainee accountancy positions).

Contract for services. A contract to engage a self-employed person to provide *ad-hoc* services, as opposed to a 'contract of service' for hiring a waged employee.

Contracted-out national insurance contributions. Class I state national insurance contributions paid by individuals who also belong to a private occupational pension scheme. Such contributions are slightly lower than the normal Class I rate.

Contracting out. An individual's decision not to contribute to a trade union's political fund, and instructing the union not to use any part of his or her union subscription for political purposes.

Control theories of motivation. Approaches to *motivation* which claim that employees typically compare their actual job situations with desired standards and then behave in ways intended to reduce discrepancies.

Convenor. The senior *shop steward* in a company or major division of a firm.

Core workers. Permanent full-time employees, usually super-annuated.

Counselling. Assisting employees recognise and accurately define their own problems, find solutions, or learn to live with a situation.

Coverdale training. A self-discovery group training method that focuses on the emotional aspects of intra-group behaviour.

CRAMP approach to training. A fivefold classification of the personal competencies that trainees are said to need to develop during an instructional programme (i.e. comprehension, reflex response, attitude formation, memorising, and procedural learning).

Criterion behaviour. All the tasks, procedures, techniques and skills that a trainee should have mastered by the end of a course.

Criterion-referenced assessment. Evaluation of a trainee's abilities against his or her capacity to complete particular specified duties at a predefined level of competence.

Critical incidents. Specific examples of an employee's exceptionally good or bad performance considered in a *performance appraisal* exercise.

Decision band method. A *job evaluation* technique that ranks jobs according to the amounts of responsibility and decision making they carry.

Demarkation disputes. Conflicts between different unions and/or grades of employee within the same organisation regarding which tasks should be completed by which category of worker. For example, is changing a light bulb an electrician's job or a cleaner's?

Differential bonus scheme. A wage incentive system whereby workers' remunerations rise by very large amounts for increased output at high levels of efficiency, but by low amounts for improvements at low levels of efficiency.

Dilutees. Unskilled workers employed to complete jobs previously undertaken by trained and skilled employees.

DISC test. A psychological test developed from research on American soldiers in the 1920s. It purports to identify four basic aspects of test subjects' personalities: dominance, influence, submission and compliance.

Discouraged workers. Unemployed workers who remain out of work for longer than is objectively necessary because of depression caused by repeated rejections from job applications, resulting in their ceasing to look for work, even when the labour market has improved substantially.

Discovery learning. An approach to training that requires trainees to ascertain for themselves the basic principles of their jobs and how best to complete them.

Distributive negotiation. Bargaining over the distribution of shares in a fixed amount of resources.

Division of labour. Breaking work into small and simple units that can be completed quickly by unskilled operatives.

Dynamic adaptive testing. Tests of achievement, intelligence or other mental ability whereby the difficulty of the questions asked automatically increases as test subjects continue to give correct answers.

EAT (Employment Appeal Tribunal). A court that hears appeals against the decisions of *industrial tribunals* and the government *Certification Officer*. It is chaired by a High Court judge who sits with two lay members, and may only consider appeals on questions of law (not points of fact).

Element of competence. According to the *NCVQ*, a description of an action, behaviour or outcome which a person should be able to demonstrate, or a piece of knowledge.or understanding of what should be done in a workplace situation that a person needs to possess in order to complete a certain type of work proficiently.

Embezzlement. Theft from an employer.

Emolument. Any wage, salary, fee, profit or perquisite.

Employer-led standards. Criteria for evaluating the contents of training courses laid down by employers in a certain industry or group of occupations, normally through industry *lead bodies*.

Empowerment. The process of giving an employee the right to take executive decisions within certain specified limits, but requiring that person to assume full responsibility for his or her actions.

End-loaded wage agreement. A negotiated pay deal which provides a relatively modest wage increase on conclusion of the agreement followed by further substantial amounts towards the end of the period covered by the bargain.

Equity theory. An approach to *motivation* which suggests that employees' perceptions of how they are treated relative to (*i*) their efforts, and (*ii*) other workers, are primary determinants of the enthusiasm they apply to their jobs.

ERG (existence, relatedness and growth) theory. A restructuring of Maslow's *hierarchy of needs*.

Ergonomics. Analysis of the relationships between people and their physical working environments and of how the latter can be adopted to meet human needs and capabilities.

Ethnic minority. A group distinguished from others by a combination of shared customs, beliefs, traditions and characteristics derived from a common or presumed common past, even if the distinctions are not biologically determined.

Euro-executives. Geographically mobile, multi-lingual EC managers capable of quickly adapting to the culture and business methods of any EC country.

***Ex-gratia* payment.** An *ad-hoc* payment made without accepting any responsibility for the possible existence of a legally-binding obligation.

Exchange theory. The proposition that the structure of interpersonal relations depends primarily on the rewards (e.g. compliments or gestures of affection) exchanged, and the costs (e.g. humiliations, rebukes, etc.) incurred during social interactions.

Executive search. Use of external consultants to identify and confidentially approach potential candidates for senior management positions.

Exit interview. An interview conducted with a resigning employee in order to establish his or her reasons for leaving, hence enabling the firm to implement measures to prevent other workers resigning for similar reasons.

Expectancy theory. An approach to *motivation* which suggests that an individual's behaviour depends on his or her self-selected goals and what the person has learned or believes will help achieve them.

Expert system. A computer-software package that mimics the problem-solving methods of a human expert.

Face validity. The property of certain selection tests that they create the impression of measuring attributes directly relevant to the jobs for which candidates are being tested (e.g. a test for selecting trainee accountants might include questions that refer to practical financial situations).

Facilitating questions. Interview questions intended to ease the flow of conversation. Examples are friendly remarks phrased as questions, general questions not related to the job, or a summary in question form of previous comments.

Factor comparison method. An approach to *job evaluation* that seeks to identify the presence of certain common factors within jobs (e.g. mental ability, skill and physical requirements, responsibility, working conditions).

False negatives. Trainees who fail assessments not because they are incompetent but rather through faults in the assessment process. 'False positives', conversely, are trainees who pass an assessment which objectively they should have failed.

Fast tracking. Accelerated promotion systems whereby certain employees are placed on training, planned experience and management development programmes, and then presented with specific targets the attainment of which automatically leads to promotion.

Faults analysis. Investigation of the types of mistake commonly made by employees while undertaking certain kinds of duties.

Featherbedding. Use by employees of rules and working practices that cause overmanning and/or reduced output.

Felt fair methods. *Job evaluation* techniques that apply overall general assessments to the grading of employees' duties, in contrast to using analytical methods.

Field review. A method of *performance appraisal* in which a personnel officer interviews heads of department about their subordinates' qualities and then prepares appraisal reports (rather than heads of department doing this personally).

Force field analysis. Investigation of the elements most resistant to change within an organisation.

Forced-choice rating scale. A *performance appraisal* checklist comprising ordered pairs of statements from which the assessor is required to tick the alternatives considered most descriptive of the appraisee's performance.

Formative assessment. Evaluation of a trainee's performance using assessments that provide feedback to the trainee on his or her progress and which help the trainee correct mistakes and remedy weaknesses.

Frame of reference. All the attitudes and psychological influences that determine how a person perceives events and issues.

Friend. In industrial relations, a person who accompanies a worker to a grievance or disciplinary interview.

Frustration. Feelings of anguish that result from interference with an individual's attempts to achieve his or her self-established objectives.

Functional analysis. A means for determining performance standards for *units of competence* in National Vocational Qualifications (NVQs). A 'function' in this context is a 'role expectation', i.e. an activity described in terms of what is expected of its outcomes (e.g. 'providing information', or 'performing calculations').

Functional job analysis. Categorisation of jobs according to two main criteria: nature of the work performed (contacts with other people, data analysis, environmental conditions, etc.), and the personal traits deemed necessary in the individual completing the job (aptitudes, intelligence, temperament, and so on).

Gatekeeper. Someone who communicates with the outside world on behalf of an organisation, who gathers information from external sources and who in consequence of being able to alter or withhold this information, can significantly affect the organisation's decisions.

Generic skills. Skills that apply to a wide range of activities and hence are easily transferred from one job or occupation to others.

Genuine material factor. A legitimate reason for men and women not receiving equal pay for work of equal value.

Genuine occupational qualification. A legitimate reason for discriminating in favour of one of the sexes or a particular *ethnic group* in an employment situation (e.g. recruiting only Chinese waiters to work in a Chinese restaurant).

Golden handcuffs. Arrangements whereby firms withhold significant payments to senior employees until the latter have remained with their employing organisations for certain minimum periods. The aim is to prevent the *headhunting* of top managers.

Grandfather system. In *performance appraisal*, the practice whereby a manager's assessment of a subordinate is sent to the appraising manager's own boss for review and comment.

Grapevine. An informal and unofficial collection of communication channels that disseminate news and rumours within an organisation.

Green labour. School leavers or other fresh recruits who do not possess work experience.

Group cohesion. The extent to which the members of a group co-operate, share common goals, and possess common attitudes and perspectives.

Group norms. Shared perceptions of what constitutes correct behaviour, of how work should be completed, and of proper attitudes towards management and other workers.

Guarantee payments. Payments available to workers under the Employment Protection (Consolidation) Act 1978 for lay-offs of up to five days during any three-month period.

Half-life survival rate. The average period that elapses before half a particular group of recruits, all of whom started at the same time, leave the firm.

Halo effect. The situation that arises when interviewers wrongly assume that because certain job applicants possess one desirable characteristic (e.g. attractive physical appearance) they must be equally worthy in several other areas.

Hay-MSL method. A job evaluation technique that breaks jobs down into three basic factors: know-how, problem solving, and accountability.

Headhunting. Another term for *executive search*.

Hersey–Blanchard model. A leadership theory which asserts that managers should adjust their leadership styles according to subordinates' work experience, levels of ability, and willingness to accept responsibility.

Hierarchy of needs. According to the American psychologist A.H. Maslow, a rank order of needs which individuals attempt to satisfy sequentially. There are five levels: physiological, security, affection, esteem and *self-actualisation*.

Horizontal fast track. A planned experience job rotation scheme intended to give selected employees numerous postings – all at the same level of responsibility – thus enabling them to acquire quickly the experience and broader perspectives needed for senior management positions.

House party method. Employee selection through observing how candidates interact with each other at an assessment centre.

Human resource accounting. Systematic measurement, analysis and recording of the costs and financial benefits of hiring and utilising human resources (e.g. estimation of recruitment and training costs, assessment of the effects of staff development programmes, investigation of the consequences for output of various types of wage incentive system, etc.).

Hygiene factor. An element of the working environment which, if it is satisfactory, will not be noticed but which, if it is unsatisfactory, will demotivate workers. However, the adequacy of a hygiene factor will not of itself motivate employees.

Impingement pay. Additional payments to employees who work during their contractual holiday entitlements.

Incapability. A reason for fair dismissal. Examples are incompetence, and incapacity for work caused by ill health or injury.

Indenture. A special contract of employment for an *apprentice*.

Independent trade union. A trade union not controlled by an employer or subject to interference by an employer *via* the latter's provision or withdrawal of financial support.

Indirect discrimination. Unfair race or sex discrimination resulting from the imposition of a special requirement for the occupancy of a job (e.g. insisting that job applicants be over six feet tall, which automatically discriminates against the great majority of women).

Indirect labour. Workers who do not contribute directly to the production of goods. Examples are secretaries, cleaners and maintenance workers.

Industrial engineering. The application to industrial operations of analytical techniques such as work study, quality control, network analysis and production planning.

Industrial relations. All the rules, practices and conventions that govern interrelations between managements and organised labour.

Industrial Tribunal. A three-person court comprising a qualified lawyer plus two lay members (each representing one of the two sides of industry – i.e. employers' associations and trade unions) that hears cases concerning unfair dismissal, health and safety at work, violations of equal opportunities legislation, and related employment matters.

Initiating structure. A leadership style that involves close supervision of subordinates and extensive application of the *division of labour*.

Inner directedness. Personal qualities associated with creativity, individualism and independence. This contrasts with 'other directedness' which involves conformism and easy submission to external influences.

Input-driven learning. Training that follows a preset syllabus, using predetermined training methods. The aim is to guarantee that learners acquire certain knowledge and/or abilities.

Instrumental attitudes. Employee orientations towards work that focus on pay and job security rather than on job satisfaction or the quality of working life.

Instrumentality. In motivation theory, how a worker perceives the correlation between reward and performance.

Integrative negotiations. Bargaining situations in which the parties seek common positions on issues.

Interactive video. A training film which outlines the background to a stimulated interpersonal communication situation and then leaves the trainees to specify how he or she would deal with critical aspects of the problems depicted.

Interview funnel. A method for conducting employment interviews which begins by asking broad, open-ended questions and then systematically narrows down the scope of the questions asked, eventually focusing on specific job related topics.

Intrinsic reinforcement. In *classical* and *operant conditioning*, *reinforcement* caused by positive inner feelings that result from performing a particular activity.

Inventory, personal. A test intended to measure a person's characteristics in a certain dimension (e.g. personality, intelligence or vocational interests). Personal inventories differ from conventional tests in that they do not have pass/fail cut-off marks. Their sole purpose is to enable participants to identify their own strengths and weaknesses.

Involuntary absenteeism. Non-attendance at work through factors entirely beyond an employee's control (e.g. bad weather leading to transport difficulties).

Ipsative tests. Psychometric tests that require candidates to express a preference from several specified alternatives outlined in each question.

Item information. Data on employees which describes their personal biographical details, qualifications, training courses attended, etc.

Job characteristics model. A means for evaluating the impact of *job enrichment* on employee attitudes and behaviour. The psychological consequences of the measures taken are predicted and then compared with actual changes in workers' perceptions and attitudes.

Job depth. The degrees of decision making and control over choice of working methods exerted by an employee while completing a job.

Job enlargement. The process of giving a worker a wider variety of tasks to perform, all at approximately the same level of difficulty.

Job enrichment. Allocation to a worker of additional responsibilities and/or more difficult and complex tasks in order to make his or her job more interesting.

Job evaluation. Analysis of the characteristics of jobs so as to rank them according to their relative value. It focuses on the elements of each job rather than the personal attributes of job occupants.

Kaizen system. A form of *quality circle* based on a cycle of 'planning, doing, checking and actioning'.

Kinaesthetics. In *motion study*, the study of the body movements needed to perform work.

Knowledge-based assessment. Evaluation of a trainee's possession of knowledge, rather than his or her ability to apply knowledge in a work situation.

Knowledge of results. Feedback given to trainees regarding their level of performance.

Labour stability index. A labour-turnover measure which shows the proportion of a firm's employees with more than one year's service.

Lead body. A committee comprising representatives of professional bodies, government departments and employers' associations concerned with a particular industry or occupation. The role of a lead body is to work out criteria for measuring the competence of employees in that industry or occupation in order to devise National Vocational Qualifications (*NVQs*) for its workers.

Leapfrogging. Constantly escalating pay awards in various industries as unions in each industry use the immediately preceding pay awards obtained by unions in other industries as the basis for their own claims for wage increases.

Learned helplessness. The situation that arises when an

individual who is unemployed for a long period 'learns' that it is futile applying for any more jobs.

Learner-centred learning. Training which seeks to impart only the knowledge and skills that trainees need to learn, rather than sticking rigidly to institutional syllabuses.

Learning family, creation of. The grouping together of training and job experiences into broad occupational categories so that trainees learn a variety of skills within a particular 'family' (e.g. 'manufacturing and assembly'). This should enable them to transfer the *skills* acquired in one job to others in the same family.

Like work. Jobs done by men and women that are broadly similar in terms of the work involved and the effort, *skill* and knowledge needed for their completion.

Local collective bargaining. *Collective bargaining* to determine pay and working conditions in particular workplaces.

Lock-out. A firm's decision to bar employees from entering their place of work, normally in retaliation for workers having taken industrial action.

Lump labour. Workers who offer their services as self-employed sub-contractors rather than as 'employees' to enable employers to avoid paying national insurance and/or assume any other legal obligations.

Managerial grid. A technique of management training intended to assist managers identify their leadership style and hence improve their managerial effectiveness. Managers are categorised according to their concern for production and concern for subordinates' welfare.

Managerial ideology. Beliefs held by some senior managers which inwardly support and legitimise their elite status within organisations.

Manifest need theory. The proposition that most human needs are learned rather than inherited and come to be felt only when triggered by events in external environments.

Maturity curve. A graph showing the median salaries of various groups of workers against their average age, thus enabling a firm to forecast its future salary bills as the average age of its workforce increases.

Measured-day work. A wage-payment system whereby employees must produce a prespecified daily output for a fixed daily wage.

Mediation. Attempts to settle an industrial dispute through the intervention of a third party who informs each side of the views and requirements of the other.

Mentor. A senior manager who provides help, encouragement and psychological support to a favoured subordinate so as to promote the latter's career development.

Merit rating. Appraisal of the performances of manual and clerical workers.

Method study. Analysis of working methods in order to simplify procedures and eliminate duplication of effort.

Methods time measurement (MTM). A form of *predetermined motion time system* based on published tables of *standard times* used to predict the periods in which basic operations should be completed, given various working environments.

Moonlighters. Employees who simultaneously hold more than one job, often without any one employer knowing the individual is also working elsewhere.

Motion study. Analysis of the human body movements needed for work.

Motivating factor. According to F.Herzberg, something responsible for creating satisfaction at work, as opposed to a *hygiene factor*. Examples of motivators in the *two factor theory* are recognition, interesting work, responsibility, and prospects for promotion.

Motor responses. Limb and other body movements that result from receipt of messages from the brain.

Motor skills. *Skills* needed for repetitive manual activities.

Multi-skilling. Working systems in which employees regularly exchange and share tasks. No job is undertaken exclusively by a single individual.

National Executive Committee (NEC). The highest level of authority in a trade union. Under the Trade Union Act 1984, every member of a union's NEC must be elected by the entire union membership.

Natural justice. Rules that courts expect employers to apply when implementing disciplinary procedures. Examples are informing an accused person of the full details of complaints, allowing the worker to be represented by a third party, not prejudging the issue, etc.

NCVQ (National Council for Vocational Qualifications). A government body set up to implement a national framework for vocational qualifications and to determine national standards of occupational competence.

Negligence. Failure to exercise the amount of care that an average reasonable person would exercise in a given situation. For negligence to be legally actionable there has to exist a duty of care, a breach of that duty by the negligent person, and resulting damage.

Networking, employment. Organising a business in such a manner that employees work from home, communicating with head office *via* a computer, telephone, and occasional visits.

Non-compliance award. Additional compensation awarded by an *industrial tribunal* to an unfairly dismissed worker whose employer refuses to take back that person.

Norm-based assessment. Evaluation of a trainee's abilities in comparison with other trainees, rather than against his or her capacity to complete certain prespecified tasks successfully.

NTTF (National Training Task Force). A government agency responsible for co-ordinating the activities of the *Training and Enterprise Councils (TECs)*.

Objective knowledge. Knowledge obtained by a worker in consequence of his or her employment in a particular firm and is therefore the intellectual property of the employing organisation, not the worker.

Occupational analysis inventory. A job-analysis method which categorises work activities and conditions under five main headings: information received, mental activities, observed behaviour, work outcomes, and work contexts.

Occupational personality questionnaire. A personality test similar to the *16PF test* but specifically related to occupational requirements, rather than to general personality characteristics.

Occupational standards. Performance or quality standards recognised by an industry, profession or training organisation as necessary for the satisfactory completion of work.

Official dispute. An industrial dispute formally sanctioned by a trade union.

Open question. An interview or written question to which any response may be given.

Operant conditioning theory. The proposition that learning occurs mainly through trial and error. According to the theory, behaviour that leads to reward will tend to be repeated, and vice versa. Hence, actual behaviour is regarded as being determined by its perceived consequences.

Organisational behaviour modification (OBM). Application of the principles of *operant conditioning theory* to organisational problems.

Organisational climate (culture). The totality of the attitudes, norms, beliefs and perspectives shared by the majority of the members of an organisation.

Organisational development. Analysis of the adequacy of a firm's organisation structures, communication networks, authority and responsibility systems, etc., and the implementation of measures for improving them.

Originating application. A form completed by an aggrieved person who wishes to initiate a case in an *industrial tribunal*.

Other directedness. See *inner directedness*.

Outplacement. Assistance given by firms to workers who are about to be made redundant, in an attempt to help them find other jobs. Outplacement activities include career counselling, informing suppliers and customer businesses of workers' availability, and *psychometric testing* intended to discover workers' aptitudes for alternative types of work.

Paired comparison method. A technique of *job evaluation* which involves the stepwise comparison of the characteristics of several jobs until a consistent hierarchy emerges.

Path-goal theory. A leadership theory which suggests that effective leadership requires managers to clarify to subordinates the actions they must take to obtain various rewards (higher wages, promotion, access to training, etc.).

Pay anomalies. Large differences in the remuneration levels of various occupational groups whose work, nevertheless, requires similar inputs of skill, effort, responsibility, educational qualifications and decision taking.

Pendulum arbitration. A wage *arbitration* method whereby management and union each submit to a third party a figure they believe appropriate for this year's pay increase. The arbitrator then chooses one figure or the other; there are no negotiations or haggling.

Perception. The mental processes through which individuals interpret sensory inputs such as sight, sound, smell, taste, etc.

Performance appraisal. Analysis of an employee's recent successes and failures, personal strengths and weaknesses, and suitability for promotion or further training.

Performance-based assessment. Evaluation of a trainee's knowledge, *skills* and competence while he or she is actually undertaking work-based tasks.

Performance criteria. In *NVQs*, definitions of expected levels of ability for *elements of competence*. Criteria relate to 'outcomes' in terms of what trainees need to be able to do, rather than to the process of learning.

Peripheral workers. Casual and/or part-time employees hired and fired according to a firm's immediate short-term requirements.

Person specification. A written description of the ideal candidate for a vacant position.

Personal effectiveness. Aspects of occupational competence determined by personal attributes rather than job knowledge (e.g. maturity, initiative, or self-confidence).

Personality. The totality of an individual's attitudes, perspectives, beliefs, values, motives, dispositions, mental and other personal characteristics.

Pickets. Striking workers who stand at the entrances of their firms in order to try and persuade fellow employees and others not to enter the premises.

Plant bargaining. Another term for *local collective bargaining*.

Pluralism. The view that the best way of avoiding industrial disputes is to recognise from the beginning that the two sides of industry (management and workers) necessarily possess conflicting interests, so that formal procedures are necessary for resolving (inevitable) disagreements.

Power. The ability to change the attitudes or behaviour of other people. Power can be exerted by unofficial as well as official leaders.

Predetermined motion time (PMT) system. A *motion study* technique which assumes that every job can be broken down into standard body movements for which average completion times have already been tabulated.

Predictive validity. The desirable property of a selection test that it generates high test scores among candidates who subsequently succeed in the job for which they were tested.

Pre-hearing assessment. A sitting of an *industrial tribunal* convened if a superficial examination of the facts of a situation indicates that one of the parties is bound to lose the case. Its purpose is to warn the appropriate party that its case is legally groundless.

Preliminary hearing. A sitting of an *industrial tribunal* convened to establish whether it has the authority to hear a case (e.g. whether a worker claiming unfair dismissal has completed the statutory period of continuous employment necessary to be able to register a claim).

Prescribed diseases. Industrial diseases the victims of which are automatically entitled to receive state industrial injury benefit.

Primary group. A group whose members regularly come into face-to-face contact.

Primary mental abilities. Aspects of intelligence involving spatial ability, numerical ability, memory, inductive reasoning, speed of perception, and verbal fluency.

Principal executive committees. The key decision-making committees of a trade union. Under the Trade Union Act 1984, every voting member of a principal executive committee must be elected by the union's entire membership.

Proactive inhibition. The situation that arises when a person's past learning inhibits his or her ability to learn new things (e.g. a two-finger typist who has difficulty learning how to touchtype). 'Retroactive inhibition', conversely, means that freshly acquired skills interfere with a trainee's capacity to apply previously learned methods.

Procedural agreements. Agreed procedures concerning rules, methods and institutions to be used for settling management/union disputes.

Process theories. *Motivation* theories which examine the thought processes underlying individual propensities to behave in certain ways.

Product skills. Skills that can be measured quantitatively (e.g. the ability to type at 40 words per minute). This contrasts with 'process' skills, which do not have quantifiable outcomes (e.g. organisational ability).

Productivity bargaining. Management/union negotiations concerning the introduction of radical changes in working methods in exchange for a package of output-related pay increases.

Profile information. Data extracted from employee records to enable a firm to define the main characteristics of typical incumbents of various types of position.

Programmed learning. Instructional materials that present trainees with a series of small units of information ('frames') each immediately followed by a list of questions that have to be answered prior to attempting more advanced work.

Progressive discipline. Increasingly severe penalties imposed on errant employees for persistent latecoming, unauthorised absence, substandard work, etc. For example, the first offence might result in a verbal warning, the second in a written warning, followed by deductions from pay, suspension and, ultimately, dismissal from the firm.

Protective award. Payments of wages for up to 90 days ordered by an *industrial tribunal* to employees whose union has complained that a firm has not followed statutory procedures when declaring the workers redundant.

Psychometric tests. Tests which attempt to measure the psychological dimensions of job applicants or current employees. Examples include intelligence tests, personality tests, and tests of individual *motivation*.

Psychomotor skills. *Skills* which require the co-ordination of thought and physical action.

Quality circle. An employee discussion group that meets periodically to consider, analyse and resolve quality and production control difficulties.

Quality of working life (QWL). The totality of human satisfactions at work. Determinants of QWL include working conditions, extent of participation in management decision making, interpersonal relations, and the *organisational climate* of the employing business.

Range statements. Descriptions of the activities, processes, equipment and contexts to which NVQ *elements of competence* apply.

Ranking system. A non-analytical method of *job evaluation* which involves an overall assessment of jobs rather than attempting to quantify the particular elements of each position.

Rating, work study. A work study officer's subjective assessment of the degree of effort an employee is putting into his or her work.

Receptor processes. The mechanisms through which individuals sense cues and stimuli from their external environments.

Recognised trade union. Any independent trade union with which an employer is prepared to bargain over employment matters. Once recognised, a union enjoys certain legal rights (e.g. to appoint *safety representatives*).

Record of achievement. A document issued to a school leaver listing his or her achievements and progress within and outside the classroom, including activities not tested by formal examinations.

Red circling. The practice following the completion of *job evaluation* exercises of continuing to pay current salary levels to individuals whose jobs have been downgraded. However, a lower rate will be paid to employees who eventually replace red-circled workers.

Reference groups. Informal groups against which individuals evaluate their attitudes, beliefs, feelings and behaviour.

Reinforcements. Rewards (positive reinforcement) and punishments (negative reinforcement) that motivate people to behave in certain ways.

Reliability of assessment. The extent to which an assessment method generates consistent results over time and among assessors.

Reliability of selection tests. The extent to which selection tests generate consistent spreads of results when repeated on different groups of people.

Repetitive strain injury (RSI). Upper limb disorders (e.g. cramp or tenosynovitis) resulting from prolonged work at a keyboard.

Reportable accidents. Accidents causing death or more than three days' absence from employment. By law such accidents must be reported to the Health and Safety Executive.

Respondent. An employer who defends an action in an *industrial tribunal*.

Retroactive inhibition. See *Proactive inhibition*.

Role. A total and self-contained pattern of behaviour typical of a person who occupies a particular social position.

Safety officer. A manager appointed by a firm to be responsible for implementing its health and safety policies.

Safety representative. An employee selected by his or her trade union to deal with workplace health and safety. Duties of a safety representative include the inspection of premises, liaison with outside inspectors, and the investigation of hazards, accidents and dangerous occurrences.

Salary attrition. Cost savings resulting from long delays in replacing highly-paid employees who leave the firm.

Secondary actions. Industrial actions (e.g. picketing) taken against firms (such as suppliers or major customers) which are not directly involved in a trade dispute.

Secondary rewards. *Reinforcements* that are earned and not connected with characteristics innate to the individual. Examples are recognition, job satisfaction, social approval, pay rises, etc.

Self-actualisation. The highest level of need allegedly felt by a human being, i.e. the need to fulfil one's potential to the maximum level.

Self-managed learning. Training courses in which participants are themselves responsible for deciding what they need to know and, in liaison with an instructor, for selecting appropriate learning methods.

Shop steward. A lay workplace trade union representative.

Single status. The situation in which all grades of management and other workers share the same canteen, use the same car park, wear similar clothes, and enjoy equal access to *superannuation* and other fringe benefits.

Single table bargaining. Negotiating situations wherein the terms and conditions of an entire category of employee (e.g. manual workers) are settled at a single sitting.

Single union agreement. A situation in which management only recognises one trade union for the purpose of *collective bargaining*.

Situational interview. An employment interview which asks questions about how the candidate would handle specific incidents likely to arise in the course of the vacant job.

[Sixteen] 16 PF test. A widely used personality test which assumes the existence within test subjects of 16 clusters of behavioural factors (e.g. emotional stability, intelligence, assertiveness, etc.).

Skill. A capacity to perform a task competently, normally involving a co-ordinated sequence of mental and/or physical activities.

Skills analysis. Observation and recording of the methods used by a competent, skilled and experienced worker while completing tasks. Its aim is to analyse these methods as a basis for training other workers.

Skills inventory. A listing of all the qualifications, competencies and work experiences possessed by a firm's employees in order to inform management of all the alternative jobs that its current workforce is capable of undertaking.

Skittle effects. The consequences of training one group of workers for the training needs of others. For example, training manual workers in new skills could necessitate extra training for their supervisors, which in turn could require better trained middle managers, etc.

Soft criteria. Subjective judgmental criteria used in employee selection, as opposed to 'hard' criteria involving factual information.

Special compensation. A form of compensation awarded by *industrial tribunals* to workers unfairly dismissed for joining or refusing to join a trade union.

Speculative training. Another term for *training for stock*.

Spent conviction. A criminal conviction which the offending person is not obliged to disclose – even if asked to do so – following the expiry of a certain period after the imposition of a fine or the offender's release from prison.

Staff association. An association of employees (which is not a trade union) formed to represent workers' interests in a company.

Stakeholder. A person or group with a vested interest in the behaviour of a business.

Standard time. The period needed by a competent, experienced and motivated worker to complete a task, allowing for contingencies and employee relaxation.

Status congruence. Consistency of opinion among the members of a group regarding the status assigned to each participant.

Stereotyping. The attribution to an individual by other people of a number of characteristics assumed typical of the group to which the person belongs.

Substantive agreement. A negotiated agreement which relates to pay, working hours, holiday entitlement or some other specific term of condition of employment.

Summary dismissal. Dismissal on the spot, without notice.

Summative assessment. An evaluation of a trainee's performance on a course, undertaken purely for recording purposes (e.g. to qualify for the award of a certificate), rather than to help the trainee identify personal strengths and weaknesses and hence improve his or her work.

Sunlighter. A person who continues in full-time employment beyond the normal age for retirement.

Superannuation schemes. Company pension schemes, normally requiring both the employer and the employee to contribute about six per cent of the employee's salary to a central fund.

Synchropay. A suggested means (never implemented) for avoiding *leapfrogging*. Under the scheme all unions and employers would negotiate annual pay deals on the same day each year.

Systematic training. A term used to describe logical, analytical approaches to training, involving the identification of training needs, planning and implementing programmes, and the careful evaluation of the effectiveness of courses.

Task and finish system. A wage payment scheme whereby employees receive a fixed wage but are allowed to leave work as soon as an agreed task has been completed (as happens with some local authority refuse collectors, for example).

Team spirit. High motivation within a group resulting from feelings of loyalty, *group cohesion*, effective leadership and extensive interaction among group members.

Theory X and theory Y. Assumptions about human nature supposedly held by managers. Theory X assumptions are that workers are naturally lazy and must be coerced into working hard; theory Y assumptions assert that individuals are naturally industrious, may be relied upon to exercise self-direction and do not require close supervision.

Theory Z. A term coined by W. Ouchi to describe the Japanese approach to management. According to Ouchi, this involves long-term employment, seniority-based promotion, intense socialisation of recruits, production orientation, employee participation in decision making and great concern for the quality of output.

Threshold agreements. Pay deals whereby employees' wages automatically increase by a predetermined amount whenever the rate of inflation exceeds a certain level.

Time span of discretion method. A technique of *job evaluation* which relates employees' remunerations to the time periods that elapse between checks or evaluations of their work. The longer the intervals, the greater the level of responsibility assumed to be involved in the job.

Total loss control. An approach to accident prevention and consequent losses to production. It involves the systematic analysis of potential hazards, safety training, safety audits, spot checks, and the development of reporting procedures.

Trade dispute. A dispute between an employer and workers which is immune from civil liability, i.e. the workers or unions involved cannot be sued for breach of contract or conspiracy to induce a breach of contract.

Training and Enterprise Councils (TECs). Government-appointed bodies consisting of local business people charged with the task of identifying training needs in various geographical areas and then contracting training providers (e.g. local colleges) to deliver courses corresponding to specifications laid down by the area TEC.

Training for stock (speculative training). Training undertaken in anticipation of new *skills* requirements and/or cyclical upturns in the economy.

Transactional leadership. A leadership style based on the provision to subordinates of the resources they need and on helping subordinates complete their duties. This differs from 'transformational' leadership, which seeks to motivate workers to look beyond mundane short-term work requirements.

Transfer of learning. The ability to transfer competencies learned in one situation to others. For example, someone who has learned one wordprocessing package can usually pick up very quickly how to operate another.

Tripartism. The proposition that government, the Trades Union Congress and the Confederation of British Industry should jointly determine national industrial relations (and perhaps even economic) policies.

Two-factor theory. A motivation theory that distinguishes between 'motivators' and '*hygiene factors*'.

Two-way communications. Communications that involve a response from message recipients.

Unconditioned stimulus. A stimulus that naturally evokes a response (e.g. a presentation of food to a hungry dog, causing the dog's mouth to water).

Unfair dismissal. Dismissal of a worker who is covered by the Employment Protection (Consolidation) Act 1978, for anything other than incapability, genuine redundancy, gross misconduct or some other substantial reason.

Union density. The percentage of employees who belong to a trade union in a particular workplace, firm or industry.

Unit of competence. A collection of NVQ *elements of competence*.

Unitarism. The belief that management and workers have identical interests and thus may be expected naturally to work as a team and in a harmonious manner towards the achievement of common objectives.

Utility analysis. Estimation of the monetary costs and benefits of various techniques of employee selection so as to compare alternative recruitment strategies. Costs include job advertising, the effects of underperformance by a badly-selected person, and the replacement costs of unsatisfactory workers who are dismissed or resign. Benefits encompass the ability to promote satisfactory recruits, improved organisational performance, *group cohesion*, etc.

Valence. The strength of a person's desire for a particular outcome or occurrence of a certain event.

Vertical job enlargement. Another term for *job enrichment*.

Vertical loading. Another term for *job enrichment*.

Vestibule training. Training that takes place in a room specially set up to replicate the conditions of a workplace.

Vicarious liability. A legal doctrine which requires employers to assume general responsibility for breaches of contract, common law or statutory obligations committed by employees in the course of their employment.

Victimisation. Unfavourable treatment of an individual because he or she complains of being denied a statutory right or helps another person complain about such treatment.

Wage drift. The tendency of locally negotiated wage rates to rise above minimum levels determined nationally by panels of unions and employers' associations.

Wage–effort bargain. A person's perception of how much work is to be done for an agreed wage, including the effort put into the job as well as the number of hours of employment.

Wastage curve. A graph showing the proportions of a firm's employees who resign in various age categories. Normally the highest wastage rates occur among young workers and those approaching the normal age of retirement.

Work-factor method. A *motion study* technique which analyses the times needed to perform operations in terms of body member used, distance travelled, extent of manual control needed, and weight or resistance encountered.

Work-profiling system. A method for generating *person specifications* based on answers to questionnaires issued to job occupants. Jobs are analysed according to the time spent on various duties, the importance of each task, the work environment, organisational involvement, and job autonomy.

Work to rule. Refusal by employees to undertake any tasks not strictly covered by their contracts of employment.

Wrongful dismissal. Dismissal without proper notice or in breach of a clause in a worker's contract of employment.

Zero-sum bargaining. A negotiating situation in which each party trades concessions to the extent that total gains and losses add up to zero.

Index